WINNING ON YOUR INCOME TAXES

WINNING ON YOUR INCOME TAXES

1982 Edition

Dennis Kamensky

CRAGMONT PUBLICATIONS • SAN FRANCISCO
DISTRIBUTED BY GROSSET & DUNLAP • NEW YORK

WINNING ON YOUR INCOME TAXES

Copyright © 1982 by Dennis Kamensky

All rights reserved, including the right
to reproduce this book, or parts thereof,
in any form, except for the inclusion of
brief quotations in a review.

Edited by Charles W. Bowman, J.D., LL.M.

First printing January, 1982
Manufactured in the United States of America

Published by
Cragmont Publications
185 Berry Street, Suite 5834
San Francisco, California 94107

Distributed by
Grosset & Dunlap Publishers
New York

Grosset & Dunlap Order No. 0-448-12329-0

Library of Congress Cataloging in Publication Data

Kamensky, Dennis, 1948-
  Winning on your income taxes.

  Includes index.
  1. Income tax—United States.   I. Title.
HJ4652.K33   343.7305'2   81-19405
ISBN 0-89666-016-8 (pbk.)   347.30352   AACR2

To
Marilyn, Adam, and Crissy

This publication is designed to provide accurate and authoritative information on preparation of federal income tax returns and planning for tax savings. It is sold, however, with the understanding that the publisher and distributor are not engaged in rendering legal, accounting, or other professional service. If legal or other expert assistance is required, the services of a competent professional person should be sought.

—Based on a Declaration of Principles
jointly adopted by a Committee of the
American Bar Association and a Committee
of Publishers and Associations

Contents

Introduction 13

**PART I
DON'T BE AFRAID—YOU *CAN* WIN!**

1 Raising Your Tax Consciousness 17
   The Fear—and How to Conquer It 17
   The IRS—Knowing the Opposition 18
   Norms—Staying Within Them 19
   Tax Audits—How to Win Them 19

2 Preparing to Win 23
   Is Tax Preparation an Art or a Science? 23
   Who Should Prepare Your Tax Returns? 24
   How Important Is Recordkeeping? 26
   Who Should File—and When? 27

3 Adopting Tactics to Win 29
   Collecting Everything You Need 29
   Entering Information 29
   Entering Numbers 30

**PART II
PREPARING THE RETURN—
FILING STATUS & EXEMPTIONS**

4 Form 1040—The Heading and Filing Status 33
   The Heading 36
   Filing Status 37

5 Exemptions 41
   Other Dependents 42
   Exemptions, Filing Status, and Tax Consciousness 43

**PART III
DETERMINING YOUR GROSS INCOME**

6 Lines 7—10 of Form 1040 47
   Wage Income Versus Self-Employment Income 47
   Wages, Salaries, and Tips 48
   Interest Income 50
   Your Best Interests 51
   Dividends 53
   Refunds of State and Local Income Taxes 54
   Alimony Received 54

7 Profit or Loss from a Business or Profession................................55
  How and When to Use Schedule C 55
  Planning for Self-Employment Income 56
  The Heading of Schedule C 56
  Part I of Schedule C—Income 59
  Part II of Schedule C—Deductions 61
  Depreciation 63
  Using Schedule C-2 63
  Accelerated Cost Recovery System 65
  Completing Schedule C 68
  Using Schedule C Properly 69
  Schedule SE—Self-Employment Social Security Tax 70

8 Capital Gain or Loss—Schedule D..72
  Short-Term Capital Gains and Losses 71
  Nonbusiness Bad Debts 72
  Long-Term Capital Gains and Losses 72
  Reporting Short-Term Capital Gains and Losses 73
  Reporting Long-Term Capital Gains and Losses 74
  Calculating Amount of Capital Gain or Loss 77
  Computation of Alternative Tax 77
  Computation of Capital Loss Carryovers 77
  Electing out of Installment Method 77
  Using Schedule D Effectively 77

9 Sale or Exchange of Real Estate...79
  Sale or Exchange of a Principal Residence—Form 2119 79
  Computation of Gain and the Adjusted Sales Price 82
  Computation of Gain to Be Postponed and the
     Adjusted Basis of the New Residence 83
  Computation of Exclusion, Gain to Be Reported, and
     the Adjusted Basis of the New Residence 84
  Exchanging Personal Residences 84
  Selling Rental Property—Form 4797 84
  Deferring Capital Gains on Rental Property 87
  Installment Sales—Form 6252 87
  Which Method Is Best? 88

10 Lines 13—17 of Form 1040..91
  Capital Gain Distributions 91
  Supplemental Gains or Losses from Form 4797 91
  Capital Gains and Investments 91
  Fully Taxable Pensions and Annuities 92
  Partially Taxable Pensions and Annuities 93
  Supplemental Income—Schedule E 93
  Computing Rental Income or Loss 101
  Tax Advantages of Rental Property 101
  Using Your Equity 102
  Income or Losses from Partnerships, Estates,
       Trusts, or Small Business Corporations—Part II
       of Schedule E 103

11 Lines 18—21 of Form 1040..105
    Farm Income or Loss—Schedule F 105
    Unemployment Compensation 105
    Other Income 106
    Total Income 107

PART IV
DETERMINING YOUR TAXABLE INCOME

12 Adjustments to Income..111
    Moving Expenses—Form 3903 111
    Foreign Moving Expenses—Form 3903F 115
    Employee Business Expenses Form 2106 115
    Education Expenses—Parts II and III of Form 2106 123
    Payments to an Individual Retirement Account 125
    Payments to a Keogh Retirement Plan 126
    Interest Penalty on Early Withdrawal of Savings 126
    Alimony Paid 126
    Disability Income Exclusion—Form 2440 126
    Other Adjustments—Line 29 of Form 1040 128
    Total Adjustments 128
    Adjusted Gross Income 128

13 Itemized Deductions—Schedule A...129
    Itemizing or Taking the Standard Deduction 129
    Filling Out Schedule A 131
    Medical and Dental Expenses 131
    Taxes 134
    Interest Expenses 135
    Contributions 136
    Casualty or Theft Losses 138
    Miscellaneous Deductions 140
    Summary of Itemized Deductions 143

PART V
DETERMINING YOUR TAX

14 Computing Your Tax Liability..147
    Tax Tables 147
    Tax Rate Schedules X, Y, and Z 147
    Income Averaging—Schedule G 147
    Filling Out Schedule G 149
    The Maximum Tax 152
    Your Tax and Additional Taxes 152

15 Tax Credits..155
    Contributions to Candidates for Public Office 155
    Credit for the Elderly—Schedules R and RP 155
    Credit for Child and Dependent Care Expenses—Form 2441 159
    Using Form 2441 Properly 161
    Investment Tax Credit—Form 3468 162
    Business Energy Tax Credit 165
    Rehabilitation Expenditure Tax Credit 165
    Foreign Tax Credit—Form 1116 166

　　　　　Work Incentive Tax Credit (WIN) 166
　　　　　Jobs Credit—Form 5884 166
　　　　　Residential Energy Credit—Form 5695 166
　　　　　Your Total Tax Credits 168

16 Other Taxes...169
　　　　　Self-Employment Tax—Schedule SE 169
　　　　　Minimum Tax—Form 4625 169
　　　　　Alternative Minimum Tax—Form 6251 169
　　　　　Tax from Recomputing Prior Year Investment Tax
　　　　　　　Credit—Form 4255 169
　　　　　Social Security (FICA) Tax on Tip Income Not Reported
　　　　　　　on Form 4137 171
　　　　　Uncollected Employee Social Security Tax on Tips 171
　　　　　Tax on an Individual Retirement Account—
　　　　　　　Form 5329 171
　　　　　Advance Earned Income Credit Payments Received 171
　　　　　Total Tax 171

17 Payments of Tax...173
　　　　　Refund or Balance Due 173
　　　　　Penalties and Exemptions—Form 2210 173
　　　　　Amount Paid with Form 4868 174
　　　　　Excess FICA or RRTA Tax Withheld 174
　　　　　Credit for Federal Tax on Special Fuels
　　　　　　　and Oils—Form 4136 or 4136-T 174
　　　　　Regulated Investment Company Credit—Form 2439 174
　　　　　Total Payments 174

18 The Bottom Line...175
　　　　　Total Federal Income Tax Withheld 175
　　　　　Estimated Tax Payments 175
　　　　　Earned Income Credit 175
　　　　　Your Check or Money Order 176
　　　　　Signatures 176

PART VI
OTHER RETURNS, FORMS, AND CONSIDERATIONS

19 State and Local Tax Returns..181

20 Additional Tax Forms..183
　　　　　Form 1040ES—Estimated Tax Payments 183
　　　　　Form 1040X—Amended U.S. Individual Tax Return 183

Appendix: Forms and Schedules—A Summary.....................................187

Index..191

Table of Illustrations

Form 1040 34-35	Form 2106 118-119
Form W-2 49	Form 2440 127
Schedule B 52	Schedule A 130
Schedule C 57	Statement of Theft or
Schedule C-1 60	Casualty Loss 139
Form 4562 66-67	Schedule G 150
Schedule D 75-76	Schedule R 156
Form 2119 80	Schedule RP 157
Form 4797 85-86	Form 2441 160
Form 6582 89	Form 3468 163-164
Schedule E 94-95	Form 5695 167
Form 3903 112	Schedule SE 170
Form 3903F 116	Form 1040X .184-185

Introduction

As wise old Ben Franklin said, nothing in life is certain except death and taxes. While ultimately there is very little we can do about death, there are a great many things each of us can do to reduce our own income taxes. The goal of this book is to raise the "tax consciousness" of the American people. It is the hard-working wage earners, the owners of small businesses, and the professionals who bear the greatest burden of our tax system. It is to this large group of people that this book is dedicated.

A tax book intended for middle income people is long overdue. Many tax guides deal with the problems faced by the very rich. They talk about the exceptions to the exceptions to the exceptions to the rules. They deal mostly with problems faced only by a few people and they ignore the real problems that the vast majority of American taxpayers face. The language of this book is plain and simple. We will deal only with the tax problems and sources of income that are shared by the majority of taxpayers.

Our tax system can treat us fairly or it can be very unfair, depending on how each individual uses it to his or her own specific advantage.

In the United States, income tax collection is based on a system known as voluntary compliance. That means that each individual, rather than the government, is responsible for his or her own tax return. It is up to each taxpayer to file tax returns, to report income received during the year, and to claim lawful deductions. There can be two taxpayers, living next door to each other, working at similar jobs, having the same number of family members, and yet each may pay a totally different amount of tax even though each reports all income. Why? The answer lies in the fact that one of these taxpayers is using the tax system to better advantage than the other. He or she understands how our tax system operates. Voluntary compliance really means two things: one, that each individual is responsible for reporting the facts to the IRS; and two, that each individual is responsible to himself in learning about the tax system and in paying the lowest amount of taxes allowed by law.

The purpose of this book is to show the average American taxpayer how to understand the tax system and how to use it to his or her greatest advantage. Today, more than forty percent of American taxpayers overpay each year on income taxes. If we learn about the tax laws, use the ambiguities and the fine points, and begin to develop our tax consciousness, we can save hundreds, if not thousands, of dollars on our tax returns each year by preparing our own returns and by paying no more than we rightfully owe. Remember, these are dollars that may be saved or invested for the future, or spent presently to raise our standard of living.

As the famous judge Learned Hand wrote in a court opinion in 1947, "Over and over again courts have said that there is nothing sinister in so arranging one's affairs as to keep taxes as low as possible. Everybody does so, rich or poor; and all do right, for nobody owes any public duty to pay more than the law demands: taxes are enforced exactions, not voluntary contributions. To demand more in the name of morals is mere cant."

I view tax return preparation as an art, rather than a science. To me, every single tax return is different, because every single taxpayer is in a unique situation. I have personally prepared over 8,000 tax returns, and no two have been the same.

What does winning on your income taxes really mean? There are two ways that most taxpayers lose. The first way, which affects the vast majority of us, is by not understanding how the tax system works and thus not taking full advantage of all the tax laws and regulations. For example, by not knowing all of the allowable tax deductions, a taxpayer will immediately pay over to the government a good deal of money that could rightfully have been saved. The other way some people lose on their income taxes is by going overboard, by becoming "pigs." They feel that anything, even personal expenditures, can be claimed as deductions and that they can get away with it. This is sort of like stretching a rubber band continuously until it stretches so far it will either break or snap back into your face. Eventually, the IRS will catch the people who cheat. Penalties may be imposed that amount to far more money than was originally saved by filing dishonest returns. For those who commit tax fraud, prison sentences may be imposed.

What winning on your income taxes means is understanding the tax system, applying your knowledge to your own specific needs, and paying the lowest amount of taxes without being challenged by the Internal Revenue Service.

Winning also means not just filling out income tax forms, but also understanding tax planning, financial planning, investments, and money management. This tax guide will specifically go into ways you can improve your whole tax picture and your entire financial outlook. This book should be used not just during the tax season, but also throughout the year, for you should always be aware of the tax consequences of your financial activities. How you spend your money and what investments you make will determine your tax position. Throughout this book we will be pointing out not only how to prepare your tax returns, and how to save money on taxes, but also ways in which you may be able to make better investments by understanding how investments affect your taxes.

PART I
DON'T BE AFRAID—
YOU *CAN* WIN!

CHAPTER ONE

☆

Raising Your Tax Consciousness

THE FEAR—
AND HOW TO CONQUER IT

The greatest obstacle to overcome in preparing your personal income tax return is fear. The American people are led to believe that the IRS knows all and sees all. This is what I call the "1984 Syndrome." It is a well-developed game of intimidation, and it wins the government millions of tax dollars that otherwise might be claimed by taxpayers as perfectly legitimate deductions. Through the media, hearsay, and "old wives' tales," we are led to believe that one of the greatest catastrophes awaiting us is to make a mistake on our income tax returns. The IRS is portrayed as the "Gestapo" of America. Every year all kinds of media reports come out about the terrible things that the IRS has done. The message seems to be that they are after all of us. It is interesting that at the beginning of every tax season, generally in February, a prominent person will be sent to jail for tax evasion, or a particular group of taxpayers will be the subject of an announced investigation by the IRS. This type of propaganda works wonders in intimidating millions of American taxpayers. The fact is that the IRS very seldom will pursue criminal action against a taxpayer unless the taxpayer owes in excess of $25,000 in tax, or the taxpayer is a celebrity and the IRS feels that a highly visible prosecution would act as a deterrent to tax crimes by ordinary citizens. Actually, these conditions do not involve the vast majority of us. Let's not be afraid of going to jail, but rather, of overpaying income taxes year after year.

The problem arises when you sit down to fill out your tax forms, and you become afraid to claim deductions. You may have purchased a tax guide or an IRS publication, but the language used in them is very difficult to understand. Between the obscure and tedious tax terminology and the articles that you've read about the IRS, you become more confused and more scared. Professional tax preparers are at an advantage because they see so many different tax returns that they come to know the types of information that will stick out on a return and be questioned, and the information that will pass without notice. What I will attempt to do in this book, therefore, is to share my knowledge, in specific detail, as to how the IRS operates, how they set up "norms" to detect tax cheats, and how to stay within the norms in order to avoid being audited. As you will see throughout the book, these norms are quite lenient, and there are many ways to improve your tax situation while staying well within them.

How do we overcome the fear of being hounded by the IRS? To say that the IRS is really a pussycat, or to think that if we cheat on taxes we will never get caught, is not true. But, with some inside information, a basic knowledge of the tax laws and how they operate, and an understanding of what can and cannot be accomplished, we can prepare our own tax returns and save a lot of money.

When it comes to dealing with money, many of us have mental blocks. Throughout our lives, we have been taught that money, taxes, and financial matters are beyond us. We are taught that the rich get richer and the poor get poorer. Many of us have been taught to leave money management to accountants or other professionals. Many, perhaps most, Americans are not really in control of their own finances, and that is an unfortunate situation. We should be in control of all aspects of our lives. We all can take control of our money, we can make our money start working for us, and we can improve our tax positions.

There is no great mystery to making money and having money work for us. It doesn't matter if we are living in times of inflation, recession, or depression. It doesn't matter if we have a doctorate degree or just a third grade education. In fact, many of the people that I've known who have "made it" have been people who do not have college degrees. We live in one of the greatest times in history to succeed financially. There is nothing stopping us but ourselves. The knowledge is there, the opportunity is there —so let's take advantage of it.

You don't have to be a C.P.A. to do your own taxes. You don't have to take accounting classes to learn how the IRS operates, or to understand the tax forms. However, whether you prepare your taxes yourself or pay someone else to do the work, it is your legal responsibility to make sure that they are done truthfully and accurately. The best way to overcome the fear of the income tax system is to take charge of your own finances, including tax return preparation.

THE IRS—
KNOWING THE OPPOSITION

The Internal Revenue Service is a vast bureaucracy that is both understaffed and overworked. As most people merely file simple tax returns and only try to get back a small tax refund, the IRS knows very little about us. The task of collecting detailed personal information about us, even with the latest computers, is insurmountable.

Basically, information about us comes to the IRS from three sources. The first, and by far the major, source is our own past and present tax returns filed under the system of voluntary compliance. The data from all past tax returns are entered into their computers, which are used to cross-check returns very quickly. Any discrepancies or outstanding changes from year to year may trigger a tax audit. It is therefore wise to keep copies of all your past tax returns for reference purposes.

The second basic source of information is the W-2 forms reporting wages paid to you that are sent to the IRS by your employer, or the similar 1099 forms that are used for self-employed persons or independent contractors. These forms contain a very limited amount of information, including only the name of your employer, gross wages, taxes withheld, and sometimes tips, union dues, or sick pay. They don't even show the dates of your employment or your occupation.

The third source is reports provided by banks, brokerage houses, or corporations. This information tells the IRS how much you have received in dividends, investment income, or interest income. For example, each of your savings accounts will generate a statement to the IRS of the total amount of interest earned during the year.

So what does the IRS really know about us? Very little. To a great extent we control the information the IRS receives by what we put down on our tax returns. Without specific checking, as in a tax audit, the IRS doesn't even know if we are really married, divorced, or separated, or whether we have two or twenty children. The point is that, since there are millions and millions of American taxpayers, detailed information cannot be gathered without an intensive search of the records of every single one of us. And that would be utterly impossible.

What all this means for the average taxpayer is that we should not be afraid of doing our own taxes and should realize that the IRS is not "big brother." I'm in no way advocating reporting false information on tax returns, but don't be afraid to take advantage of every pertinent tax form, procedure, and loophole, and, wherever possible, to use our understanding of the system to decrease our tax bills.

The key word here is tax *avoidance,* not tax *evasion.* Tax avoidance is perfectly legal. It is no more than "so arranging one's affairs as to keep taxes as low as possible."

Tax evasion, on the other hand, involves some kind of deceit or a deliberate attempt to cover things up and conceal the truth. Obviously there is a fine line between the two concepts, but that works to our advantage. In other words, the IRS is not after us, just our money. It's not worth the time and trouble to the IRS to go after the average taxpayer unless blatant tax evasion is involved. When we hear about someone getting arrested for tax fraud, it is usually someone who owes the government a great deal of money, and the case must be worth the great effort required to prosecute it. As we discuss the fine points of the tax laws and some of their ambiguities, keep that in mind.

In the past few years a number of people have begun revolting against the IRS and the income tax in general. I'm totally against most of the tactics employed in this form of revolt. By putting down false informaton on a tax return, or by not filing tax returns, people are leaving themselves open to prosecution and a jail sentence. The IRS has and will come down very hard on these people. I'm advocating understanding the tax system, using it, and not in any way breaking the law. If Richard Nixon can make three million dollars in taxable income and pay only $600 in taxes legally and without going to jail, then each of us can also save money. The same laws that apply to Presidents apply to all of us.

NORMS—
STAYING WITHIN THEM

In order to determine who should be audited, the IRS has established a series of norms for tax returns. These norms are based on amounts shown on tax returns in various specific categories. For each type of deduction, certain norms have been established, based on level of income, type of job, filing status, number of dependents, sources of income, previous tax returns, and geographic location. The IRS computers are programmed to pick up any returns on which the figures exceed these norms in specific areas, generally two or more. The computers give a certain mathematical rating to the various parts of your return, and if the rating goes above a set figure based on the above criteria, then it is popped out. Since the IRS is so understaffed and the nature of tax filing so confusing and ambiguous, these norms are fairly high. In other words, there are ranges of numbers, or norms, and as long as the numbers on your tax return fit within these ranges you probably will not be audited.

TAX AUDITS—
HOW TO WIN THEM

There are many misconceptions about audits, what they are, why they come about, and what happens during one. An audit is basically a questioning of the information that has or has not been put down on a tax return.

Many returns are redone immediately after they are received by the IRS and put into the computer. Usually this occurs when a mathematical or procedural error is detected. The computers automatically refigure the return and recompute the tax. A statement is sent to the taxpayer with a computerized list of the corrections made. This is not an audit, and having this happen means that there will probably be no audit of the return for that year. In fact, it has been my experience that when a mathematical or procedural error is made on a tax return, it is very unlikely that a regular audit will take place. It seems that the computers may be set up first to find mathematical or procedural errors and then, using the system of norms, to pick out returns to be audited from the remaining error-free returns. The point here is that just by getting a computerized sheet from the IRS saying that you made an error does not mean that you are being audited, or under investigation, or any such thing.

A real tax audit does not come about usually until nine months to a year and a half after the tax return has been filed. You may have already received your tax refund and spent it. In fact, there are instances when audits do not occur until after two or even three years after a tax return has been filed. The basic statue of limitations bars the IRS from forcing a taxpayer to pay more tax if no action has been taken within three years after a tax return is filed. However, there are many exceptions to this rule, and there is no statute of limitations at all in the case of a false return, a willful attempt to evade tax, or where no return has been filed. In some cases the IRS puts a great deal of pressure on taxpayers to waive the statute of limitations so that they may have more time to complete an investigation.

There are two basic ways that audits come about. The first and by far the most common is when something on the return sticks out—in other words, when certain amounts are well above the specific norms that have been established by the IRS. There may have been some questionable deductions taken, or some very high amounts that are inconsistent with the rest of the tax return. (The word *consistency* is a key to doing taxes effectively, and we will be spending a good deal of time discussing this). This type of audit can be avoided as already mentioned by sending in proof (always send in a photocopy—never the original) with the return. For example, let's say you have a medical deduction of $4,000 with an income of $10,000. That seems to be relatively high, given the amount of income. Just send in a photocopy—never the original—of the receipt with the tax return and write "see attached" next to the amount on Schedule A, Itemized Deductions. This probably will prevent an audit immediately.

The number of tax returns audited is generally between six and eight percent of all the returns filed. Obviously, this is a very small percentage. This illustrates the great latitude that the IRS gives us on our tax returns.

The second basic reason for a tax audit is random selection. Each year the IRS randomly selects a very, very small number of t   eturns to audit. The purpose of these audits is not so much to collect money as it is to help establish the norms for future years. In most audits the IRS will ask for information concerning two to four items. In a random audit, however, the IRS *may* go over the entire tax return.

The random audit is so rare that it affects only a handful of people each year. The IRS, though, likes people to think that random audits are a big item. That is not true. Almost all audits are caused by going above the norms established by the IRS or by taking illegal or questionable deductions. If the return looks clean, that is, consistent with most of the norms, and there seems to be no angle that the IRS can use to make some money, then the return probably will not be audited. The underlying purpose of an audit is to collect more money, and if the IRS auditor feels that it cannot be done, the IRS will not proceed.

There is an additional reason a return may be audited. It comes about because of an informer. The IRS may pay a reward of varying amounts to people who give them information about someone else's tax return. One way to avoid this is to keep your return and its information to yourself. Don't brag about how much you deducted at a party or allow others to see your returns, even if you have nothing to hide.

Let's say that you are going to be audited. What now? Don't panic, it's not really the end of the world. It won't be like all those horrible stories you've imagined and have been led to believe. First of all, the audit will almost certainly cover only a specific part of your tax return. For example, they may ask for proof of the amount of specific payments. Search your records and find the receipts or other items you need to justify the deduction in question.

It is very important to plan a strategy for the audit. Find out exactly what they want, and do not bring in other proof or information that is not being called for. Go over your records and your return, and understand every figure and total so that you can explain it to the IRS agent concisely and logically. Being prepared and being sure of yourself is three-quarters of the battle.

If a professional tax preparer has done your tax return, you should consult him or her immediately when you receive notice of an audit. Meet with the tax preparer, go over the parts of the return that are to be audited, and have everything prepared before you appear for the audit.

Dress well but conservatively for the audit. Smile, be friendly, and, above all, look firm but honest. The completeness and accuracy of all your records and receipts are, of course, very important, but so is how you dress and how you interact with the tax auditor.

Whether or not you have all of the necessary records and other proof, never admit to any dishonesty. Don't let the auditor intimidate you. With some auditors a sign of weakness indicates that they should expand the scope of the audit, perhaps even to the previous two years' tax returns. If possible, try to take the offensive. You can plan ahead to do this when you feel your return may exceed the norms and trigger an audit. For example, when one of my clients can claim many large but valid deductions and would thus get a substantial refund, I may deliberately leave out some of the deductions so as to reduce the amount of the refund. If the return is later audited, then the taxpayer can take the offensive by claiming a larger refund and thus put the auditor on the defensive.

An IRS auditor once told me that he felt that fifty percent of winning a tax audit depended upon the impression the IRS auditor had of the taxpayer. I, too, feel that a large part of winning an audit is how well the two of you hit it off, and what kind of mood the tax auditor is in.

Even if you do not have exact receipts, but can verify things orally and offer convincing explanations, you will probably win the tax audit. I have been on audits in which the taxpayer has not had any proof and yet we have still been able to win the audit. I have seen other audits in which the largest part of the time was spent talking about raising children, or how rotten the weather has been lately, or parking problems. During one audit, my client, who was an airline stewardess, sat beside the auditor's desk and noticed a butterfly print from Nigeria on the wall. After discussing the print for about twenty minutes, we got down to talking about her tax return. Inwardly, I knew the audit was over.

Another consideration to take into account when dealing with the IRS is the differences among the individual people who work there. The IRS has many agents, and with the tremendous complexity and ambiguity of tax procedures, interesting things often develop. A few years ago, a fellow tax preparer and I had a question about the Earned Income Credit. We called the IRS three different times, spoke to three different agents, and got three different answers. No wonder the IRS will not stand by any information its agents convey to the public.

Once an airline pilot was a student in a tax class I taught. He had gotten advice from the IRS as to how to fill out the previous year's tax return. There was a problem regarding how to take a charitable deduction for the time he had spent flying aircraft for charity, so he asked the agent to fill out that part of the return, which the agent did. His return was audited on that question, and he lost. He appealed and lost again. The pilot came into my class, furious, and wanted to learn how to complete his returns so that he could beat the IRS in audits. I showed him, instead, how to do his own tax returns, save money, and not be audited.

Most of the IRS agents that I have dealt with have been very nice, sincere people who had some understanding of taxes, and were generally fair to the taxpayers. In fact, the vast majority of people I have met who have been audited have been pleasantly surprised by the politeness of the agents and the absence of pressure during the audit. The worst that can happen, in reality, is that you may have to pay back a few dollars. Even so, you will come out of the experience with a better understanding of the tax system. Don't get uptight, don't fall for the exaggerations of the media about the IRS, and don't let the old wives' tales prevent you from claiming everything to which you are legally entitled on your tax return.

The keys to winning a tax audit are: one, to be prepared before you meet with the auditor; and two, to have some understanding of the tax laws. I have found it more important to have a good explanation than to have actual receipts. Don't go into an audit with the attitude that you are going to fight the IRS and somehow defeat them. Instead, go in with the conviction that you are an honest person and you are appearing to explain the figures on your tax return. It's as simple as that. Remember, the IRS knows very little about us, and the auditor is someone who is just trying to do his job and get through another working day.

There are two kinds of people who lose on their tax returns in our tax system, which allows for stretching, pushing, and a great deal of leeway. Those who don't use the system to their full advantage lose immediately. Those who go too far and try to grab too much will eventually overextend the "rubber band." It then recoils right back in their faces.

There have been all kinds of books and guides written about how to beat the tax system, but most of them are losers. They are based on gimmicks and shady deals that cause tax returns to stick out and invite an audit by the IRS. You can't win by making money and never paying *any* taxes. The system cannot tolerate that. What winning really means is to pay the least amount of taxes possible in your particular situation without being audited, and to be able to sleep very soundly at night.

People often ask, "If I am audited, does that mean that I will be audited again every year?" The answer is that it depends on what happens during the first audit. If you win the audit, the chances are very slim that the IRS will audit the same sections of your return again the next year. The reason for this is that if the IRS audits the same things twice and you win both audits, they will be open to charges of harrassing you if they audit the same things again. They can, though, audit another part of your tax return in a subsequent year. Of course, if you lose an audit on a specific tax question, and you handle the same question in the same manner on the next year's tax return, there obviously will be a greater chance of another audit.

CHAPTER TWO

☆

Preparing to Win

IS TAX PREPARATION AN ART OR A SCIENCE?

The first step to take before you begin to fill out an income tax return is to be prepared, both intellectually and emotionally. In Chapter 1 we discussed the emotional aspects of the tax system and the IRS, so now let's discuss the intellectual side of the matter. Preparing your own tax returns is like writing a gourmet recipe for a fancy cookbook. You have to know all about the ingredients and the correct procedures, but what turns food into a gourmet dish are the exquisite little touches of creative genius. For the types of income earned and deductions claimed by the vast majority of Americans, the wage earners, owners of small businesses, and professionals, most of the applicable tax procedures are fairly basic and easy to comprehend. It's only when a person gets into the very high tax brackets that all of the extremely complicated forms and procedures come into play. As we go through each of the basic forms, you will learn how to fill them out and what they all mean, in simple language. We will also discuss how to use the nuances and ambiguities of the tax system in order for you to save money.

Even in the simplest of the tax forms that taxpayers must fill out, there are many ambiguities and unclear meanings. These ambiguities and unclear meanings are there to be used for our own benefit. This is where completing a tax return becomes an *art* as well as a science. As with a gourmet receipe, the creativity we all possess can be used to turn merely filing a tax return into winning on your income taxes.

The United States income tax system is distinctly class-based and biased. The system is set up to allow the upper income groups to avoid taxes, but many of the same tax breaks for the rich can be used by the middle and even the lower income groups. The point is that you can easily use the system to your own advantage without penalty. There are few yes or no, right or wrong answers in doing a tax return. The IRS knows this fact very well, the tax system actively encourages it, and the wealthy have been taking advantage of it for many years. Now is the time for everyone to know the rules of the game. Throughout the years, I have done tax returns for some very wealthy as well as some fairly poor people. I have tried and have succeeded in using the same laws and regulations that apply in helping wealthy people to help poorer people as well.

A key word to keep in mind always when preparing your tax return is *consistency*: Consistency with regard to your previous tax returns, your past and present occupations, your filing status (married, single, or head of household), your number of dependents, and your overall income. As was stated earlier, the IRS gets most of its basic information from what you have told them on your previous tax returns. One method used by the IRS to determine whether a return is to be audited is to compare the present tax return with previous ones. When I do someone's taxes, the first thing I ask for is a copy of the previous year's tax return. As I go through the current year's return, I compare it with the previous one. If there are any great shifts or changes, a logical basis for them must exist. In other words, if your income is about the same as last year's, yet your itemized deductions are much greater, beware. Unless these deductions can be substantiated on the return itself, be prepared for a tax audit. In the case of abnormally large deductions, you can substantiate them immediately and probably prevent an audit by submitting photocopies of receipts or other proof along with the return.

There are some taxpayers who feel that they can just pick numbers out of the air and put them down on a tax return. I once tried to do a tax return for a person who wanted to put down a $21,000 amount as an interest expense deduction. His overall income was less than $15,000. Was there any basis in reality for such a figure? He could not provide any proof of payment of such an amount, yet the size of the deduction in relation to his income would almost certainly have triggered an audit. Unless proof could have been sent in with the tax return it would have been asking for trouble for him to have claimed such a large deduction.

On the other hand, most taxpayers don't take advantage of all of the legitimate, provable deductions to which they are entitled. How many teachers, or managers, go to occupation-related conferences or go on trips that are required by their jobs, yet ignore their expenses at tax time? How many blue collar workers buy tools, safety equipment, or protective clothing, yet don't deduct all or part of these costs? These are all job-related costs and can be deducted without any problem. There are many other types of deductions that are job-related, and most people do not take advantage of them. They may buy pens and pencils and other kinds of clerical necessities for their jobs, but never collect the receipts or deduct these items on their tax returns. These people really shouldn't complain that the rich do not pay their share of taxes, since they are paying more than their own share through carelessness. Take advantage of the tax system, and save money by using it!

Once you begin handling your taxes correctly, each year it becomes easier as you develop your own systems. For example, if you've never taken an employee business expense deduction because in the past you were not sure you were able to do so, but, after reading this book, you realize that you now can, by all means take advantage of it. But start off slowly. Make sure that you have the receipts and other proof for each trip that you take. Start saving receipts or keeping a diary. Millions of people are doing the same thing. The IRS will only bother you if they think that you cannot prove that you are entitled to the deductions you claim.

WHO SHOULD PREPARE YOUR TAX RETURNS?

This book is written to show you how to do your own tax return. *Should* you do it yourself? Why not have a professional prepare your returns or even let the IRS do it? If you think a professional tax preparer, by some stroke of magic, will know all of the solutions to your tax problems, you are mistaken. Anyone can prepare his or her own tax returns and do just as well or even better than a professional. In fact, a few years ago a leading consumer magazine published an article on professional tax preparation. Their findings were that private tax preparers were incorrect on 86% of their returns and that the IRS, who also will prepare your tax returns, was incorrect when preparing complicated tax returns almost 100% of the time. So you can't do much worse, and, with a little effort and some sound advice, you will probably do much better.

Nevertheless, let's discuss the various choices that you have as to who can prepare your tax returns. There are four main types of professional tax preparers. The most influential, for most Americans, is the large national tax preparation firm. These firms generally hire housewives, unemployed persons, or retired people to prepare tax returns for the public. These employees are paid very little, usually a small percentage of the fee charged to the client, or even the minimum wage. The problem is that these preparers are not tax experts. They are taught generally to simplify or minimize the returns, and are not at all concerned about obtaining the best possible results for each client. They gather some information from you and, after you leave, do the return, or have another employee do it for them. After it is finished, a more experienced preparer may go over it. It's no wonder that even the IRS has criticized one of these outfits for not obtaining all of the legitimate refunds for their clients. For the IRS to criticize this is very significant. If you should choose to go to a large chain of tax preparers, try to see someone other than the person who greets you right off the street. See if it's possible for the manager of the office to see you and do your returns. Generally a manager is more experienced and will produce better results for you. I compare the national firms with the fast food franchises—which are fine unless you are planning on a gourmet dinner.

A second type of tax preparer is a C.P.A. or other accountant. A major misconception of most people about tax preparation is that it is the same as, or similar to, accounting. That's not true. Tax preparation is a very specific field, and a knowledge of accounting does not automatically include tax expertise. You don't really need to know anything about accounting or bookkeeping to do your own taxes. The proper time to consult a C.P.A. is when you have a very unusual or complicated tax problem that involves enough money to justify fees that may range as high as $90 to $150 an hour. Hiring a C.P.A. is not necessary for most taxpayers, and it doesn't guarantee that the tax return will be done correctly or that you won't be audited, either. The only guarantee is that you'll be paying a lot of money for its preparation.

I once had a student who had gone to a C.P.A. to have her tax returns prepared. Her income was about $3,500, and the tax return was prepared on a 1040A, the so-called short form. She was charged $100 for this "service." Many C.P.A. firms hire students or inexperienced people to prepare tax returns. Their tax departments make most of their income by preparing tax returns for corporations and well-heeled individuals, and they really don't want to be bothered with ordinary individual tax returns.

Another possibility is to ask the IRS to prepare your tax return. You can go down to their overcrowded offices and wait in line for a very long time. The completed return will not have a special appearance, but you probably will end up paying too much tax, and you will still run the same risk of being audited. The IRS does not guarantee its own work any more than any other preparer does. When you sign the tax return, as you must, you are the person solely responsible for the accuracy and completeness of everything on it. The one benefit of going to the IRS is that they will do your federal return for free. However, you usually get what you pay for.

A final possibility is to have a small, independent tax preparer do your return, but you should be very careful in selecting one. Do not hire one unless you can be confident that he or she will be around throughout the year, and the next year as well. If possible, ask a friend who has consulted the same preparer before. Some of the firms of independent tax preparers can be very good, if the preparers are knowledgeable and, more importantly, are concerned about you personally. If they want to keep you as a long-term client and hope to expand their clientele through your recommendations, great. But if they are constantly changing locations or have a frequent turnover of personnel, watch out. For the most part, however, these small outfits are the most satisfactory alternative to doing your own tax returns. The key thing about hiring someone else to do your returns is service. You want the taxes done properly, you want to see the results quickly, you want them to stand by their work and to go with you in case of an audit, and you want to be satisfied with the bottom line. Paying someone to do tax returns is an investment (although it is also tax-deductible). No one would mind paying $200 or $300 if it would produce a savings of several hundreds of dollars. Unfortunately, many people will hire someone else for the task, pay a substantial fee, and get a very poor return from the investment.

One other word of caution is in order here. Consistently the worst results that I have seen are obtained when a relative or friend does a person's tax return for nothing. You will get what you pay for, if not worse. The worst returns that I have ever seen are when "Uncle Charlie," who claims to be a tax expert, has done a return.

These are the choices if you must have an outsider do your tax return. Now let's proceed to learn how to do it ourselves.

HOW IMPORTANT IS RECORDKEEPING?

Recordkeeping is a vital element of "tax consciousness." You pay taxes throughout the year, so you should also lay the groundwork throughout the year for return preparation. Tax consciousness involves being aware of and alert to receipts, deductions, income, and all other factors that affect your income taxes at any time during the year. No law states that you must keep receipts, except for entertainment expenses of $25 or more, but in case of an audit you must be prepared. If you are really interested in saving tax dollars, don't do it in a half-hearted way. Be determined and be aware of your tax position at all times. It is *your* money we are talking about, and you've worked very hard for it. If you feel that it's worth the effort to keep some of it, then do it wholeheartedly. Anything you do for yourself will be successful to the extent that you put time, energy, and intelligence into it. With income taxes, that means being aware all year long, and constantly thinking of ways to improve your tax position.

The biggest problem with recordkeeping is that when we sit down to do tax returns, the year in question has usually ended. It is too late to collect records and receipts. They should be collected and filed throughout the taxable year. We should be thinking about records whenever we buy something, or take a trip, or spend money for anything related to our job or profession. The easiest thing to do is to set aside a drawer or two, or even a large envelope, for collecting all pertinent receipts. By pertinent I mean anything that is, or looks as if it is, related to your tax return or tax position. Most receipts are not very specific, and most people do not save many, or any, of them. So, wherever possible, save them! Collect them. One suggestion is to get a rubber stamp with the name of your business or profession. When you buy something, stamp the back of the receipt and write a brief note to explain how that purchase is relevant to your job or profession. This will make it more acceptable as proof during an audit. Even if you never have to use the receipts because you are never audited, they are still valuable as records to help you determine what you are able to deduct.

Some receipts will be needed for the current year's tax return, whereas others will not be used for many years to come. For example, if you have work done on your house, and it is a personal residence, then you will not need these receipts until you sell your house. Receipts that may not be used for many years should be kept in a separate drawer or file, but be sure to keep them and use them when they are needed. In the example above, the receipts for house repairs must be kept so that you can lower the capital gain when the house is sold. Capital gains are discussed in Chapter 8 below.

A second area of recordkeeping involves ledgers. Ledgers are the first thing the IRS will check in an audit of self-employed people. It is vitally important to keep an accurate set of books for your business. You need to know exactly how well your business is doing at all times anyway, and the books will make it much easier to fill out financial statements and tax returns. In many small businesses a sole proprietor can handle the ledger himself. That is much cheaper than hiring a bookkeeper. But, whether you do it yourself or hire a bookkeeper or a professional accountant, it is essential that at all times you know exactly how much money is coming in and how much is going out, and how your business is doing.

There are some excellent publications

available that explain how to set up books for a small business or professional office. I recommend that you browse through the shelves of a book shop and select a how-to guide that fits your need for bookkeeping information.

Another important type of recordkeeping involves diaries used for job-related trips, conferences, conventions, seminars and local travel. If you are audited for travel or transportation deductions, the IRS will ask for and accept a diary as proof. This diary should be prepared by you, the taxpayer, and should have specific information as to dates, how each expense was related to your work or profession, and the total amount of expenses. I suggest, if you have job-related travel expenses, that you keep a diary in the glove compartment of your car. Every time you take a job-related trip, write down the date, how it was pertinent to your work, and the number of miles traveled. Keep an account of parking fees and tolls paid, as they are also tax deductible.

Get into the habit of keeping records, collecting receipts, and keeping diaries. Remember that when it is time to do your taxes, more than a year may have passed since you made a purchase, or took a business trip, or incurred other deductible expenses. By having complete records, you will be able to refresh your memory and take full advantage of all your legitimate deductions. Proper recordkeeping will save you money and give you peace of mind.

WHO SHOULD FILE— AND WHEN?

There are many people who will not be required to file a tax return this year. Whether or not you are required to file depends on three factors: your filing status, your total income, and the type of income that you have received. At the beginning of each tax year the IRS mails out Federal Tax Forms booklets. In the front of the booklet there is a chart that indicates exactly who is required to file or not based on the above three factors. Each year the amounts change, but generally, for a single person earning $4,000 or less or for a married couple earning $5,000 or less, no return needs to be filed. Generally, if you are self-employed and your net income (the net profit derived from subtracting all your expenses from total gross income) is $400 dollars or more, you'll have to file a tax return.

One reason for filing a tax return, even if your income is below the minimum shown on the chart, is that you may be entitled to a refund. The IRS will not automatically send you a refund, even though more money than you actually owe in taxes has been withheld from your wages and paid over to the Treasury. This is another aspect of voluntary compliance.

Another reason for filing a return is the Earned Income Credit, which will be explained in Chapter 17 below. If you feel that you can qualify for the Earned Income Credit, you must file a tax return in order to receive the money.

Another important question about filing is when to do it. Everyone knows about the April 15th deadline. The IRS, along with the mass media, scares us almost to death about the necessity of filing by midnight, April 15. Actually, you don't have to file by April 15 if you are entitled to a refund or if you owe no tax. Many people file their returns one, two or even three years late. (After three years, though, a claim for a refund is barred by the statute of limitations.) The IRS is perfectly happy to let it slide providing that the taxpayer does not owe any tax. However, if the IRS believes that you owe any amount of tax, then very quickly they will demand payment, and there will be penalties charged.

I had a client a few years ago whose salary had been garnished by the IRS. He had not filed a return for the previous three years, and the IRS thought he owed them money. In fact, he was entitled to refunds because he had gotten married, which the IRS did not know. The IRS charged him all sorts of penalties and interest, but by filing, he was able to recover some of this money. In this case, the taxpayer should have filed by April

15 of each year.

My advice is not to file late. The reason for this is that late returns may attract attention. They are more likely to be gone over closely, and an audit may result. The best time to file is during either of the two tax rushes. The first of these is during February when most wage earners get their W-2 forms and then file immediately to get their tax refunds. The second big rush, of course, is right before April 15th when the slow starters and those who owe money send in their returns. It is best to file at the times when most returns are filed so as to have your return get lost in the crowd. This is not going to prevent an audit, but it may reduce your chances of being selected for one.

To get an extension of time for late filing, you should fill out Form 4868. If you do not owe any tax or if you are entitled to a refund, a two-month extension usually will be granted automatically. If you owe money, however, you must send in the approximate amount with the Form 4868.

CHAPTER THREE

☆

Adopting Tactics to Win

Now we are ready to begin to do the return. We will proceed by going step by step through the procedures, forms, and methods in doing one single tax return. This example will cover all of the necessary information required for almost any wage earner, small business owner, or professional to do his or her complete tax return. When doing your own return, follow these procedures exactly, but disregard the information and forms that do not apply to your specific situation. The order of doing your return should be exactly as it is shown here. Using this order and method, with good preparation, you will be able to do the return quickly and efficiently.

COLLECTING EVERYTHING YOU NEED

The first step is to gather up all your records, ledgers, diaries, receipts, and tax forms. You may have to get some information from a stock broker, or finance company, or bank, or credit card company, etc. Obtain all this information beforehand. Collect all of your and your spouse's W-2s and 1099s, and be sure that you have all of the tax forms that will be required to report all sources of income and all types of deductions and credits.

Many people lose a lot of tax money each year because they are not familiar with all of the different tax forms. Be aware of which forms are pertinent to your return and get at least one extra copy of each. Tax forms are sometimes very difficult to obtain. The local IRS office usually has most of them, and you can order them from the IRS by telephone or by using the order form that is enclosed in the back of the Federal Income Tax Forms booklet that is mailed to taxpayers every January. Keep in mind that, if you order forms by mail, it may take a couple of weeks to get them.

There are instructional guides in the booklet for certain forms, and the IRS will give you its more detailed guide, entitled *Your Federal Income Tax, For Individuals*, known as Publication 17, free of charge. The main problem with IRS instructions, both in the tax forms booklet and in Publication 17, is that they are very difficult to understand. The language is technical, using IRS tax terminology, and even simple procedures are turned into difficult ones. They also cater to extraordinary tax situations that hardly ever affect most people and are therefore even more confusing. Nevertheless, get all the information you need, gather your records, get the forms and instructions, and then begin.

ENTERING INFORMATION

The tax return you actually file should be handwritten in ink, not typed or done by a computer. You should never send a photocopy of the return, or a copy showing erasures or obvious corrections. Neatness *does* count! If you have followed my advice so far, you will have gotten two copies of each tax form you need. Fill out one in pencil, correcting mistakes and changing entries as you go. When you are completely finished and satisfied with everything, copy everything in ink onto the second copy of each form.

I feel that it is very important to fill in your tax return by hand, in ink. The advantage of handwriting is to be able easily to write in additional information in margins, in between spaces, to explain things in further detail, or to show your calculations throughout the tax forms. There are going to be places where you want to write additional information, or where you want to show the IRS the various kinds of calculations by which you arrive at a specific amount. For example, under medical deductions on Schedule A, Itemized Deductions, it is good to show calculations and subtractions for medical insurance reimbursements in the left hand column next to their amounts. As we go through the specific forms you'll see how and where this should be done.

It is interesting to note here that the tax return we mentioned earlier, President Nixon's, where he made three million dollars and paid $600 in taxes, was handwritten.

Many tax preparation firms now use computers to fill out tax returns. Computerized returns have the advantage of looking very neat, being easy to read, and being mathematically correct (usually). The problem with using computers, though, is that you cannot enter explanations and calculations as you go. Since each tax return is unique, it is important to be able to point out specific things to the IRS. Only by doing your tax return by hand can you set it up exactly as you want it to be.

ENTERING NUMBERS

Numbers are an essential ingredient in a recipe in a gourmet cook book, and they must also be treated with careful consideration on a tax return. To begin with, never use cents—always round off to the nearest dollar. Fifty cents or more always should be rounded up to the next dollar, and 49 cents or less should be rounded down to the previous dollar. This treatment is not only perfectly legitimate, but in fact the IRS itself recommends rounding off to the nearest dollar. Rounding off greatly lessens the likelihood of making an unintentional mathematical error.

The appearance of your filled-out tax forms is very important. Remember, before a return is selected for audit, even when the computer picks it out, an IRS agent will first go over it. If it looks right, the auditor may simply put a tax return back. Numbers, of course, play an essential part in how that return looks. If it is at all possible, set up your numbers the same way that retail stores and businesses use them. The idea is that two different numbers that are very close in value can look much different. For example, $1,012 looks much larger than $997. A lot of small numbers can look like much less than one larger number, and the total of many small numbers may appear greater than one larger one.

Wherever it is possible, and particularly on itemized deductions, business or rental expenses and adjustments to income such as moving and employee business expenses, treat the numbers creatively. If, for example, on your medical deductions, the total of all the various medical and dental expenses is $3,004, see if it's possible to redo it and come up with a total of $2,994.00. The difference between the two numbers will hardly affect your tax bill, but the smaller number *looks* a lot better than larger one. Also, try not to come up with suspiciously round numbers such as $500 or $1,000. Making the numbers look good can stop an audit before it gets started, and still get you a refund.

PART II
PREPARING THE RETURN—
FILING STATUS & EXEMPTIONS

CHAPTER FOUR

☆

Form 1040— The Heading and Filing Status

The two basic tax return forms are the 1040 and the 1040A. Every individual who files a tax return must use one or the other. Most people think of them as the long (1040) and the short (1040A) forms. The 1040A does not allow for any supplemental schedules or forms, such as the ones for itemized deductions, adjustments to income, tax credits, business gains and losses, capital gains and losses, etc. Therefore, when you use the short form, what you are doing in reality is paying the highest possible taxes for your income level. Since you cannot take any deductions when using Form 1040A, you will have no opportunity to save money. You should *never* use Form 1040A (the short form) if you want to win on your income taxes!

When I recently ordered tax forms in preparation for the tax season, I ordered 8,000 long forms and ten short forms. The only reason for ordering the short forms was that my neighbor's parakeet likes to look at them in the bottom of his cage. The only taxpayers who possibly should ever use the 1040A form are students or unemployed people, people who have very little gross income. There's absolutely no advantage at all for anyone who has sizeable income to use it. The 1040 long form can be used by everyone, regardless of income, and everyone should use it.

Most people have been taught that either you can itemize deductions using Schedule A, and therefore use the long form, or you can simply take the standard deduction and use the short form, 1040A. This is utter nonsense, because there are many other types of tax write-offs besides itemized deductions, and the only way to take advantage of them is to use the long form. Even if your deductions do not amount to enough to make it worthwhile to itemize them, and thus it would be more advantageous to take the standard deduction, you still can save money by using and understanding the other areas of the tax system. You may be able to claim a business loss or a net loss on rental property, or claim job-related or professional business expenses, or use income averaging, etc. The main thing to remember is that all these tax-reducing provisions necessitate the use of the long form.

For professional tax preparers, the 1040 is the basic and most important tax form of all. It is both a table of contents and an index, combined. Every other tax form is supplemental to the 1040, and the bottom line amounts on the supplemental forms must all come back eventually to one of the lines on the 1040. It is essential that you become aware of all of the other types of supplemental forms. They are illustrated throughout this book. You can obtain them from the IRS and, before you do your tax returns, you should sit down and become familiar with them and know which ones you can use.

Unfortunately, much of the wording, the terms, and many of the lines of the Form 1040 are confusing or have nothing to do with most taxpayers. This causes confusion and errors, and makes people fearful of doing their own tax returns. As we go through each line, its meanings and relevance will be pointed out. Don't worry if many of the lines on your 1040 are blank—that's the way it usually is.

Form 1040 — U.S. Individual Income Tax Return 1981

Department of the Treasury—Internal Revenue Service

For the year January 1–December 31, 1981, or other tax year beginning , 1981, ending , 19   OMB No. 1545-0074

Use IRS label. Otherwise, please print or type.
- Your first name and initial (if joint return, also give spouse's name and initial) | Last name
- Present home address (Number and street, including apartment number, or rural route)
- City, town or post office, State and ZIP code
- Your occupation ▶
- Spouse's occupation ▶
- Your social security number
- Spouse's social security no.

Presidential Election Campaign
- Do you want $1 to go to this fund? .... Yes / No
- If joint return, does your spouse want $1 to go to this fund? ... Yes / No

Note: Checking "Yes" will not increase your tax or reduce your refund.

For Privacy Act and Paperwork Reduction Act Notice, see Instructions.

Filing Status
Check only one box.
1. ___ Single
2. ___ Married filing joint return (even if only one had income)
3. ___ Married filing separate return. Enter spouse's social security no. above and full name here ▶
4. ___ Head of household (with qualifying person). (See page 6 of Instructions.) If he or she is your unmarried child, enter child's name ▶
5. ___ Qualifying widow(er) with dependent child (Year spouse died ▶ 19   ). (See page 6 of Instructions.)

Exemptions
Always check the box labeled Yourself. Check other boxes if they apply.

- 6a ___ Yourself   ___ 65 or over   ___ Blind
- b ___ Spouse   ___ 65 or over   ___ Blind
- Enter number of boxes checked on 6a and b ▶ ___
- c First names of your dependent children who lived with you ▶ ....
- Enter number of children listed on 6c ▶ ___
- d Other dependents:

(1) Name	(2) Relationship	(3) Number of months lived in your home	(4) Did dependent have income of $1,000 or more?	(5) Did you provide more than one-half of dependent's support?

Enter number of other dependents ▶ ___
Add numbers entered in boxes above ▶ ___

- e Total number of exemptions claimed ....

Income
Please attach Copy B of your Forms W-2 here. If you do not have a W-2, see page 5 of Instructions.

7. Wages, salaries, tips, etc. .... 7 ____
8a. Interest income (attach Schedule B if over $400 or you have any All-Savers interest) .... 8a ____
  b. Dividends (attach Schedule B if over $400) ...... 8b ____
  c. Total. Add lines 8a and 8b .... 8c ____
  d. Exclusion (See page 9 of Instructions) .... 8d ____
  e. Subtract line 8d from line 8c (but not less than zero) .... 8e ____
9. Refunds of State and local income taxes (do not enter an amount unless you deducted those taxes in an earlier year—see page 9 of Instructions) .... 9 ____
10. Alimony received .... 10 ____
11. Business income or (loss) (attach Schedule C) .... ▶ 11 ____
12. Capital gain or (loss) (attach Schedule D) .... 12 ____
13. 40% of capital gain distributions not reported on line 12 (See page 9 of Instructions) . 13 ____
14. Supplemental gains or (losses) (attach Form 4797) .... 14 ____
15. Fully taxable pensions and annuities not reported on line 16 .... 15 ____
16a. Other pensions and annuities. Total received ..... 16a ____
  b. Taxable amount, if any, from worksheet on page 10 of Instructions .... 16b ____
17. Rents, royalties, partnerships, estates, trusts, etc. (attach Schedule E) .... 17 ____
18. Farm income or (loss) (attach Schedule F) .... ▶ 18 ____
19a. Unemployment compensation (insurance). Total received 19a ____
  b. Taxable amount, if any, from worksheet on page 10 of Instructions .... 19b ____
20. Other income (state nature and source—see page 11 of Instructions) ▶ .... 20 ____
21. **Total income.** Add amounts in column for lines 7 through 20 .... ▶ 21 ____

Adjustments to Income
(See Instructions on page 11)

22. Moving expense (attach Form 3903 or 3903F) ..... 22 ____
23. Employee business expenses (attach Form 2106) ... 23 ____
24. Payments to an IRA (enter code from page 11 ....) . 24 ____
25. Payments to a Keogh (H.R. 10) retirement plan .... 25 ____
26. Interest penalty on early withdrawal of savings .... 26 ____
27. Alimony paid .... 27 ____
28. Disability income exclusion (attach Form 2440) .... 28 ____
29. Other adjustments—see page 12 ▶ .... 29 ____
30. **Total adjustments.** Add lines 22 through 29 .... ▶ 30 ____

Adjusted Gross Income
31. **Adjusted gross income.** Subtract line 30 from line 21. If this line is less than $10,000, see "Earned Income Credit" (line 57) on page 15 of Instructions. If you want IRS to figure your tax, see page 3 of Instructions .... ▶ 31 ____

343-057-1

FORM 1040—THE HEADING AND FILING STATUS 35

Form 1040 (1981) Page **2**

Tax Computation (See Instructions on page 12)	32a Amount from line 31 (adjusted gross income)	32a
	32b If you do not itemize deductions, enter zero .... ⎫	32b
	If you itemize, complete Schedule A (Form 1040) and enter the amount from Schedule A, line 41 ... ⎬	
	Caution: If you have unearned income and can be claimed as a dependent on your parent's return, check here ▶ ☐ and see page 12 of the Instructions. Also see page 12 of the Instructions if:	
	• You are married filing a separate return and your spouse itemizes deductions, OR	
	• You file Form 4563, OR	
	• You are a dual-status alien.	
	32c Subtract line 32b from line 32a	32c
	33 Multiply $1,000 by the total number of exemptions claimed on Form 1040, line 6e ..	33
	34 Taxable Income. Subtract line 33 from line 32c	34
	35 Tax. Enter tax here and check if from ☐ Tax Table, ☐ Tax Rate Schedule X, Y, or Z, ☐ Schedule D, ☐ Schedule G, or ☐ Form 4726	35
	36 Additional Taxes. (See page 13 of Instructions.) Enter here and check if from ☐ Form 4970, ⎫ ☐ Form 4972, ☐ Form 5544, or ☐ Section 72(m)(5) penalty tax .... ⎬	36
	37 Total. Add lines 35 and 36 .... ▶	37
Credits (See Instructions on page 13)	38 Credit for contributions to candidates for public office ...	38	
	39 Credit for the elderly (attach Schedules R&RP)	39	
	40 Credit for child and dependent care expenses (attach Form 2441) ..	40	
	41 Investment credit (attach Form 3468)	41	
	42 Foreign tax credit (attach Form 1116)	42	
	43 Work incentive (WIN) credit (attach Form 4874)	43	
	44 Jobs credit (attach Form 5884)	44	
	45 Residential energy credit (attach Form 5695)	45	
	46 Total credits. Add lines 38 through 45	46
	47 Balance. Subtract line 46 from line 37 and enter difference (but not less than zero) . ▶	47
Other Taxes (Including Advance EIC Payments)	48 Self-employment tax (attach Schedule SE)	48
	49a Minimum tax. Attach Form 4625 and check here ▶ ☐	49a
	49b Alternative minimum tax. Attach Form 6251 and check here ▶ ☐	49b
	50 Tax from recomputing prior-year investment credit (attach Form 4255)	50
	51a Social security (FICA) tax on tip income not reported to employer (attach Form 4137) ..	51a
	51b Uncollected employee FICA and RRTA tax on tips (from Form W–2)	51b
	52 Tax on an IRA (attach Form 5329)	52
	53 Advance earned income credit (EIC) payments received (from Form W–2)	53
	54 Total tax. Add lines 47 through 53 .... ▶	54
Payments Attach Forms W–2, W–2G, and W–2P to front.	55 Total Federal income tax withheld	55	
	56 1981 estimated tax payments and amount applied from 1980 return .	56	
	57 Earned income credit. If line 32a is under $10,000, see page 15 of Instructions	57	
	58 Amount paid with Form 4868	58	
	59 Excess FICA and RRTA tax withheld (two or more employers)	59	
	60 Credit for Federal tax on special fuels and oils (attach Form 4136 or 4136–T)	60	
	61 Regulated Investment Company credit (attach Form 2439)	61	
	62 Total. Add lines 55 through 61 .... ▶	62
Refund or Balance Due	63 If line 62 is larger than line 54, enter amount OVERPAID .... ▶	63
	64 Amount of line 63 to be REFUNDED TO YOU .... ▶	64
	65 Amount of line 63 to be applied to your 1982 estimated tax ... ▶	65	
	66 If line 54 is larger than line 62, enter BALANCE DUE. Attach check or money order for full amount payable to "Internal Revenue Service." Write your social security number and "1981 Form 1040" on it. ▶ (Check ▶ ☐ if Form 2210 (2210F) is attached. See page 16 of Instructions.) ▶ $	66

Please Sign Here

Under penalties of perjury, I declare that I have examined this return, including accompanying schedules and statements, and to the best of my knowledge and belief, it is true, correct, and complete. Declaration of preparer (other than taxpayer) is based on all information of which preparer has any knowledge.

▶ Your signature   Date   ▶ Spouse's signature (if filing jointly, BOTH must sign even if only one had income)

Paid Preparer's Use Only

Preparer's signature ▶	Date	Check if self-employed ▶ ☐	Preparer's social security no.
Firm's name (or yours, if self-employed) and address ▶		E.I. No. ▶	
		ZIP code ▶	

343-057-2

THE HEADING

At the very top of Form 1040 is where you write in the heading. First, put in your name and address. For married people filing jointly that means putting in the husband's first name first, then his middle initial, then the wife's first name and middle initial. In the space immediately to the right of that put in your last name. Your names do not have to correspond exactly to those on your W-2 forms, but the social security numbers do have to match.

In the case of married couples filing separately, you must do two completely separate tax returns. Therefore, just put one spouse's name on top of the return, and then on line 3 you will put the other spouse's complete name. Make sure you put both spouses' social security numbers in the proper place on each return.

If your spouse has passed away during the taxable year, write in his or her name, and above it write in "deceased" and the date of his or her death. Form 1310, which you can get from the IRS, is to be filled out in order to obtain a refund for a deceased taxpayer. But also put this information onto the surviving spouse's 1040, just in case the supplemental form is lost or misplaced.

Below the line for your names are two lines for your address. Be sure to put in the address where you want your tax refund to be sent to you. For example, if you are filing a previous year's tax return, don't put in the address that you lived in during that taxable year, but rather your present address.

In the top right hand corner of the 1040 are the spaces for your social security numbers. The accuracy of these numbers is very important. Everything on your tax return is based upon social security numbers. If you leave them out, the IRS will send back the return. The IRS knows us only by these numbers, not our names or addresses, and can process returns only by the numbers. The husband's number goes on top, the wife's underneath. You will totally confuse the IRS if you do it the other way around. It's interesting that on joint returns the IRS always wants the husband on top and the wife on the bottom—an instruction they enforce with missionary zeal. Perhaps they have not read any of the latest marital happiness manuals.

Under the social security number boxes are spaces for occupation titles. I can't stress enough the importance of this information. The information you put down here is vital to a good tax return without an audit. Certain occupations allow for specific deductions. As we have stated earlier, the tax system is class-biased. Generally speaking, people with highly skilled occupations or professionals may claim more types of deductions. I am in no way advocating falsifying your job title, but look at the various aspects of your work and, without dishonesty, select a title that will allow you to take the most deductions.

Sometimes it is a mistake to glorify your occupation. For example, some people who are industrial workers may put down "foreman" or "supervisor" for their job title. Then on Schedule A, Itemized Deductions, they will claim a large amount for union dues. The mistake is that most foremen or supervisors are not union members, and this inconsistency can trigger a tax audit. On the other hand, you may have some type of technical position and put down something like "clerk" or "secretary," and then when you claim various books, educational materials, or job-related expenses, you may be audited. A classic example of this was a student in one of my tax classes who had put down "clerk" for his job title and then claimed a legitimate deduction for having a telephone, which was required by his employer. In fact, he was not a clerk but a dispatcher. He was audited for this inconsistency and error. Clerks generally are not required to have a telephone as part of their job, but dispatchers are, at least according to the norms established by the IRS.

Think carefully about your work position or profession. You also may have more than position or job. In that case put down the best occupation, i.e. the one that probably will allow the greatest number of deductions without questions being raised. You may even want to put down both job titles or occupations on this line. If you are self-employed, or if one of your occupations involves being self-employed, write in "S.E.", for self-employed. You don't have to explain the nature of the self-employed income here, because that will be done on your Schedule C, the form on which income from self-employment is reported. Remember, the key here is to be consistent with the information reported on the rest of the tax return.

There are some titles and occupational descriptions that should be avoided if possible. They include "housewife" and "student." The only good time to put down "student" is when you are being claimed as a dependent on your parents' return. This will show a consistency with what they are reporting. Housewife, written "H/W," will not allow for any type of deductions. If a housewife has any source of earned income, as from a part-time job or self-employment, write in the name of that occupation and then, of course, claim all of its allowable deductions. Again, as always, the husband's occupation goes on top and the wife's on the bottom.

Below the job occupation lines are the boxes for the Presidential Election Campaign Fund. If you check either of the "yes" boxes, the money sent to the Fund does not affect your tax return. You won't get one dollar less of a refund nor will you have to pay an additional one dollar in taxes. The money comes out of a general tax fund we all pay into. I recommend that you check "yes" in these boxes if you intend to elect to claim the Credit for Contribution to Candidates for Public Office on line 38 on page 2 of the Form 1040. This tax credit lowers your taxes directly by a maximum of fifty dollars if you are single or married, filing separately, or one hundred dollars if you are married, filing jointly. In other words, if you have contributed to a candidate for public office, you can deduct one-half of that amount as a direct tax credit. Incidentally, this tax credit is allowed even if you can't itemize, and even if you just use the Form 1040A. It is a nice little tax write-off, and if possible, use it. To be consistent, you should also check the boxes marked "yes" for the Presidential Election Campaign Fund. Then you are telling the IRS that, by contributing directly to a candidate for public office, you are a politically involved person, and by checking the one dollar amount for the Presidential Fund, you are showing a consistency throughout your tax return.

FILING STATUS

You are given a choice of five categories on lines 1 through 5 in determining your filing status. You can choose only one. The status you select will determine the tax rate that will apply in computing your tax.

Although you are placed in one category for the entire taxable year, each category is based on your status as of December 31st of that tax year. We will discuss each category and its respective hows, whys, advantages, and disadvantages.

1. Single. This status should be checked if you are not married, as of the end of the year, or are legally separated or divorced. Even if you and your spouse lived apart for the entire year, unless a decree of legal separation or divorce has been granted according to the law of your state, you cannot file as single. Many couples do not realize this and, even though they are technically married, file as two single persons. Generally, though, the IRS is not aware of this kind of personal information, and there is a very small chance of such returns being audited, as both tax returns show consistency.

If you have had a dependent relative living in your household for most of the year, you may be able to qualify for the head of household category, which is discussed below. If you do have someone living with you as your dependent, but that person is not a blood relative, then you must file as a single taxpayer. You can, however, claim that person as a dependent if he or she meets all of the qualifications for dependency. These qualifications are also discussed below.

There are basically two advantages to filing as a single taxpayer. One appears where both the husband and the wife earn a fairly high income. In that case, even with the new tax deduction that becomes effective in 1982 for married couples who both work, it is better to be divorced and for each ex-spouse to file as a single taxpayer. Always remember that the tax rates are progressive--that is, the higher your taxable income, the higher the percentage, or rate, on it will be. Therefore, when you and your spouse are working, and you file a married return (married filing a joint return or married filing separate returns), you will pay more taxes than if you are not married.

A second advantage of filing as a single taxpayer involves persons who are self-employed and their chances of being selected for audit. If your filing status is single, if you have no dependents, and if your taxable income is very low, you will have a smaller chance of being audited. In other words, the IRS doesn't expect a single person to need as much income as people with dependents and married couples. Many young people who are self-employed and single are really afraid when it comes to doing their tax returns. Their businesses may have made very little net profit and they are afraid that the IRS will not believe this. But actually, their chances of being audited are greatly reduced when their filing status is single and they have no dependents.

2. Married Filing Joint Return. This filing status should be checked if, as of December 31st, you were legally married. In the states that recognize common law marriage, the IRS will accept such a status as well. When you are married, there are two choices as to your filing status: married filing jointly, or married filing separately. It is entirely up to you to decide whether to file a joint or a separate tax return. It goes without saying that you should choose the status that will result in the lowest total tax for both spouses. When you file a joint return, you and your spouse combine everything. That means all of the income, all of the deductions, all of the credits, etc. In essence, you are doing one tax return for two people.

The main advantage in filing a joint return is enjoyed where one spouse doesn't work, or has very little income. That spouse, in effect, helps the spouse with the higher income to pay lower taxes. A problem arises where both spouses have substantial incomes. In the past few years, in more and more households, both husband and wife are working full time. Although they are now making more money, they are also in much higher tax brackets and, therefore, are paying more in taxes to the government than they would if they were filing as single taxpayers. The additional tax is known as the "marriage tax penalty." Because of this penalty, some couples have gotten divorced solely for tax reasons.

As of January 1, 1982, there will be a special deduction applicable to two-earner married couples, or couples where both husband and wife are working and filing joint returns. (Note that this does not apply to the returns you file for the 1981 taxable year.) This deduction will be calculated by taking five per cent of the amount of qualified income of the spouse with the lower income, up to a $1,500 maximum deduction. It is essential for every married couple to understand this new provision of the tax law and to take advantage of it.

Beginning in 1983, the deduction will be raised to ten percent of the amount of qualified earned income of the spouse with the lower income, up to a $3,000 maximum deduction. "Qualified earned income" excludes many items of income, such as pensions, annuities, wages earned in the employ of the spouse, and unemployment compensation. Thus, a couple in which one or both spouses are retired probably will not benefit from the new deduction.

3. Married Filing Separate Return. This filing status may be selected if you are married but you elect not to file a joint return. Here, you separate all of your income and deductions from those of your spouse. You must file two separate returns, one for each spouse. We have already discussed how to complete the headings of each Form 1040. The status of married filing separate returns will save money if both the husband and wife have considerable income and the income is about the same for each. If, for example, the husband makes $14,000 in wages and the wife $17,500, you should try doing first a joint return and then two separate ones to compare the amounts of tax figured each way.

The status of married filing separately may lower your overall taxes by allowing the spouse in the higher tax bracket to claim more deductions. In other words, the number of exemptions and some of the itemized deductions can be allocated to either the wife or the husband. For example, say you and your spouse have three children. You can give all of the exemptions for the children, or two of the exemptions, to the spouse with the higher taxable income. Since that spouse will be in a higher tax bracket, he or she will get a greater tax savings for each exemption.

In the case of large medical and dental expenses, there is generally an advantage to the status of married filing separately because of the limitations on the amount that may be deducted. Generally, as will be more fully explained in Chapter 13 below, you may deduct only the portion of your medical and dental expenses that is more than three percent of your adjusted gross income. When you file jointly, and both spouses have income, that three percent figure will be higher than when filing separately. Therefore, if you have a lot of medical deductions and can give most or all of them to one of the spouses, the one with the lower income, when he or she deducts the three percent figure, he or she will be left with a larger allowable deduction.

The disadvantages of the status of married filing separate returns are twofold. First, either both spouses have to itemize deductions, or both have to take the standard deduction. One spouse cannot itemize deductions while the other takes the standard deduction. This can really hurt your overall tax position if there are not enough deductions for both of you. Unless you are well over the minimum amount necessary to itemize deductions, so that you can allocate a large amount of these deductions to either the husband's or the wife's returns, you may lose money. A second disadvantage may arise where the Tax Credit for Child and Dependent Care Expenses is involved. You cannot take that tax credit if your status is married filing separate returns. You must file a joint return.

In the community property states, Arizona, California, Idaho, Louisiana, Nevada, New Mexico, Texas and Washington, the status of married filing separate returns has a different wrinkle. Since by law in these states all income and expenses of a married couple are legally considered to be shared equally, there generally is no advantage to filing separate returns.

There are other advantages and disadvantages to the status of married filing separate returns in specific cases. To determine which status is better in your case, you should figure your tax under each status and file under the one in which you pay less to the government. The difference in tax savings should repay you for the extra time spent.

4. Head of Household. The filing status of head of household has a distinct advantage over the filing status single for an unmarried person. To qualify for the status of head of household the following conditions must be met:

• You have to be unmarried at the end of the tax year, or legally separated, or you must not have lived with your spouse for the entire year. If you have not lived with your spouse for the entire year, in order to qualify for the status of head of household, a child or children must have lived with you in your household for the entire year, but not necessarily as your dependent.

• You must have maintained a household, you must have contributed over one-half of the costs of maintaining this household, and your household must have been the main residence of at least one relative for the entire year. The costs of maintaining the household include rent, mortgage interest, taxes, upkeep, and repairs. In other words, you maintain your own house and a relative must have lived in it for the entire year. There is an exception if the relative is your mother or father who qualifies you as a head of household. Parents must be considered your dependents, but they do not have to live in the same household for the year. A rest home or home for the aged is acceptable, or for that matter any other home for which you pay more than half the cost of maintaining.

• If it is your unmarried child, grandchild, foster child, or stepchild that qualifies you as a head of household, that person does not need to be your dependent. In other words, as long as that child is living in your household, even if your ex-spouse is claiming him or her as a dependent, you can still qualify for the head of household filing status. Any other relative must also qualify as your dependent. If a person lives with you who is not a relative, but is still your dependent, you have to file as a single taxpayer, and cannot claim the status of head of household.

Many single taxpayers consider themselves to be the head of a household, just because they're by themselves and maintain their own house. This is incorrect for purposes of determining filing status. In fact, thousands of people wrongly select this filing status each year. It's interesting to note here that many of these people get away with it, but some get caught. In such cases, the IRS computer often simply redoes the tax return and sends a letter of explanation.

The advantage of filing as a head of household is simple. The tax rate is lower than for the status of single. Also, as a head of household, with children that qualify you for the status, if your income is lower than $10,000 you may also qualify for the Earned Income Credit and be able to get additional money from the government. This credit is discussed later in Chapter 15.

5. *Qualifying Widow[er] With Dependent Child.* In the year that your spouse passes away you can choose the status of married filing joint return, but for the next two years after that, if you have dependent children living at home or as full-time students, you may be able to choose the status of qualifying widow(er) with dependent child. Write in the year your spouse died in the space for it on line 5, and when you figure your tax, use Tax Table B or Tax Rate Schedule Y, the same as for the status of married filing joint return, rather than the table or schedule for the status of single. The advantage of this filing status is, again, a lower tax rate, but remember, you have to have one or more dependent children to qualify.

A further point about filing status should be made here. The key, as in many other areas of return preparation, is consistency. If you claim the status of head of household on your tax return, and your ex-spouse does the same, using the same child to qualify, then both of you may be audited. Remember, that whatever you put down on your tax return, there should be nothing else, and no other tax return, to contradict it. The IRS may not know who does or does not live in your household or for how long, but if there are inconsistencies in your return and with other present and past returns, they may decide to audit you in order to find out the truth. In order to prevent this, be prepared and be consistent.

Here are two simple illustrations of how the filing status operates:

John earns $20,000, claims no deductions, and has no other income. Here is how his tax would be different under two tax filing statuses:

Single: $3,829

Head of household: $3,548

Joe earns $11,000 and Mary earns $9,000. Again, there are no deductions and no other income. They are not sure if they are really married or not (it seems the judge who married them might have been an impostor):

Married Filing Joint Return $2,739 tax

Married Filing Separate Return:

Joe's tax $1,619   Mary's tax $1,127

Total $2,746

Single:

Joe's tax $1,382   Mary's tax $972

Total $2,354

Well, let's hope the judge really was an impostor.

CHAPTER FIVE

☆

Exemptions

Exemptions are similar to tax deductions and are given for people and their special needs. They are based on specific qualifications for dependency, and for age and blindness. For each exemption you get a tax deduction of $1,000. This doesn't mean that you get back $1,000 more in refunds or pay $1,000 less in taxes, but, rather your taxable income is lowered by that amount. Depending on the particular tax bracket you are in, you will save a corresponding amount in taxes. For example, if you are in the 35% tax bracket and have a tax deduction of $1.00, you save 35 cents. If you are in the 50% tax bracket, for every dollar deduction you claim, you save 50 cents. Therefore, if you are in the 35% tax bracket, for each exemption you can claim you save approximately $350 in taxes.

On *lines 6a and b* of the Form 1040, check the boxes that apply to you and your family. If you are filing a joint return, be sure to place an "X" or a check mark in boxes 6a, for yourself, and 6b, for your spouse. If your filing status is married filing separate return, then just check "yourself" in box 6a. Everyone is entitled to claim himself as an exemption; therefore, everyone should have box 6a checked. If either you or your spouse is over sixty-five as of December 31st of the taxable year, then check the "65 or over" box(es), and you'll gain one or two additional exemptions, which means, in effect, another $1,000 or $2,000 tax deduction. Remember, if your spouse died during the taxable year, you may still file a joint tax return and, therefore, you can check both "yourself" in line 6a and "spouse" in 6b.

A third set of boxes has to do with the extra exemption given for blindness. Again, it is based on the situation as of December 31st of the taxable year. If either you or your spouse is totally blind, or has 20-200 vision in the better eye even with corrective lenses, or if the widest diameter of the visual field is not greater than twenty degrees, then you can qualify for this exemption. Be sure to attach to your tax return a statement from your physician or optometrist describing the specific visual impairment involved. Once such a statement is filed with the IRS, you do not need to send another one for each year the same exemption is claimed.

Line 6c deals with dependent children who may live with you. A dependent child is one who is under nineteen, or one over nineteen who has income under $1,000 for the taxable year, or one who is a full-time student (meaning one who has attended school for at least *five months* out of the year, no matter how much income he or she has made). The term "child" applies also to stepchildren, adopted, and foster children. A grandchild who has lived with you all year may also qualify here.

In this category you cannot claim a partial exemption or credit. Thus, a child born December 31, 1981 is a full exemption for the entire taxable year (a "tax baby"), and a child born on January 1, 1982 cannot be claimed at all in 1981 (let's call him or her an "IRS baby"). You can claim a deduction for all of the medical expenses incurred during the pregnancy in 1981, but you cannot claim the child as an exemption until you do your 1982 tax returns. If a child dies during the year, a full exemption may be claimed for the entire year. Finally, write in line 6c the first names of all of the dependent children who have lived with you or are at school during the year.

OTHER DEPENDENTS

Line 6d deals with "other dependents," whether or not they are your relatives. This section can be very confusing and is a common source of error. In order to claim other dependents besides your spouse and children who live with you, certain criteria must be met. These are:

• The Support Test. You must have furnished more than half the dependent's total support for the year. This includes food, clothing, medical expenses, etc. If you are paying child support, and this amount is greater than one-half of the child's total support, then even if the child did not live with you at all during the tax year, you could claim him or her as a dependent. Often there may be a multiple support agreement in which several people support one dependent. For example, four children may share in supporting their elderly mother. None of the children is furnishing more than half of the total support, but only one child can claim the mother as a dependent. In this case, the children should reach an agreement among themselves to decide who can claim the mother as a dependent for tax purposes. Form 2120, the Multiple Support Declaration, should be filled out and signed by each child who will not claim the exemption and sent in along with the tax return of the child who will claim the exemption. This gives the right to claim the exemption to only one person, but each year a different child may claim the parent as a dependent, so long as new Forms 2120 are completed and filed. Remember that the taxpayer who has the higher taxable income is in a higher tax bracket and, therefore, gets a greater tax savings with each deduction. Thus, in the case of a multiple support agreement, it's usually best to give the exemption to the taxpayer who has the higher taxable income.

• The Gross Income Test. The dependent to be claimed must have less than $1,000 in reportable, gross income for the year. This figure does not include income that is tax-exempt, such as social security payments, health insurance proceeds, etc. Again, if the dependent is under nineteen years of age or is a full-time student, the gross income test doesn't apply.

• The Member of Household or Relationship Test. If a person lives with you for the entire year, excluding brief absences, he or she need not be a relative to qualify as a dependent. For example, in states that do not recognize common law marriage as a legal marriage, one of the partners who does not have the minimum $1,000 income may be claimed on line 6d as an "other dependent," instead of a "spouse."

• The Citizenship Test. Your dependent must be a United States citizen, resident, or national, or a resident of Canada for some part of the taxable year. Thus, foreign exchange students may not qualify as dependents.

• The Joint Return Test. If an "other" dependent is planning to file a joint return, then you cannot claim that person as a dependent. For example, say your daughter marries on December 31st, has income over the minimum necessary for filing a return, and even has lived with you through December 30. However, she will be filing a joint return with her husband, a return that treats her as married for the entire year. You therefore cannot claim her as a dependent on your tax return. If neither she nor her husband is required to file a tax return, however, you may then claim her as a dependent.

On *line 6d* fill in all the information required in each of the boxes for each of your other dependents. Write in their full names, their relationship to you (if not related, write in "none"), the number of months they have lived in your household, whether or not they had income of at least $1,000, and whether or not you provided more than one-half of their support. Note that on Form 1040 the IRS provides spaces for only two "other dependents." Some taxpayers mistakenly believe that, since there are only two spaces, they can claim only two other dependents. This is not so. If you have more than two other dependents, simply write in "see attached," and include with the return a separate sheet of paper showing all the information that the IRS requires. However, on line 6d, fill in the total number of other dependents in the box provided on the right-hand side. Now, add all of the numbers in the boxes to the right-hand side of the exemptions section. Put the total number of the exemptions claimed on *line 6e*. This number will be used multiplied by $1000 on line 33 of Form 1040 in order to arrive at your taxable income.

EXEMPTIONS, FILING STATUS AND TAX CONSCIOUSNESS

The main things to keep in mind when claiming exemptions are that you can prove that you legitimately may claim these people as exemptions that no one else will claim the same persons as an exemptions on a tax return for the same year. The IRS carefully watches for such errors, and when they are found, both you and the other taxpayer claiming the same exemption will be audited. You then must prove which of you is legally able to claim the exemption by having provided over one-half of the person's support.

The point is to be aware through a raised tax consciousness of the possibilities for claiming exemptions, and to work out among the parties concerned the one taxpayer who will be able to benefit the most from the exemption. Proper planning can be very advantageous. For example, when divorced parents both desire to claim their children, or when brothers and sisters all wish to claim dependent parents, the taxpayer with the most taxable income will gain the most in being able to claim additional exemptions. In the case of divorced parents, if one ex-spouse is not working and has no taxable income, then it is to the working ex-spouse's advantage to be able to claim the children as dependents. If the working ex-spouse is paying sufficient child support, perhaps he or she could claim the children as dependents by agreement with the non-working ex-spouse. As long as there are no contradictory claims, there will be no problem with the IRS.

When clients come to me who are recently divorced or about to be divorced, I always ask them first, "Are you still on speaking terms?" It is so much easier when ex-spouses are still communicating and can sit down and work out tax problems to their mutual advantage. Someone with very little or no taxable income will gain nothing by claiming an exemption for a child, but by allowing the taxpayer with the higher income to claim the exemption, a sizeable tax savings will result. An agreement to share the tax savings might be the answer. In this way, both taxpayers are winning.

The filing status of head of household also can be used to benefit two different parties. One ex-spouse can adopt the status of head of household while the other can claim the children as his or her dependents, using the filing status of single. In such a case, one ex-spouse is getting the benefit of the tax reduction that comes with the filing status of head of household, while the other is claiming $1,000 exemption for each of the children. Remember, when your own children live with you, you don't have to claim them as dependents. Your ex-spouse can claim them as dependents, but you can still benefit by using the head of household filing status. However, do not forget that the person who claims a child as a dependent must pay for more than one-half of the support for the child.

Where there is more than one dependent child, both parents may be able to claim the head of household filing status if each claims a different child as his or her dependent. A few years ago, a divorced couple came to see me after having lost in an audit on the question of head of household filing status. They had two children and had made an agreement whereby each child lived with each parent alternately for a period of one year. They would exchange the children in September of each year. On their subsequent tax returns, each then claimed the head of household filing status. At the audit, the IRS stated that since each child did not live with each parent for an entire year, the parents could not qualify for the status of head of household. Since the parents lived in the same school district anyway, I advised them simply to change the date they traded the children from September to January 1st of each year. By doing that, each child then lived with each parent for an entire taxable year, and each parent was able to file in the status of head of household and, thus, save hundreds of dollars in taxes. This is another example of how, by understanding the tax system, and by developing your tax consciousness, you can save a great deal of money.

A word of caution should be given here about filing under the head of household status. When a man files under that status and dependent children live with him for the entire year, he faces a greater chance of being selected for a tax audit by the IRS. Be sure that you have all the necessary documentation to support the status, such as a statement by your ex-spouse acknowledging the status, and always be prepared to prove your entitlement to the status of head of household.

In conclusion, there are two things to remember when dealing with filing status and number of exemptions. They are: One, that the tax rate is progressive, and Two, that the taxable year for individuals almost always begins on January 1 and ends on December 31, the same as the calendar year. (A *fiscal* year, used by businesses and the Federal Government, may begin on the first of any month.) The progressive tax rate means that you should always try to give the most deductions to the taxpayer with the higher taxable income. If you are married and filing separate returns, the spouse with the higher taxable income should get the greater deductions, and, if possible, the larger number of exemptions.

As for the taxable year, if you are planning to be married, or are contemplating a divorce, you should remember your tax position in making these plans. Of course, I realize that there are many other reasons for getting married or divorced besides taxes. However, where both spouses have high taxable income, divorce will probably produce a tax benefit. If possible, you should try to arrange for a decree of divorce or legal separation to become final during the year of higher taxable income. Remember, though, it is unlawful to obtain a divorce only for tax purposes. How the IRS could prove wrongdoing, however, I have no idea, unless it were to become an annual ritual for a couple.

As for your marriage plans, you may want to wait until the next taxable year to tie the knot. I have a client, a physician, who was planning to marry another physician. This joining in wedlock, while possibly made in heaven, was also an IRS delight. Since they were planning to marry at the end of the year, I convinced them to wait until the following January. By doing so, they saved thousands of dollars in tax, at least for one taxable year.

PART III
DETERMINING YOUR GROSS INCOME

CHAPTER SIX

☆

Lines 7—10 of Form 1040

An income tax return is much like a financial statement. In essence, what you are doing when you file a tax return is balancing your tax books for the year. On one side is income from various sources; and on the other side are deductions or expenses. The difference between the two is the amount of your taxable income. You then compute your tax liability for the year, based on the amount of taxable income. You may then have to add to the tax, as computed, certain other taxes, or subtract from it any tax credits to which you are entitled. The difference between the amount you have paid in to the government during the taxable year and your total tax liability will determine "the bottom line." The amount on the bottom line will be either a refund or the balance due to the IRS. The point to be made here is to understand the different components that go into figuring the bottom line. If you can make changes to lower your taxable income, or add to your tax credits, then you will lower your tax liability. In this chapter we will discuss lines 7 through 21 of the Form 1040. We are going to calculate your "total income." As you'll see, this involves a lot more than just putting down your total wages.

Before we enter any money amounts, a few more words of explanation are necessary. First, there are some types of income that are not taxable and should not be reported on Form 1040. Some examples of non-taxable income are social security benefits, welfare payments or benefits received, life insurance proceeds, child support payments received, disability payments received, scholarships and grants, gifts, bequests, inheritances (the taxes on an inheritance have already been paid by an estate before you receive it), and accident and health insurance proceeds. Amounts of income from these sources that you have received during the year are not to be listed on your return. They can be used later on, however, when you itemize, on Schedule A, the general sales tax you have paid. You should add such amounts to your income to determine what your sales tax deduction should be for the year.

WAGE INCOME VERSUS SELF-EMPLOYMENT INCOME

The majority of Americans are wage earners. That means that most of us work for somebody else, are paid a salary, and have taxes taken out, or withheld, from our paychecks throughout the year. Whenever we receive a paycheck, the net, or take-home pay, is a lot lower than the gross. Because the law requires it, the employer has subtracted from our gross pay federal taxes, state taxes, social security taxes (called FICA), and, perhaps, several other things. After the taxable year is over, usually in late January or early February, we receive a W-2 statement from our employer. This statement tells us exactly how much in wages we were paid, and shows the total amounts of taxes that were withheld.

Some people are not paid on this basis. Instead, they are considered self-employed. They may own their own business, whether it is a sole proprietorship, a partnership, or a corporation, or they may have an arrangement with a company to pay them on a commission basis or as an independent contractor, which is different from a salary. At the end of the year, instead of receiving a W-2 statement, these people receive a Form

1099. This form will tell them only the gross amount of money they were paid by a company during the year.

There is a tremendous tax advantage to being self-employed, because tax is not withheld from each paycheck. People who are self-employed pay lower taxes than wage earners because self-employed people pay taxes on only the net profit of a business, that is, all the income minus all the expenses. Wage earners, on the other hand, pay tax on the gross, or total, amount of income they receive. The tax system is also set up to allow the self-employed person to claim many more deductions for business-related expenses. We will go into the specific advantages of being self-employed when we discuss Schedule C in Chapter 7 below.

The point is that wage earners pay the greatest amount of taxes. In this class-based system, they are at the bottom. However, there are many wage earners who can become self-employed. There are two ways of doing this.

One way is to quit your job and set up your own business. While this may seem like a drastic step, in the long run it may be the most important and best step you ever take. As long as you work for someone else, you'll never really win on your income taxes. Having your own business is both risky and nerve-racking, but if you are interested in making a lot of money, it's the only way to go.

A second way of becoming self-employed involves keeping your present position, but changing your job status. In certain situations you may be able to work out something with your present employer to change your job status from that of a wage earner to that of an independent contractor. For example, I had a client who worked for a cable television company and was paid on a W-2, salaried basis. He went to the management of his company, and they agreed to change his status to that of a 1099, self-employed, independent contractor. He was paid exactly the same total amount but no taxes were taken out. He was then considered self-employed. instead of paying taxes on his gross wages, he set up his own business, and his tax was based on his net profit. He was also able to write off many, many more expenses as business expenses. This change enabled him to save a few thousand dollars in tax each year.

Another example of a wage earner becoming self-employed was a lawyer who worked for a construction company. He got the company to agree to pay him on a commission basis, per job. Again, since he was considered self-employed, he was able to benefit greatly on his taxes. If a change of status is possible for you, you really should look into it. Consult your employer to see if it can be done.

WAGES, SALARIES, AND TIPS

There are five copies of every W-2 statement. Your employer keeps one, and you receive three copies, two to be filed with your federal, state, or city tax returns, and one to keep for your own records. The fifth copy (copy D) goes directly from your employer to the IRS. Thus, when your tax return is filed, the IRS supposedly already has a copy of all of your and your spouse's W-2 statements. It is important for all taxpayers to realize this. Some people seem to think that if they've made less than a certain amount of money, the IRS doesn't know about it, and they won't have to include it on their tax returns. This is not true. The IRS gets information from all of your employers about all of your wage and salary income. It is therefore essential to put down the total of the amounts that all of your various W-2 statements contain.

If, however, you lose your W-2 or don't receive it in time to file your tax return, you can file a substitute W-2 statement. There is a form available from the IRS for this purpose, or you can make one up using a blank piece of paper and signing it to verify it. Be certain, of course, that the exact figures of income and taxes withheld are stated. Every company by law must furnish you a W-2 statement and keep exact records of wages paid and amounts withheld. Before doing your tax return you need to know these exact amounts of wages paid and taxes withheld. If necessary, you can also calculate these amounts by adding up all your wage stubs. I would advise you not to begin to do your tax return until you have gathered all of your W-2 forms or all of the necessary wage and tax information you need.

Now let's look at the W-2 statement itself. The first thing to notice is the social security number. Be sure that it is correct. This will determine whose W-2 it is and who gets credit for the amount of tax withheld. Remember, all tax information is based on social security numbers. In box number nine of the W-2 form you will find the amount of federal tax withheld. This is the total amount that has been taken out of your paychecks and sent to the federal government to pay your federal tax liabilities.

Box number ten, entitled "wages, tips and other compensation," contains the gross amount of money the company has paid you for the year.

Box number eleven, entitled "FICA employee tax withheld," is the amount that was paid in to the social security system by yourself and your employer. There is a limit to the amount that is paid in for each year. For 1981 the limit is $1,975.05 for each taxpayer. Each year the limit is raised. You should look up the maximum amount for each taxable year. The information can be found in the instructions for line 59 of Form 1040 in the Federal Income Tax Forms booklet. Be aware that any amount over that limit is refundable. Some companies, and even the Federal Government, do not pay into the social security system. Therefore, there will be no amounts for employees of such institutions in boxes three and four. I find it very interesting that people who work for the Social Security Administration do not pay into the fund. Federal employees have their own fund which is partly supported by our tax money.

Box number thirteen entitled "total FICA wages" contains the total amount of wages used as the base for the amount of social security taxes that were withheld. This total amount is also limited each year. For example, the limit in 1981 is $29,700 in wages.

The rest of the boxes on the W-2 statement deal with state and local taxes withheld, any state disability insurance (SDI) amounts withheld, and, on some W-2's, amounts paid for union dues. All of these amounts are deductible on Schedule A of your federal tax return, so be very aware of them.

Now that we understand what the amounts on the W-2 mean, let's see what we should do with them. First, gather all your W-2 statements. If you are married and filing a joint return, gather all of your spouse's statements as well. In some cases there may be several of them, depending on how many employers you and your spouse have had during the year. Now, on a sheet of paper make four columns. The columns should be: 1-wages; 2-federal withheld; 3-state withheld; 4-FICA withheld. List all of the amounts in each of the separate columns and total them.

The total amount in the wages column goes onto line 7 of the Form 1040. If you are married, filing separate returns, each spouse's total wages goes on his or her individual 1040. The total amount of federal taxes withheld will then go onto line 55 on page 2 of the 1040. The total amount of state taxes withheld goes on the state tax return, which should be done right after you finish doing the federal tax return. (If you live in a state where there is no state income tax, smile and ignore the last sentence.)

The total amount of FICA taxes that were withheld should be looked at carefully. If you or your spouse had more than one employer and your combined wages were greater than the FICA limit for that year, then check the FICA column and see if more than the legal maximum of FICA taxes was taken out. Anything over that limit is refundable as a tax payment and will come back to you. Any amount that is over the limit is placed on line 59 on page 2 of Form 1040, entitled "excess FICA and RRTA tax withheld." I strongly advise that you do your tax return in the exact method outlined here. By using this method you won't lose any excess taxes that were paid into the government, or any excess FICA contribution.

Remember, line 7 on Form 1040 is for W-2 wage and salary income only. Do not mistakenly put any other type of income there. If you have been paid on a commission basis or as an independent contractor, you are self-employed, and that income is reported on Schedule C and on line 11 of Form 1040. It does *not* go onto line 7 of the 1040. Taxpayers who put self-employed income on line 7 lose the benefits of being self-employed.

INTEREST INCOME

Many people confuse interest income with the interest expenses that they have paid out during the year. The two are completely different and should *never* be combined. Interest income is money that you receive. Interest expenses are monies that are paid out and reported as itemized deductions on Schedule A. Interest income is taxable and must be declared on line 8a of Form 1040. It includes interest that is earned on bank and savings & loan accounts, and interest on credit union accounts. Sometimes credit unions call these amounts "dividends," but they are really interest income and must be reported as such. Also included is interest earned from tax refunds, from bonds after the bonds have been cashed in, and from loans or personal notes that you may hold, including interest that is being paid to you by a relative or another person, interest from an installment sale, or interest on a mortgage that you are holding. Be sure to gather all the total interest amounts from each and every source.

For the 1981 taxable year you can exclude, and thus not pay taxes on, the first $200, or $400 if filing a joint return, of interest and dividend income. For the first time in history the government is giving a small tax break to people who earn interest income. Also, there is a new provision, effective October 1, 1981, that allows people to exclude up to $1,000, or $2,000 on a joint return, of interest income from a special bank account known as a "tax-exempt savings certificate," otherwise called an "All-Savers Certificate." If you ordinarily keep several thousand dollars in savings, or if you are in at least the 25% tax bracket, you should ask your banker to explain the tax-exempt savings certificate to you. Every possible tax break should be explored, and this one will be available only for a short time.

There are some other types of interest income that are tax-exempt, or non-taxable. A surviving spouse who is a beneficiary of a life insurance policy and who elects to receive the proceeds in installments can exclude up to $1,000 in interest earned per year. Also, interest paid on certain state, local, and municipal bonds is tax-exempt, as is certain tax-exempt interest from mutual funds.

On line 8a of Form 1040, put in the total of all interest income received during the year. If the total is under $200, or $400 if you are filing jointly, and if you have no dividend income, on line 8c put the total amount of interest income. Then, on line 8d, put in either $200 or $400, depending on your filing status, and on line 8e, put "0." If the total is over $400, then you'll have to fill out Schedule B, which is found on the back of Schedule A. Part I of Schedule B, on the left-hand side, is where you record the name of each source of interest income and the amount received. You may have many different sources. List each one, each amount, and then total the amounts. The total amount of interest income is recorded on line 2 of Schedule B, and this amount is also put on line 8a of Form 1040.

If you have received interest income in 1981 from an All-Savers Certificate, you must fill out line 1c on Schedule B, even if the interest income is under $400. Simply list each All-Savers Certificate payer and the amounts received.

Then, on line 1e of Schedule B, put in your exclusion, a non-taxable amount. That exclusion is up to $1,000 for single taxpayers or married persons filing separate returns, or $2,000 for married couples filing joint returns. Subtract line 1e from line 1d, and put the remainder, if any, on line 1f.

If you received more than $400 in interest or dividend income during the taxable year, you are required to answer questions 9 and 10 in Part III of Schedule B.

A mistake some people make in reporting interest income is to leave out some or all of it. Remember that the IRS gets an exact record from banks and all other payers of all the interest that you've received. It is a foolish mistake to try to hide interest income. In fact, it is one of the main ways to trigger a tax audit. If the IRS learns that you have failed to report interest income, they may suspect that it could be productive to audit several areas of your tax return.

YOUR BEST INTERESTS

The interest rate that you actually receive from savings accounts or other investments can be very deceiving. For example, let's say that you have $10,000 in a money market account that is paying 16% interest. If you are in a 50% tax bracket and filing a joint tax return, you'll actually earn a lot less than 16% interest. You would earn $1,600 in interest income, but $700 of that money is going to go to the government. Of the $1,600 of interest earned, the first $400 will be excludable from income. The remainder, $1,200, is fully taxable, and, in the 50% tax bracket, that means that $600 will be paid in taxes. Here, you are not earning 16% interest, but actually only 9% interest. Depending on each taxpayer's tax bracket for the year, the actual rate of interest earned will vary.

In the case of someone in a high tax bracket, it may pay to put money in municipal bonds that are tax-exempt, or in the new tax-exempt savings certificates from which you can exclude up to $1,000 or $2,000 of interest earned. These accounts, as this book is being written, are paying approximately 11% interest, but as we've seen, someone in a higher tax bracket will end up with more money left over after taxes are paid.

On the other hand, taxpayers in lower tax brackets, such as people who are retired, would benefit the most by putting their money where they can earn the highest possible interest. Using the same example as above, but with a 20% bracket instead of a 50% bracket, the result is much different. In that case only $240 would go to the government, and the taxpayer would in fact earn over 13% interest.

For years the wealthy have been able to avoid paying taxes on interest income by setting up trusts and putting accounts in their children's names and social security numbers. As we have seen, a dependent child can earn up to $1,000 in interest without having to pay taxes on it, or even having to file a tax return. By setting up trusts, the interest income can be distributed to taxpayers who have lower taxable incomes. The higher the taxable income, the higher the tax bracket and the percentage of

Schedules A&B (Form 1040) 1981 **Schedule B—Interest and Dividend Income** OMB No. 1545-0074 Page **2**

Name(s) as shown on Form 1040 (Do not enter name and social security number if shown on other side) | Your social security number

Part I — Interest Income

If you received more than $400 in interest or you received any interest from an All-Savers Certificate, you must complete Part I and list ALL interest received. Also complete Part III if you received more than $400 in interest. See page 8 of the Instructions to find out what interest to report. Then answer the questions in Part III, below. If you received interest as a nominee for another, or you received or paid accrued interest on securities transferred between interest payment dates, please see page 20 of the Instructions.

Name of payer	Amount

1a Interest income (other than qualifying interest from All-Savers Certificates).

1b Total. Add above amounts .....
1c Qualifying interest from All-Savers Certificates. (List payers and amounts even if $400 or less.) See page 20 of Instructions.

1d Total. ......
1e Exclusion (See page 20 of Instructions).
1f Subtract line 1e from line 1d.
   Caution: *No part of the amount on line 1f may be excluded on Form 1040, line 8d .*
2 Total interest income (add lines 1b and 1f). Enter here and on Form 1040, line 8a ....

Part II — Dividend Income

If you received more than $400 in gross dividends (including capital gain distributions) and other distributions on stock, complete Part II and Part III. Please see page 9 of the Instructions. Then answer the questions in Part III, below. If you received dividends as a nominee for another, please see page 21 of the Instructions.

Name of payer	Amount

3

4 Total. Add above amounts ......
5 Capital gain distributions. Enter here and on line 13, Schedule D. See Note below ...
6 Nontaxable distributions (See Instructions for adjustment to basis)
7 Total (add lines 5 and 6) ......
8 Total dividend income (subtract line 7 from line 4). Enter here and on Form 1040, line 8b ....

Note: *If you received capital gain distributions for the year and you do not need Schedule D to report any other gains or losses or to compute the alternative tax, do not file that schedule. Instead, enter 40% of your capital gain distributions on Form 1040, line 13.*

B

Part III — Foreign Accounts and Foreign Trusts

If you received more than $400 of interest or dividends, OR if you had a foreign account or were a grantor of, or a transferor to, a foreign trust, you must answer both questions in Part III. Please see page 21 of the Instructions.

	Yes	No
9 At any time during the tax year, did you have an interest in or a signature or other authority over a bank account, securities account, or other financial account in a foreign country?		
10 Were you the grantor of, or transferor to, a foreign trust which existed during the current tax year, whether or not you have any beneficial interest in it? .... If "Yes," you may have to file Forms 3520, 3520–A, or 926.		

For Paperwork Reduction Act Notice, see Form 1040 Instructions.   343-059-1

income that must be paid to Uncle Sam.

One last point about interest income should be stressed. I think it's absolutely essential that we put our money to work for us. After all, we work very hard for it, and it's about time it started working for us. Before you put your money in savings accounts, Treasury Bills, money market funds, etc., determine what your actual return on investment is going to be. If that return is lower than the rate of inflation, then, in fact, you are losing money. I have told clients that it would be better to go out and buy a $500 oil drum and fill it up with gasoline today than to take their money and put it into a bank savings account.

The way our system works, most people work for their money and relatively few have their money work for them. Let's look at what these few are doing and follow their example. High interest rates can be very misleading, as we have seen, and with today's inflation rate it may be better in the long run to put your money into other investments. Alternative investments include real estate, antiques, rare coins, gold, silver, and precious stones. Throughout the book we will be discussing the advantages and disadvantages of each of these types of investments.

DIVIDENDS

On *line 8b* of Form 1040, you record the total amount of dividends received. Dividends are money that you receive out of the earnings and profits of a corporation in which you own stock. You are sent a Form 1099-DIV from the corporation or from your stockbroker at tax time. If the total amount of dividends plus the total amount of interest received on line 8a is under $400, put that figure in line 8c. *Line 8d* is explained above in the discussion of how to report interest.

Be careful with dividend amounts. The dividends on certain stocks are not taxable, or only partially taxable, and there are other kinds of dividends that can be treated as income from capital gains which are only 40% taxable. It is essential here to check carefully each dividend, and to call the corporation or your stockbroker, if necessary, in order to find out exactly what is taxable, and how much, and how it is to be reported on your tax return. This should be done before you prepare your tax return. In fact, it should be done before the tax season. Don't wait until the last moment to get this information.

For the 1981 taxable year only, the dividend exclusion, i.e., the amount that is not taxable, has been doubled and has been combined with the new interest exclusion. For single taxpayers, the first $200 of interest and dividend income is not taxable, and for married persons filing joint returns, the first $400 of interest and dividends received is excludable, regardless of which spouse received the income. Also, if you reinvest the dividends on certain utility stocks, the first $750, or $1,500 on a joint return, is excludable.

If the total amount of dividends and interest received by a married couple filing a joint return is more than $400, then you must fill out Schedule B, Part II, on the right-hand side of page 2 of the form under the heading "Dividend Income." On the spaces provided under *line 3*, list the source of each dividend, such as AT&T, General Motors, etc., and the amount of dividends paid by each source. Then add all the amounts and put that total on *line 4*. *Lines 5 and 6* on Schedule B have to do with capital gain distributions and non-taxable distributions. As we have already mentioned, information about such special distributions is obtained from the 1099-DIV statement furnished by the corporation or your stockbroker. Put down the total of all capital gains distributions on line 5. The amount of capital gains distributions is only 40% taxable, and either goes directly onto line 14 on page 1 of Form 1040, or is reported on Schedule D, Capital Gains and Losses.

Line 6 on Schedule B is for non-taxable distributions, i.e., dividends that are considered not taxable. Since the gross amounts of dividend income appear on the spaces below line 3, the total amount of non-taxable distributions must be entered on line 6. It is very important to determine which of your dividends are non-taxable before you fill out Schedule B. For example, a few years ago all dividends received by shareholders of the Pacific Gas & Electric Company were non-taxable. It would be a foolish waste of money to pay tax on such dividends, but many people make the mistake of doing so. Remember, the IRS will not point out this kind of error.

On *Line 7* of Schedule B, add lines 5 and 6 and subtract that total from line 4. The remainder is the total amount of dividends before exclusion. Put that total on line 8b on page 1 of Form 1040. Line 8d is for the amount of the interest and dividend exclusion to which you are entitled, up to $200 for single people and up to $400 for a married couple filing a joint return. Line 8e on Form 1040 is the difference, the taxable amount of interest and dividend income.

REFUNDS OF STATE AND LOCAL INCOME TAXES

Line 9 of Form 1040 is irritating to many people, with good reason. You are asked to put down the amount of money you received as a refund from your state or city tax return of the previous year. This applies *only* if you itemized deductions on Schedule A to your federal tax return the previous year and used the gross amount of state or local income taxes that were withheld as a federal tax deduction. If you did so, then any amount you may have received as a refund of such state or local income taxes for the previous year must be declared on line 9 as taxable income. This sounds terrible but, since the IRS allowed you to deduct the gross amount of state or local taxes that was withheld last year, they are really only asking you to pay tax this year on the difference between what you deducted from federal taxes last year, and what you actually paid in tax to the state or city.

It is possible to use this provision to your advantage. For example, if this year's taxable income is going to be much greater than next year's, you could send in a large amount of estimated taxes to the state. This amount would then be deductible on your federal tax return, and since this year you will be in a higher tax bracket, a larger deduction will save you a greater percentage of taxes. Then, next year, you will have to declare and pay tax on the refund you received from the state; but since your taxable income will be lower, you will be in a lower tax bracket. The result, therefore, will be that you pay less federal income taxes overall.

ALIMONY RECEIVED

All alimony that you *receive* during the tax year is to be declared on *line 10* of Form 1040. *Child support* is not taxable and therefore does not have to be reported. When you are divorced, your property settlement agreement or support agreement should clearly state whether amounts paid by one ex-spouse to the other are to be treated for income tax purposes as alimony or child support. This is one of the stickiest points in negotiating settlements because alimony payments may be deducted by the ex-spouse who pays them, but child support payments may not be deducted. Assuming the ex-spouse who is ordered to make payments of either kind is in the higher tax bracket, a tax savings would result from agreeing to classify all or most of such payments as *alimony*, so that they may be deducted from the larger taxable income. The ex-spouse who receives alimony must pay tax on it but, presumably, is in a lower tax bracket to begin with. There are, of course, vital non-tax considerations in these matters, and a lawyer should be consulted before a change in classification of support payments is made.

CHAPTER SEVEN

☆

Profit or Loss from a Business or Profession

HOW AND WHEN TO USE SCHEDULE C

Schedule C is the form used for declaring a profit or loss from a business or profession. It can be used by sole proprietors, or one-person enterprises, only. If you are involved in a partnership, joint venture, etc. you cannot use Schedule C. Instead, Form 1065 is to be filed by the partnership, and you must fill out Schedule E, which is discussed in Chapter 10 below. Schedule C is used by self-employed people who have their own businesses, or who are paid commissions, or who are considered self-employed professionals or consultants. It is not to be used to report any W-2 wage or salary income.

For our purposes, there are two types people who should use Schedule C. The first type is the taxpayer whose main source of income is derived from self-employment, although he or she may also have some W-2 or other type of income. For these taxpayers, Schedule C is by far the most important part of their tax return. If you fall into this category, you must be well prepared. Your books and ledgers must be complete for the year, and by the time you are ready to file your tax return, you should have a very good understanding of your basic tax position. Throughout the year, at least once a month, you should go over the books to see how the business is doing and to project what your total profit or loss will be at the end of the year. Also, you probably will have been making quarterly estimated tax payments, along with quarterly state sales tax statements and payments, if applicable to your business. Even if you have a professional accountant or bookkeeper, you should be aware of how your business is doing. By the time you start to prepare your tax return, the taxable year in question is already over and it is too late to change things. Actually, you should be planning now for next year's tax return.

The second type of person who should use Schedule C is the taxpayer who has self-employed income as a secondary source. These are people whose spouses may be earning either W-2 or Schedule C income, or they may have salaried jobs as the main source of income, or they may only work part-time as self-employed individuals. There are many, many people who have self-employment income on the side. Some examples are teachers who tutor outside school, housewives who take care of children or do babysitting, people who sell various products on a commission basis as a secondary source of income, secretaries who do typing or research for extra income, nurses who practice after their hospital shifts are over, carpenters or mechanics who moonlight, people who sell firewood, do photography, raise worms, sell tropical fish, breed dogs or horses, etc.

Many people ignore or try to hide this type of income. There are two reasons why that may be a mistake. One is that it is illegal, and the IRS may come after you for not declaring it. If you sell something or perform a service for someone and he itemizes that expense on his own tax return, the IRS may audit him. Your name may come up, and the IRS agent could start an investigation into your own tax returns. The IRS believes very strongly that for every deduction claimed there should be a corresponding item of income declared.

The other reason for declaring all self-employment income is that it can actually improve your tax position. Most small businesses lose money in the first few years of operation. Your small, sideline operation can be used to claim a tax loss on Schedule C, and that will result in lower taxable income and a lower tax bracket. Also, if you are paid as a consultant or on a commission basis, you can greatly lower your *net* earnings by using Schedule C. For example, I had a client, a teacher, who also did consulting work on the side for the school district. He was paid on a commission basis for his consulting work, and the school district reported the total commissions paid on Form 1099. In years past, he had just taken the total amount from the Form 1099 and declared it on his Form 1040 under "other income." Therefore, he was paying taxes on the gross amount of his commissions. Besides being technically incorrect, he was paying way too much tax. When I prepared his return, I put that income on a Schedule C, set him up as a self-employed professional, which, in fact, he was, and then deducted *all* of the expenses he incurred in earning that income. After we finished, his net profit was much lower and, therefore, he paid a very small tax on that income.

Many people have small businesses on the side and, in fact, lose money each year. Because they don't understand the tax system, they don't realize that they can deduct business losses and, therefore, lower their taxable income. For example, if someone earns $20,000 a year and is in the 35% tax bracket, a business loss of $1,000 would in fact save that person $350 in income tax.

In conclusion, be aware of the benefits of the tax loss, and keep good records.

PLANNING FOR SELF-EMPLOYMENT INCOME

One problem with secondary sources of income reported on Schedule C is whether there is a legitimate business or profession, or just a personal hobby. "Hobbies" are for your personal pleasure and, therefore, expenses connected with them are not tax-deductible. It is essential that you can prove that it is a real business and not a hobby.

If possible, get a business license. Most states require licenses for almost every activity, but they are usually fairly easy to obtain. Get one if you can. The next thing to do is to advertize. Put an ad in the local paper, flea market, trading post paper, etc. Save the paper and cut out your ad for future reference. You can also have business cards and flyers printed, and you should keep some of them with your tax records. Be sure to include your telephone number on your ads and business cards so you can deduct telephone expenses on Schedule C. Also, you should open a business checking account and begin to set up business books or ledgers. The point here is to be professional, prepared at all times for any questions from the IRS, and totally thorough, in order to dispell any suspicion that your sideline is just a hobby. Whether you do tutoring, or raise worms or tropical fish, you are engaged in a legitimate business, and, therefore, all income must be reported and all business-related expenses must be deducted. The same principles apply to General Motors.

For each business or profession that you engage in, you need to fill out a separate Schedule C. If your spouse also earns any self-employment income, a separate Schedule C must be filled out for that business, as well. Nothing is wrong if there are two or more Schedules C included with your tax return.

THE HEADING OF SCHEDULE C

The main thing to remember in filling out Schedule C is that, legally, all expenses are deductible in earning, or *trying* to earn, self-employed income. *All* related expenses are deductible, even if you don't make a profit. This allows for a great deal of leeway, and can be used to save you a lot of tax money.

PROFIT OR LOSS FROM A BUSINESS OR PROFESSION 57

SCHEDULE C (Form 1040)
Department of the Treasury
Internal Revenue Service

Profit or (Loss) From Business or Profession
(Sole Proprietorship)
Partnerships, Joint Ventures, etc., Must File Form 1065.
▶ Attach to Form 1040 or Form 1041. ▶ See Instructions for Schedule C (Form 1040).

OMB. No. 1545-0074

1981

08

Name of proprietor | Social security number of proprietor

A Main business activity (see Instructions) ▶ _____ ; product ▶ _____
B Business name ▶ _____
C Employer identification number
D Business address (number and street) ▶ _____
   City, State and ZIP Code ▶
E Accounting method: (1) ☐ Cash   (2) ☐ Accrual   (3) ☐ Other (specify) ▶ _____
F Method(s) used to value closing inventory:
   (1) ☐ Cost   (2) ☐ Lower of cost or market   (3) ☐ Other (if other, attach explanation)   Yes | No
G Was there any major change in determining quantities, costs, or valuations between opening and closing inventory? . .
   If "Yes," attach explanation.
H Did you deduct expenses for an office in your home? . . . .

Part I   Income

1 a Gross receipts or sales **1a**
  b Returns and allowances **1b**
  c Balance (subtract line 1b from line 1a) **1c**
2 Cost of goods sold and/or operations (Schedule C–1, line 8) **2**
3 Gross profit (subtract line 2 from line 1c) **3**
4 a Windfall Profit Tax Credit or Refund received in 1981 (see Instructions) **4a**
  b Other income (attach schedule) **4b**

5 Total income (add lines 3, 4a, and 4b) . . . . ▶ **5**

Part II   Deductions

6 Advertising		29 a Wages . .	
7 Amortization		b Jobs credit	
8 Bad debts from sales or services .		c WIN credit	
9 Bank service charges		d Total credits	
10 Car and truck expenses		e Subtract line 29d from 29a .	
11 Commissions		30 Windfall Profit Tax withheld in 1981	
12 Depletion			
13 Depreciation (see Instructions) .		31 Other expenses (specify):	
14 Dues and publications		a	
15 Employee benefit programs . .		b	
16 Freight (not included on Schedule C–1) .		c	
17 Insurance		d	
18 Interest on business indebtedness		e	
19 Laundry and cleaning		f	
20 Legal and professional services .		g	
21 Office supplies and postage . . .		h	
22 Pension and profit-sharing plans .		i	
23 Rent on business property . . .		j	
24 Repairs		k	
25 Supplies (not included on Schedule C–1) .		l	
26 Taxes (do not include Windfall Profit Tax, see line 30)		m	
		n	
27 Travel and entertainment . . .		o	
28 Utilities and telephone		p	

32 Total deductions (add amounts in columns for lines 6 through 31p) . . . . ▶ **32**
33 Net profit or (loss) (subtract line 32 from line 5). If a profit, enter on Form 1040, line 11, and on Schedule SE, Part II, line 5a (or Form 1041, line 6). If a loss, go on to line 34 . . . . . **33**
34 If you have a loss, do you have amounts for which you are not "at risk" in this business (see Instructions)? . . ☐ Yes ☐ No
   If you checked "No," enter the loss on Form 1040, line 11, and on Schedule SE, Part II, line 5a (or Form 1041, line 6).

For Paperwork Reduction Act Notice, see Form 1040 Instructions.

Now, let's go over the form itself, line by line. At the top, write in the name of the proprietor, either yourself or your spouse. To the right, write in either your own or your spouse's social security number.

Line A. "Main business activity" means the type of work you did in earning the self-employed income. Examples would be sales, service, consultant, teacher, writer, etc. In other words, what is the general business activity? "Product," on the right half of line A, refers to what you sold or what you did. Examples of products would be hardware or record albums, or tutoring, or tax preparation. For a writer, the product would be books and publications.

Line B. For "business name," put in the name of your business, or at least your own name. Do not leave it blank.

Line C. "Employer I.D. number" is for businesses that employ people and have applied for and gotten an I.D. number, which is registered with the government. If you do not have one, just leave it blank. If you have completed the Form SS-4, but haven't yet received the number, write in "applied for."

Line D. Your "business address" is the place where you conduct your business. It can be a place that you rent, or one that you own. It can also be your home address, even if you are not deducting expenses for business use of your home. Again, do not leave this blank. If you do not conduct your business in any specific place, just put in your home address.

Line E asks you to check the appropriate box for the accounting method that you use in figuring your self-employment income and expenses on Schedule C. There are basically two types, the cash method and the accrual method. Under the cash method you deduct expenses when they are paid, and take in income when it is received. Under the accrual method, you record income when it is *earned,* even before it is received. Expenses are deducted when they are *payable,* even if they have not been paid. The cash basis of accounting is generally the easier method to use, although the accrual method must be used in most businesses that carry inventories. Consult a good book on small business bookkeeping or discuss the matter with an accountant before you determine which method is better for your business.

Line F asks you to check the appropriate box for the method of inventory valuation you use. Many small businesses do not carry inventories. If yours does not, just write in "N/A," not applicable. If you do have an inventory in your business, the simplest method of valuation is the cost method, specified by checking box number 1.

Line G. Again, if you do not carry an inventory of goods for sale, this question does not apply to you. The answer here should be no. If you do carry an inventory, its value at the end of last year should be the same amount as for the beginning of this year. If that is not the case, the IRS wants you to attach an explanation.

Line H. Deductibility of expenses of an office in the home has become a big controversy in the last few years. Recently, the IRS really tried to crack down on people claiming business use of their home. They virtually eliminated the deduction for wage earners. In the case of self-employed people, you can still deduct home office expenses, but be very careful. By checking "yes" on line H, I feel you are greatly increasing your chances of being audited. Be sure the part of your home you are claiming is: permanent; where you conduct all your business; and the place where money transactions occur. If you are going to deduct home office expenses, then you have to prorate the portions of your house that are personal and the portion that is used for business. For example, if you have a four-room house and you use one room for your business, then one-fourth of the expenses of the house would be your home office deduction.

If you own your own home, all mortgage interest and property taxes are already deductible as itemized deductions on your Schedule A. Therefore, you can deduct only the allowable portion of the amount of principal payments on a home loan as an expense of your home office. The problem is that, if you own your own house, almost all of your monthly mortgage payments, in the early years, go to interest, which is already tax deductible. You'll probably wind up with a very small deduction for home office expenses. Since the deduction will increase your chances of being audited, it may not be worth it.

If you are renting a personal residence, and you use part of it in your business, then you can deduct the applicable percentage of your total monthly rent as a business expense.

If you do have an office or workplace in your home, it may be advisable to try to separate the office physically from the rest of the house. For example, if you can create a separate entrance to the office with its own separate address, it would no longer be a home office, but a separate place of business. You would then be able to check "no" on line H, and to treat the expenses as if you conducted business at a separate address.

PART I OF SCHEDULE C—INCOME

Line 1a. "Gross receipts or sales" asks for the total amount of self-employment income that you took in during the taxable year, whether you sell products, or do tutoring, or are in a service business.

Line 1b. "Returns and allowances" is a subtraction from your gross receipts or sales for money that has been returned to clients or customers after those fees or sales were recorded. If gross receipts or sales on line 1a includes any amount that has been returned, then you would subtract the amount or amounts that you had to return here.

On *line 1c,* put in the amount of the difference between lines 1a and 1b.

Line 2. The "cost of goods sold and/or operations" refers primarily to retail sales businesses and manufacturing enterprises. If your business does not involve any sort of inventory, simply skip line 2 and go on. Generally, businesses that involve providing a service to the public do not have inventories, but businesses that involve selling a specific product do. The cost of goods sold determines the total expenses of the products that are then sold. The cost of goods is not part of the gross profit on a sale, and should be subtracted from gross receipts. In order to determine the cost of goods sold, you have to fill out Schedule C1, on page 2 of Schedule C. Let's now turn over Schedule C and look at Schedule C1.

Schedule C1, line 1. The "inventory at the beginning of the year" is as of January 1 of the taxable year. If you start a business during a taxable year, the amount here should be zero. For example, if you started a business in July, as of January 1 of that year, your inventory would have been zero.

Line 2a. "Purchases" refers to all of the items that you have purchased for your inventory during the year. For example, if you own a record shop, it would include all the records, 45s, 33s, and 78s, that you've purchased during the year.

Line 2b. Any inventory items that were taken for personal use must be subtracted from the total amount of purchases. Remember, it is very basic to tax law that anything spent for personal use is not deductible. However, everything spent for business use is tax-deductible. Thus, if you take home fifty of the records from your shop's inventory and keep them for your family's use, the cost of those records must be subtracted on line 2b.

Lines 3, 4 and 5 deal with other costs related to inventory. I generally try to avoid putting down any of these expenses here. It is usually better to deduct the costs of labor, materials and supplies under Part II on page 1 of Schedule C (discussed in detail below). If you do put down any amounts here, don't duplicate them on page 1, as you can't deduct any amount twice.

On *line 6,* simply add all the amounts on lines 1, 2c, 3, 4 and 5.

Line 7. "Inventory at end of year" is as of December 31 of the taxable year. If you've sold or closed your business during the year, then the amount on line 7 would be zero.

Schedule C (Form 1040) 1981 Page **2**

SCHEDULE C–1.—Cost of Goods Sold and/or Operations (See Schedule C Instructions for Part I, line 2)

1 Inventory at beginning of year (if different from last year's closing inventory, attach explanation) .	1	
2 a Purchases	2a	
b Cost of items withdrawn for personal use	2b	
c Balance (subtract line 2b from line 2a)	2c	
3 Cost of labor (do not include salary paid to yourself)	3	
4 Materials and supplies	4	
5 Other costs (attach schedule)	5	
6 Add lines 1, 2c, and 3 through 5	6	
7 Inventory at end of year	7	
8 Cost of goods sold and/or operations (subtract line 7 from line 6). Enter here and on Part I, line 2 . ▶	8	

SCHEDULE C–2.—Depreciation (See Schedule C Instructions for line 13)

Complete Schedule C–2 if you claim depreciation ONLY for assets placed in service before January 1, 1981. If you need more space, use Form 4562. If you claim a deduction for any assets placed in service after December 31, 1980, use Form 4562 to figure your total deduction for all assets; do NOT complete Schedule C–2.

Description of property (a)	Date acquired (b)	Cost or other basis (c)	Depreciation allowed or allowable in prior years (d)	Method of computing depreciation (e)	Life or rate (f)	Depreciation for this year (g)
1 Depreciation (see Instructions):						
2 Totals					**2**	
3 Depreciation claimed in Schedule C–1					**3**	
4 Balance (subtract line 3 from line 2). Enter here and on Part II, line 13 . . . . ▶					**4**	

SCHEDULE C–3.—Expense Account Information (See Schedule C Instructions for Schedule C–3)

Enter information for yourself and your five highest paid employees. In determining the five highest paid employees, add expense account allowances to the salaries and wages. However, you don't have to provide the information for any employee for whom the combined amount is less than $50,000, or for yourself if your expense account allowance plus line 33, page 1, is less than $50,000.

Name (a)	Expense account (b)	Salaries and wages (c)
Owner		
1		
2		
3		
4		
5		

Did you claim a deduction for expenses connected with:	Yes	No
A Entertainment facility (boat, resort, ranch, etc.)?		
B Living accommodations (except employees on business)?		
C Conventions or meetings you or your employees attended outside the North American area? (see Instructions) . .		
D Employees' families at conventions or meetings?		
If "Yes," were any of these conventions or meetings outside the North American area?		
E Vacations for employees or their families not reported on Form W–2?		

Line 8. The difference between the amount on line 6 and the amount on line 7 is the cost of goods sold or of operations. This amount is transferred to line 2 on page 1 of Schedule C, under Part I. Now let's return to page 1 of Schedule C.

Part I, line 3 Your "gross profit" is the difference between the cost of goods sold and your total income.

On *line 4a*, if you received any Windfall Profit Tax Credit or Refund, put in the amount received.

Line 4b, "Other income" refers to amounts related to your business or profession that have not been included on line 1 as gross receipts or sales. For example, if you own a bar that has a jukebox and, under line 1, you included all of the income from liquor sales, you could put the amount of income you received from the jukebox on line 4b, and then attach an explanation to the IRS. In some businesses it makes sense to separate one source of income from another. In others, it makes no difference.

I have a client who has an engineering consulting business. He also teaches engineering classes, and has written articles and pamphlets about engineering. On his tax returns, we put the income from the classes, articles, and pamphlets on line 4a and attach a schedule explaining them. The reason for doing this is that there are certain deductions he can take for his teaching and writing, and another type he can take for his consulting work. We want the IRS to be aware of the difference, and also to be alerted to the fact that he is going to take both types of deductions. Thus, even though all of these items of income are related to one specific business, we separate them in order to clarify the different deductions for the IRS.

Line 5 is for the total amount of income, which reached by adding lines 3, 4a, and 4b.

PART II OF SCHEDULE C—DEDUCTIONS

On *lines 6 through 31*, enter all of your various business-related deductions. The IRS provides a list of different categories for these deductions on Schedule C, but it may not be sufficient for your specific business or profession. It is important to classify all of your business expenses into specific categories. You should never lump different business expenses into a single category. Always remember that many low numbers look better than a few high ones. Also, never use the category "miscellaneous." On lines 31a through p you can put in all of the necessary additional categories you need. It's important to do this, and don't feel limited to the categories that the IRS offers.

Most of the categories listed in Part II are fairly self-explanatory, but some are more important than others and deserve going into in greater detail.

The first area is that of "transportation." There is no such category listed on Schedule C, so use the blank lines under line 31. I suggest that you do not use line 10, "car and truck expenses," or line 27, "travel and entertainment," to declare your transportation expenses. Those lines are frequent targets of tax audits. I also suggest that you separate local from out-of-town transportation expenses. Thus, under the category "other expenses," use one line for local transportation and another for out-of-town transportation. Local transportation refers to expenses incurred while driving around town during the working day. Out-of-town expenses would include overnight trips, air or train fares, car rentals, hotel, motel, and food costs.

There are two methods that can be used in determining the cost of local transportation, such as auto expenses. The first, and simplest, method is to figure the total mileage that you put on your car while on official business. You are allowed to deduct 20 cents per mile for the first 15,000 miles, and 11 cents per mile thereafter.

The other method of determining auto expenses involves the actual out-of-pocket costs of gas and oil, repairs, insurance, and maintenance, plus depreciation of the automobile. If you elect to use this method you need to keep exact records of the amounts you spend on all of these various expenses.

Therefore, it is essential that you maintain these records throughout the year, save receipts, and keep a diary or ledger in the car. Figure your expenses according to both of these methods, and use the one on Schedule C that will give you the greater deduction.

Under out-of-town transportation, put down all of your business-related travel expenses. Records are extremely important here. These expenses may include air fares, car rentals, seminar or convention costs, materials and supplies, meals and lodging, gratuities, etc. If part of a trip is devoted to personal pleasure, that amount is not deductible. You can deduct only the amounts that are directly related to your business or profession.

On a separate line under section 31, "other expenses," write in the total amount of tolls and parking expenses. This includes all bridge and tunnel tolls and parking fees, but not parking tickets.

There may be many types of "other" business expenses that relate specifically to the particular business you are engaged in. Examples are protective clothing, gifts, promotional expenses, and business luncheons.

Here's an example of how a business expense works. Say you buy a box of good cigars and then deduct that expense on Schedule C. If you are audited by the IRS, the auditor will ask you if you smoke cigars. If you answer "yes," then you probably will not be able to deduct the cigars. If you answer "no," then it appears more likely that you are using the cigars to help develop your business, and they then become tax-deductible. The same can hold true for tickets to baseball or football games, if you use them to entertain clients and to enhance your business. This is the type of business entertainment that large corporations have been deducting for many years, and the rest of us can take advantage of it as well.

Let's look at some of the other categories of deductions. Under "bad debts" on line 8, the IRS is referring to bum checks you've received, or clients who have reneged on obligations, or amounts of money you've lost because of non-payment of loans.

Line 12, "Depletion," refers to an allowance, or deduction, for taxpayers who own economic interests in mineral deposits, oil and gas wells, or standing timber. A certain percentage, usually about 20 to 25% of the total income you've received from such investments, is tax-deductible. This depletion amount goes on line 12 under Part II.

Under the category "telephone," on line 28, remember that you can deduct only business-related telephone expenses, not personal expenses. If you work out of your home, I suggest that you get a separate telephone number and use it for business only. In that way you can deduct all of the bills for that phone, and, in case of an audit, there would be no problem in showing the amount of telephone expenses that were business-related.

Under the category marked "taxes" on line 26, put down all all the sales taxes you've paid during the year and, if you own the building where your business is located, the property taxes that you've paid during the year.

Under "utilities" on line 28, if you work out of your house, put down only the amount of utilities expense that is related directly to your business. In other words, if one-fourth of your house is used for business, then you can put in one-fourth of the total utility bills that you paid during the year. It is a good idea to show the proration to the IRS, so on the dotted line next to the word utilities, write in "at 1/4."

Line 31. If you've hired help for your business, be sure to separate the amounts that you paid in wages, meaning W-2 wages, from commissions and contract labor. If you have salaried employees, then the amount you pay them is called wages. It is your duty to withhold quarterly federal, state, and local income taxes, and social security taxes from such wages. Put the total of these wages on line 31. If they are paid on a commission basis, they are considered self-employed, and if you have paid them more than $600, or the applicable minimum amount, during the year, you are required to send a Form 1099 to the IRS and furnish a copy to the independent contractor. If you've hired independent contractors, they are, in effect, subcontractors to you and your business. Write in the term "contract labor" on one of the lines under item number 31, "other expenses," and then put in the total amount that you paid them during the year.

DEPRECIATION

On *line 13,* under Part II of Schedule C, is the word "depreciation." This term seems to scare many taxpayers and to cause them a great deal of confusion. Therefore, we will discuss this deduction in detail.

The term "depreciation" means decreasing in value through deterioration. It applies to material or equipment that are used totally or partially for your business or profession and have a useful life of more than one year. Some things that you buy for your business last only for a year or less, such as pens, paper, small tools, clothing, etc. You can generally deduct the total amount of such items each year under Part II of Schedule C. Other items that you purchase will last longer than a year, such as automobiles, trucks, buildings, furniture, major tools, specialized equipment, etc. These items have a useful life in the business of more than one year, and, therefore, must be depreciated over a period of time. For example, if you purchase a camera for your photography business, it will last for more than one year, and you cannot deduct its total cost in the year you purchased it. In a sense, you have to prorate its cost over its useful life, over the period of years that it will be used for your business. That's called depreciating the camera. Let's say that the camera will last for five years before it has to be replaced. You would then depreciate it over a five-year period.

For items that are used only partially for your business or profession you can depreciate only the amount, a percentage of the total cost, that directly applies to the business use. For example, say you use your personal car for business travel. You must determine how much of the time the car is used for business and how much of the time it is used for personal purposes. If you determine that 60% of the time the car is used for business and the rest of the time it is used for personal purposes, then, on Schedule C, you can depreciate 60% of the car's cost over the vehicle's useful life. You cannot depreciate the other 40%.

Also, if you've just started a business during the taxable year, you have to prorate depreciation to reflect the fraction of the year the items were in use. If, for example, you started your business in September and transferred your personal car to business use at that time, you could only depreciate the car for September through December.

USING SCHEDULE C-2

Use Schedule C-2 on page 2 of Schedule C to report depreciation *only* if you do not claim a depreciation deduction for any assets placed in service after December 31, 1980. If you want to claim depreciation for items placed in service during 1981—and you almost certainly will—use Form 4562.

For depreciating items placed in service in 1981, see the discussion of accelerated cost recovery system, below.

Now let's look at Schedule C-2. The information asked for is the same as that requested on Part II of Form 4562.

Column (a) is fairly self-explanatory. Describe each of the properties that you are going to depreciate. For example, write in the name and model of each car and truck. In the case of photographic equipment, it's a good idea to put in the brand name and specify whether it's a lens or camera body, etc. Try to be as specific as possible.

Column (b) asks for the date on which you acquired each item. If you acquired the item before you started the business, put in the date that it was originally acquired. You can only depreciate an item during the years it is used in your business. You cannot depreciate it over any year occurring before the business began.

Column (c) asks for the total cost or other

basis of each item being depreciated. If you acquired it other than by purchase, for example as a gift or an inheritance, then put down the exact value of the item at the time you received it. For example, if you inherited a building that is now used as your store, determine its value at the exact time that ownership passed to you, and put that amount in Column (c).

Column (d). For "depreciation allowed or allowable in prior years," total all the amounts that you have deducted in prior years for each item. Remember that each item will eventually become depreciated out. You can't take more in total depreciation deductions on an item than its original cost. If you have never taken a depreciation deduction for a particular item in any previous year, put a zero in column (d). Certain items, such as automobiles, have a salvage value, which is the dollar amount that an item will be worth at the end of its useful life, or, in other words, when it has been completely depreciated. This amount, which you must determine, for property placed in service prior to 1981, cannot be depreciated. Salvage value is determined when you first acquire the property. For property that has a useful life of three years or more, you can substitute 10% of the cost of the item for the actual amount of salvage value, if the percentage amount is lower. Also, if you estimate that the salvage value is going to be less than 10% of the cost or adjusted basis of the property, then you don't have to subtract any amount for salvage value.

Colulmn (e). For items placed in service before January 1, 1981, there are several methods of computing depreciation. A detailed discussion of the finer points of these methods is beyond the scope of this book, so I suggest that you refer to a good manual on bookkeeping techniques in order to determine which method is best for you.

Remember, you should use ACRS depreciation methods, described in the next section of this chapter, for items placed in service January 1, 1981 or later.

The following paragraphs briefly describe the most commonly used depreciation methods for property placed in service *before* January 1, 1981.

The simplest and most commonly used method is called "straight-line depreciation." In this method, you simply divide the cost or other basis in Column (c) by the useful life in Column (f). In other words, if an item costs $5,000 and the useful life is five years, the allowable depreciation would be $1,000 per year. This method is called "straight-line" because, in each year the deduction will be the same amount. In effect, the basis of the item is reduced on a straight line.

There are other methods of depreciation, including forms of accelerated depreciation. One type of accelerated depreciation is "declining balance," or "d/b." For example, in 125% declining balance depreciation, you divide the cost of an item in Column (c) by the useful life in Column f, and multiply the quotient by 125%. That figure becomes the amount of the depreciation deduction for the current taxable year. The deduction will be higher in the first year than it would be using the straight line method. For the second year you must subtract the amount of depreciation taken for the first from the cost of the item in Column (c). That lower figure is again divided by the total useful life, and the quotient multiplied by 125%. The balance is declining, and, therefore, in the earlier years you are taking greater amounts of depreciation.

On new property purchased for your business, you can take the highest allowable form of accelerated depreciation, the double declining balance, or 200% declining balance, method. According to that method, you again divide the item's cost by its useful life, but you then multiply the quotient by 2. In other words, you are taking 200% of what the first year's deduction would be under the straight-line method of depreciation.

Another form of accelerated depreciation is called the sum of the years'-digits method. Under this method, you figure the depreciation of property by subtracting the salvage value from the cost, and multiplying the result by a different fraction each year. The denominator of the fraction always remains the same. It is the sum of all the numbers between zero and the number of years of the useful life of the item. For example, if an item has a useful life of three years, you would add 3 + 2 + 1, for a total of 6. The numerator of the fraction is the number of years remaining in the useful life of the item, including the year for which the deduction is being figured. The number decreases by 1 every year. The fractions for an item with a three-year useful life would change as follows: the first year, the fraction would be 3/6; the second year, 2/6; and the last year, 1/6. The sum of the years-digits method is similar to the declining balance method, in that both methods will result in a greater deductible amount in the first years of the depreciation schedule.

Column (f). The life, or rate, of depreciation is what *you* determine to be the useful life of each item used in your business or profession. In depreciating business property, there is a gray area in determining the life or rate. You, the taxpayer, will ultimately determine an item's life or rate. The determination is based upon how long you feel the item will be useful to your business. The shorter the life, the greater the amount of the depreciation deduction for each taxable year. The longer the life, the lower the deduction for each taxable year, but you will be able to continue deducting amounts for depreciation for more taxable years. One important factor to keep in mind in determining the life or rate of depreciation is how long you plan to stay in a particular business. If your business is not going to last very long, you should try to shorten the life of each item. If you plan to be in business for a long time, then a longer life may be more advantageous to you. Large depreciation deductions may be wasted in the beginning years of a business, when profits are usually low to begin with.

Column (g) asks for the amount of the depreciation deduction you will be taking for each item this year. This amount is determined by the cost of the items, their life or rate, and the method of computing the depreciation, as has been explained above.

ACCELERATED COST RECOVERY SYSTEM

A new system of depreciation is available for property purchased after December 31, 1980, and is known as the Accelerated Cost Recovery System, or ACRS. Under this system, the cost of items, such as automobiles and light-duty trucks may be recovered in three years, and the cost of most other equipment may be recovered in five years. These lives are much shorter than those allowed in previous years. Items such as furniture and fixtures can be depreciated over a life of five years. Trucks, tractors, and other heavily used equipment can now be depreciated over three years. And buildings, which used to be depreciated over twenty to forty years, can now be depreciated over fifteen years.

In effect, for the years 1981—1984 most items can be depreciated under the 150% declining balance method, and then you can switch to the straight line method later on. Under ACRS, there is no problem with the IRS associated with changing over from accelerated to straight-line depreciation.

Also, under ACRS, the salvage value subtraction has been eliminated. You now can write off the entire cost of an item.

In 1985 you will be able to use the 175% declining balance method, and in 1986 and thereafter, the 200% declining balance method will be acceptable for all items used in a trade or business.

You may still elect to adopt the straight line method of depreciation for property purchased in 1981 and thereafter. For property purchased prior to 1981, the old depreciation rules still apply.

For reporting ACRS depreciation, use Part I of Form 4562.

Let's take a look at how ACRS works. The depreciable property is assigned to one of six different categories, listed in Column A of Part I on Form 4562. Three-year property includes automobiles and light-

Form 4562
(Rev. September 1981)
Department of the Treasury
Internal Revenue Service

Depreciation

▶ See separate instructions.
▶ Attach this form to your return.

OMB No. 1545-0172
Expires 12/31/82

Name(s) as shown on return | Identifying number

▶ Generally, you must use the Accelerated Cost Recovery System of depreciation (ACRS) for all assets you placed in service after December 31, 1980. Report these assets in Part I, lines 1(a) through 1(f).
▶ You may elect to exclude certain property. Report this property in Part I, line 2.
▶ Use Part II for assets you placed in service before January 1, 1981, and certain other assets for which you cannot use ACRS.
▶ Filers of Schedule C (Form 1040), Schedule E (Form 1040) and Form 4835 should see the instructions for those forms before completing Form 4562.

Part I — Assets placed in service after December 31, 1980

A. Class of property	B. Date placed in service	C. Cost or other basis	D. Recovery period	E. Method of figuring depreciation	F. Percentage	G. Deduction for this year
1 Accelerated Cost Recovery System (ACRS) (See instructions for grouping assets):						
(a) 3-year property						
(b) 5-year property						
(c) 10-year property						
(d) 15-year public utility property						
(e) 15-year real property—low-income housing						
(f) 15-year real property other than low-income housing						
2 Property subject to section 168(e) (2) election (see instructions):						

3 Totals (add amounts in columns C and G) . . .
4 Depreciation from Part II, line 3 . . . .
5 Total (add column G, lines 3 and 4). Enter this amount on the depreciation expense line (where it applies) of your return . . . .

See Paperwork Reduction Act Notice on page 1 of the separate instructions.   343-168-1   Form **4562** (Rev. 9-81)

PROFIT OR LOSS FROM A BUSINESS OR PROFESSION 67

Form 4562 (Rev. 9-81) Page 2

Part II Assets placed in service before January 1, 1981 and other assets not qualifying for ACRS

A. Description of property	B. Date acquired	C. Cost or other basis	D. Depreciation allowed or allowable in earlier years	E. Method of figuring depreciation	F. Life or rate	G. Depreciation for this year
1 Class Life Asset Depreciation Range (CLADR) System Depreciation					▶	
2 Other depreciation (for grouping assets, see instructions for Part II):						
Buildings						
Furniture and fixtures						
Transportation equipment						
Machinery and other equipment						
Other (specify)						

3 Total (add amounts in column G). Enter here and in Part I, line 4 . . . .

343-168-1

duty trucks. Five-year property includes most office equipment and other items used in generating business income. Mobile homes are in the ten-year category, and real estate falls into the fifteen-year category.

Regular ACRS. ACRS depreciation can be taken in its regular form, which is accelerated, or as straight-line depreciation. For regular ACRS depreciation of personal property used in your business, the following table is used:

Recovery Year	Property Class		
	3-Year	5-Year	10-Year
1	25%	15%	8%
2	38%	22%	14%
3	37%	21%	12%
4		21%	10%
5		21%	10%
6			10%
7			9%
8			9%
9			9%
10			9%

Under the ACRS accelerated depreciation method a light truck, for example, that cost $10,000 when bought in 1981 would be depreciated as follows: $2,500 depreciation in 1981, $3,800 in 1982, and $3,700 in 1983.

Straight-Line ACRS. You may elect to use the straight-line ACRS method instead of the regular, accelerated ACRS method if you wish to extend the depreciation over a longer period of years or if you want to take higher depreciation deductions down the line than you could under accelerated depreciation. For each class of property, you have the option of chosing one of three recovery periods (similar to useful life) for each item. The allowable recovery periods for personal property are as follows:

3-year property .... 3, 5, or 12 years
5-year property .... 5, 12, or 25 years
10-year property .... 10, 25, or 35 years
15-year property .... 15, 35, or 45 years

It probably seems odd that "three-year property" can be depreciated over three, five, or twelve years, but that's the way it is done.

In straight-line ACRS depreciation, you can take only one-half the cost recovery amount the first year. And in the year *following* the last year of the recovery period, you again take one-half the cost recovery amount.

Are you confused? It really isn't too complicated. Say you buy a $500 machine in 1981 and want to depreciate it over a five-year recovery period using straight-line ACRS. Your depreciation deductions would be: $50 in 1981, $100 each year from 1982 through 1985, and $50 in 1986.

If you dispose of an item before the end of the recovery period, you may not claim cost recovery, or depreciation, for it in the year of disposition.

COMPLETING SCHEDULE C

Next, total all the amounts on Schedule C-2 or on Form 4562, whichever you used. Then put the total first onto the appropriate lines of the depreciation form or schedule you are using, and then onto line 13 of Schedule C.

On *line 32,* on Page 1 of Schedule C, total all of your various deductions. Then subtract line 32 from line 5, and the result will be your net profit or loss. On tax returns, losses are always enclosed in parentheses, for example (319). Never use minus signs or the word "subtraction."

Line 33. The net profit of your business is the amount that you will pay taxes on. If this is your only source of income, it will be the amount of your taxable income for the year. If it is a secondary source of income, a loss will help your overall tax position by lowering your taxable income. The tremendous tax advantage that self-employed people have is that their taxes are based on their net profit or loss. Wage earners, on the other hand, must pay taxes on their gross wages.

By law, if an activity shows losses on line 33 for more than two out of five years, the IRS may classify the activity as a hobby rather than a business engaged in for profit, and you will not be able to deduct net losses from that activity from your other income. In my opinion, you should not show net losses for more than three consecutive years. The reason is that, after the third year of showing a net loss, you run a great risk of being audited.

For people whose self-employment income is the main part of their tax return, showing a net loss is an attention-getter. If this should happen to you, be prepared for a tax audit.

Your net gain or loss should also be related to the Schedules C you have filed in previous years. Remember, the IRS has a record of all your previous tax returns. Any large changes from year to year may trigger an audit, so you should be ready to substantiate them. Be sure that you can prove all of your deductions, and be able to show how they are related to your business or profession.

Do not omit any of your gross receipts or sales in declaring your income on Schedule C. Some people feel they can hide a good part of their income by simply not declaring it. The failure to declare all of your income constitutes tax fraud, and could eventually lead to criminal charges being filed against you. The IRS can obtain a record of all of the checks that have passed through all of your bank accounts, so you can't hide income for long. The key thing here is not to hide *any* income, but to use the tax system to your advantage. The tax system allows you to deduct all of your expenses that relate to your business. You have to declare all of your income, but through legitimate deductions, you can lower your net profit. There are many businesses that take in over $200,000 in gross income each year, but after all of their deductions are subtracted they may show only $10,000 or $15,000 net profit, or they may even show a net loss.

USING SCHEDULE C PROPERLY

There are a number of tax questions that taxpayers frequently ask about expenses of their business. One is, which method of depreciation should be used? To answer this, you have to have a good idea as to how long you are going to stay in a particular business and what its net income will be in the future.

If you know that you will only be in business for a short time, you may want to use the most accelerated forms of depreciation, such as double declining balance. Under that method, you will recover the cost of your business property in the shortest period of time. Also, if you feel that in the current taxable year, and perhaps the next year, too, you will receive higher than average income, then, again, you would want to use accelerated depreciation to offset your high income. In other words, in the years that you have the highest gross income, you want to be able to take the greatest amount of deductions.

When you are planning to operate a business over a long period of time, or when you see greater net profits in future years, then you may want to use the straight-line method of depreciation. In such cases, you need to take deductions later on down the road, and, using the straight-line method, you will not be using up all of your deductions right away, which is what occurs under methods of accelerated depreciation.

Another question many taxpayers have is, should I buy or lease a car? The answer to that involves your overall tax bracket, and whether you can get a better deal on buying a car or leasing one. Generally, taxpayers in the lower tax brackets will not benefit from leasing a car. Leasing usually costs more than buying, but all of the lease payments can be deducted as a business expense if the car is used solely for your business. If you purchase, you can only depreciate the cost of the car over a period of three or more years. With leasing, you spend more money, but you also get a larger tax deduction, which only matters if you are in a very high tax bracket. In a low tax bracket, it definitely would not pay to lease. Another advantage to buying rather than leasing is that the Investment Tax Credit may be available when you buy. This credit is discussed in Chapter 15.

Always keep this in mind: Don't spend a dollar to save fifty cents in taxes. If you do so, you will lose the other fifty cents anyway. Spend your money wisely, i.e., spend it in order to make more money. It's better to make $20,000 and pay taxes on it than to lose $20,000 in order to get some sort of tax write-off. You should buy equipment for your business only when the business needs it to increase your net profit, not because you could get a tax deduction. One of the things that destroys many, many businesses is too much overhead. That often includes equipment that isn't really needed and employees who are not producing. Strive to maximize your profits and avoid negative cash flows.

SCHEDULE SE—COMPUTATION OF SELF-EMPLOYMENT SOCIAL SECURITY TAX

If the amount on line 33 of your Schedule C, the net profit, is over $400, then you must fill out a Schedule SE, "Self-Employment Social Security Taxes." This form is also used for computing social security taxes on income from farm self-employment, partnerships, joint ventures, or service as a minister, a member of a religious organization or a Christian Science practitioner. If your net profit is over $400 from any of these sources, you are subject to paying social security tax on that income.

This form is a perfect example of how the IRS needlessly complicates forms and uses language to confuse taxpayers. Most of the material on this form is over-worded and doesn't apply to the vast majority of self-employed people. Let's go through it from the point of view of someone who is self-employed and has shown a net profit of more than $400 on Schedule C. If you have farm self-employment income, or need additional information, order the instructions for Schedule SE from the IRS.

Take the amount from line 33 on Schedule C and put it on line 5a under Part II on Schedule SE. If you have any partnership income or losses, put that amount on line 5b. Then add the amounts on lines 5a through 5e and put the total on line 6, line 8, line 12b, and line 13. On line 15a, put in the total amount of "FICA" wages you received, if any, from your W-2 Forms. If you do not have any W-2's, put in "0" on line 15a. Subtract the amount, if any, on line 15b from the amount on line 15a and put the difference in line 15c.

On *line 16,* subtract line 15c from line 14. The printed amount on line 14 is the total amount of wages subject to social security taxes. For 1981, that amount is $29,700. If you already had $29,700 in FICA wages, the amount on line 16 would, therefore, be "0." You would not be subject to paying any more social security taxes.

On *line 17* put down the amount from line 13 or line 16, whichever is the smaller one.

On *line 18* you compute the self-employment tax. This is done very simply. Multiply the amount on line 17 by .093 (9.3%), the rate of the self-employment tax. There is a maximum limit to this figure printed on line 18. For example, the maximum in 1981 is $2,762.70. That is the highest amount of social security self-employment taxes that any one taxpayer has to pay. Put the amount from line 18 onto line 48 on page 2 of Form 1040.

Schedule SE is reproduced on page 170.

CHAPTER EIGHT

☆

Capital Gain or Loss—Schedule D

Schedule D is used for reporting capital gains and losses. This schedule deals with capital gains and losses on stocks, bonds, and other capital investments, as well as gains—but not losses—on personal assets, such as your personal car, home, or jewelry. In this chapter we will go over Schedule D in detail.

Capital gains and losses is the most difficult and confusing area in tax law for most taxpayers. The language used on these forms is quite technical. Most laymen have seldom, if ever, come into contact with many of these terms in any other context. But, like most tax forms, a lot of the information asked for does not apply and many lines need not be filled in. Also, once we translate the difficult technical terms into everyday language, you will be able to gain an overall understanding of the subject of capital assets. Then, you'll see what the IRS is talking about and you won't have too much trouble filling out the forms.

First, what is meant by capital gains and losses? Capital is money used for investment. The investment can be in stocks, the most common type of capital investment, or real estate, or even in investment-quality stones, jewelry, paintings, antiques, etc. The point here is that you are investing, which means you are taking some kind of risk with your money. The risk is that you may make money on an investment, but you may also lose some, or all, of it. Our tax system gives taxpayers a special tax break when they keep investments for a certain period of time as a reward for taking this risk.

There are two types of capital gains and losses, short- and long-term. Short-term gains or losses occur when a capital asset is sold within one year of its purchase. Long-term gains or losses occur when the asset is owned for longer than one year. It's important to note here that capital gains and losses occur only when the investment is sold or traded. When you first make an investment, usually nothing has to be reported on your tax return. It is only when it is sold or traded that you have to report information about a capital investment on your tax return.

SHORT-TERM CAPITAL GAINS AND LOSSES

A short-term capital gain or loss results from the sale of an asset that is owned for one full year or less. For example, on March 12, 1981 you buy 100 shares of the XYZ Corporation, and on January 12, 1982, you sell them. Since you did not own the stocks for more than one year, the sale would produce a short-term gain or loss. A short-term gain is 100% taxable, just like wage or salary income. Similarly, a short-term loss is 100% tax-deductible.

You determine whether there is a gain or a loss by simply taking the cost of the item, plus any fees or commissions you paid to acquire it, and subtracting the amount you sold it for, minus any fees or commissions you paid to sell it. For example, you buy 100 shares of XYZ Corporation for $10 a share, for a subtotal of $1,000. You also pay $100 in commissions to your stockbroker.

Therefore, the total amount of your investment is $1,100. Then, six months later, you sell all 100 shares for $2,000, plus a $200 brokerage commission, receiving $1,800. You have made a $700 net short-term gain on your investment. That $700 is 100% taxable, which means that, if you have no other capital gains or losses during the year, $700 will be added to your gross income. If you are in the 35% tax bracket, then 35% of that $700, or $245, would go to the government in taxes. It is important to remember that even though the short-term gain is 100% taxable, 100% of the gain does not go to the government, but only that percentage of the gain that corresponds to the tax bracket you are in.

The same thing holds true for short-term capital losses. For example, if you sell corporate stocks for $1,100 and they cost $1,900 six months earlier when your bought them, then you would have a short-term capital loss of $800. That loss would be 100% tax-deductible, but there is a maximum limit of $3,000 per taxable year on the amount of capital loss you can deduct. In other words, if you have a $5,000 capital loss, then you can deduct only $3,000 of that on the current year's tax return. If the $5,000 is a short-term capital loss, then you would report a loss of $3,000 on this year's tax return, and carry over the remaining $2,000 short-term capital loss to the next year's tax return. In other words, you are able to deduct 100% of short-term losses, but you may have to spread the deduction over a period of time if the losses exceed $3,000.

NONBUSINESS BAD DEBTS

Although loans are not usually capital assets, nonbusiness bad debts are treated in the same way as short-term capital losses. Business-related bad debts, however, are deducted directly from gross income. A nonbusiness bad debt arises from a loan to someone or a company or firm which, due to unforeseen circumstances, will never be paid back. You must wait until the debt becomes worthless, that is, after legal proceedings or bankruptcy, before it may be claimed as a deduction on your tax return. For example, you loan $5,000 to Mr. Smith, who promises to pay you back in three months. Then, Mr. Smith mysteriously winds up in Rio. You can't reach him or contact him, and he has no property in the United States. In order to be able to deduct this bad debt, you would have to take some action to try to get the money back. If you file a criminal complaint and the District Attorney states that you probably never would get the money back, then in that year you would be able to deduct the bad debt. In such a case, I would send in a copy of the District Attorney's signed statement with the tax return. The IRS likes to audit bad debts. Wait until the debt is worthless, and be certain that you can back up your case for claiming it.

LONG-TERM CAPITAL GAINS AND LOSSES

Long-term capital gains and losses occur when assets are sold or traded after being held for at least a year and a day. When you make a capital investment, such as buying corporate stocks or real estate, you should mark the date on the calendar that is exactly one year and one day from the date of purchase. In that way, you'll always be sure how long you have held the asset, and you will know when to sell it in order to take long- or short-term gains or losses.

I prepared tax returns a few years ago for a man who had invested a good deal of money in the stock market, and had sold out for a large gain. He wasn't aware of the difference between long- and short-term capital gains and losses when he sold the stock, which was two weeks before the one-year holding period was up. Because it was considered short-term, he had to pay taxes on 100% of the gain. By doing this, he lost approximately $12,000 in taxes. It is always critically important to know exactly when you've purchased a capital asset, and when you have held it for a year and a day.

Long-term capital *gains* are only 40% taxable. That means that you pay tax on only 40% of the gain. For example, if you make $800 from buying and selling 100 shares in XYZ Company, you would have to pay taxes on only $320, or 40% of the $800 gain, if you held the shares for at least a year and a day. Furthermore, if you are in the 35% tax bracket, you would add only $320 to your gross income, and you would have to pay only 35% of that amount, or $112, to the government.

Long-term capital *losses* are 50% tax-deductible. That means that if you've held an asset for a year and a day or longer, and you lose money when you sell it, you can deduct only one-half of the total loss. Thus, if you lose $800 from buying and selling 100 shares of XYZ company, you would only be able to deduct $400 from your gross income. Obviously, if you are going to lose money on a capital investment, you want it to be a short-term loss so that you are able to deduct 100% of it.

The $3,000 annual limitation on deduction of capital losses also applies to long-term losses. If, for example, you have a $10,000 long-term capital loss, which allows a $5,000 total deduction, you would be able to deduct only $3,000 on the current year's tax return, and $2,000 on the next year's.

REPORTING SHORT-TERM CAPITAL GAINS AND LOSSES

Part I of Schedule D is used to report short-term capital gains and losses. On *line 1, Column a*, write in the kind of property you invested in and a description of it, for example, "100 shares of General Motors common stock." Your share certificate will contain the proper description. In *Columns b and c* put in the exact date it was acquired and the exact date it was sold. If you inherited stocks, under Column b put in the exact date that you inherited them.

In *Column d* put down the gross sales price of the asset minus the expenses of the sale. For example, if you sold stock and had to pay a broker's commission and sales tax, subtract the commission and sales tax from the sales price of the stock, and put that amount in Column d. In the case of assets such as real estate or jewelry, there may be expenses such as legal fees, travel, telephone calls, commissions, etc. involved. All of those expenses are subtracted from the gross sales price.

In *Column e*, state how much the asset originally cost you. Again, that means the actual purchase price of the item, plus any commissions or fees, etc. that you paid in order to buy it. In the case of an asset that was inherited, its cost is its value on the open market on the exact date you acquired it. For example, say that on March 5, 1972, you inherited 500 shares of General Motors stock. If necessary, you could contact a stockbroker to find out exactly how much General Motors stock was selling for on that date.

Column f. If the amount in Column e, the basis, is greater than the amount in Column d, the selling price, you have suffered a loss. Remember that on tax returns, losses are always written in parentheses, for example (4,982).

In *Column g*, put down the gain, if Column d is greater than Column e. Note that for each capital gain or loss you have to fill out a separate line under Columns a through g. Each and every sale or exchange of a capital asset must be done in this manner. You may have to contact your stockbroker to get all the necessary information for each of your stocks that was sold during the year. You should do so as soon as possible after the close of the taxable year.

Line 2a on Schedule D deals with gains from the sale or exchange of a principal residence held for one year or less. If you have sold your house during the year, simply put in the total from line 7 or 11 of Form 2119, which we will discuss in detail in Chapter 9.

Line 2b is for reporting short-term capital gain from an installment sale. Fill out Form 6252 as described in Chapter 9, and put in the amount of this year's capital gain on line 2b of Schedule D.

On *line 3*, put in the net amount of any short-term gains or losses you received from partnerships or fiduciaries. If you are a member of a partnership, a partnership return on Form 1065 should have been filled out already, and you should have been provided with a copy of Schedule K-1, which will show your share of the partnership's capital gains or losses. That amount from Schedule K-1 goes here, on line 3.

"Fiduciaries" refers to estates or trusts. If

you receive short-term gains or losses from either, put the amount on line 3.

On *line 4*, simply add the amounts on lines 1, 2 and 3 under Columns f and g.

On *line 5*, combine the amounts on line 4, Columns f and g, and put the amount, either a net gain or a net loss, on line 5.

Line 6 asks for short-term capital loss carryovers. As stated earlier, a capital loss carryover occurs when you have more than $3,000 in capital losses in any one year. On your previous year's tax return, you should have already computed the carryover amount for the current year. Simply put in the amount of the short-term loss carryover from the previous year on this year's tax return, on line 6.

Line 7 is the total of your net short-term gains or losses which is calculated by combining lines 5 and 6.

REPORTING LONG-TERM CAPITAL GAINS AND LOSSES

Under Part II of Schedule D, you report long-term capital gains and losses arising from the sale or exchange of assets that have been held for more than one year. On *line 8*, do the same thing that was done on line 1 for short-term capital gains and losses. Put in the kind and description of each asset, the date acquired, the date sold, the selling price, the basis, and whether you had a gain or a loss. Again, this has to be done for each asset that was sold or traded during the taxable year.

On *line 9a*, put in the amount of gain from the sale or exchange of a principal residence that was held for more than one year. This amount can be found on line 7, 11, or 18 of Form 2119, to be discussed in Chapter 9.

On *line 9b*, put in the amount from Form 6252, as discussed in Chapter 9, for long-term capital gain from an installment sale.

Line 10 is for long-term gains or losses from partnerships or fiduciaries. As described above in the discussion of line 3, this amount would be shown on Schedule K-1.

On *line 11*, total the amounts on lines 8, 9 and 10 under Columns f and g.

On *line 12*, combine the amounts on line 11 under Columns f and g and enter the net gain or loss.

Line 13 asks for capital gain distributions, which are amounts of money that you may have received from a corporation. The difference between a dividend and a capital gains distribution is that a dividend comes from the corporation's earnings and profits, whereas a capital gains distribution does not. The only time most people ever receive this item of income is when they have paid money into a profit-sharing plan at work and then leave that particular company. The corporation would then return their investment plus the capital gain, if any, on that investment. The amount in excess of the contribution would be considered long-term capital gain. If you receive a capital gains distribution from a corporation, it is required to furnish you with a statement showing the amount. That amount goes onto line 13 of Schedule D, or directly onto line 13 of Form 1040. You should put the amount of capital gain distributions on line 13 of Schedule D, rather than directly onto line 13 of Form 1040 if you have more than $3,000 of capital losses. The reason for this is to be able to deduct all of the capital losses in this tax year instead of using a capital loss carryover to the next year. In other words, if you have $5,000 in losses and $5,000 in capital gain distributions on line 13 of Schedule D, you can offset the two amounts and, in effect, deduct the $5,000 loss totally in this tax year. If you had entered an amount only on line 13 of Form 1040 instead, the $3,000 limitation on deductions for capital losses would force you to carry the remainder of the loss over to future years.

On *line 14* of Schedule D, put in long-term capital gains from the sale of rental properties or property used in a trade or business. The amount is calculated on Form 4797, which we will discuss in Chapter 9, below.

On *line 15*, enter your share of net long-term gains from "Subchapter S" corporations, if any. As with partnerships, you should receive a Schedule K-l from the Subchapter S corporation indicating your

CAPITAL GAIN OR LOSS—SCHEDULE D

SCHEDULE D (FORM 1040)
Department of the Treasury
Internal Revenue Service

Capital Gains and Losses
(Examples of property to be reported on this Schedule are gains and losses on stocks, bonds, and similar investments, and gains (but not losses) on personal assets such as a home or jewelry.)
▶ Attach to Form 1040. ▶ See Instructions for Schedule D (Form 1040).

OMB No. 1545-0074

1981
14

Name(s) as shown on Form 1040 | Your social security number

Part I — Short-term Capital Gains and Losses—Assets Held One Year or Less

a. Kind of property and description (Example, 100 shares 7% preferred of "Z" Co.)	b. Date acquired (Mo., day, yr.)	c. Date sold (Mo., day, yr.)	d. Gross sales price less expense of sale	e. Cost or other basis, as adjusted (see instructions page 23)	f. LOSS If column (e) is more than (d) subtract (d) from (e)	g. GAIN If column (d) is more than (e) subtract (e) from (d)
1						

2a Gain from sale or exchange of a principal residence held one year or less, from Form 2119, lines 7 or 11 . . . .
  b Short-term capital gain from installment sales from Form 6252, line 19 or 27 . . .
3 Enter your share of net short-term gain or (loss) from partnerships and fiduciaries .
4 Add lines 1 through 3 in column f and column g . . . . ( )
5 Combine line 4, column f and line 4, column g and enter the net gain or (loss) . .
6 Short-term capital loss carryover from years beginning after 1969 . . . . ( )
7 Net short-term gain or (loss), combine lines 5 and 6 . . . .

Part II — Long-term Capital Gains and Losses—Assets Held More Than One Year

8						

9a Gain from sale or exchange of a principal residence held more than one year, from Form 2119, lines 7, 11, 16 or 18 . . . .
  b Long-term capital gain from installment sales from Form 6252, line 19 or 27 . . .
10 Enter your share of net long-term gain or (loss) from partnerships and fiduciaries .
11 Add lines 8 through 10 in column f and column g . . . . ( )
12 Combine line 11, column f and line 11, column g and enter the net gain or (loss) . . . .
13 Capital gain distributions . . . .
14 Enter gain from Form 4797, line 5(a)(1) . . . .
15 Enter your share of net long-term gain from small business corporations (Subchapter S) . . . .
16 Combine lines 12 through 15 . . . .
17 Long-term capital loss carryover from years beginning after 1969 . . . . ( )
18 Net long-term gain or (loss), combine lines 16 and 17 . . . .

Note: Complete this form on reverse. However, if you have capital loss carryovers from years beginning before 1970, do not complete Parts III or V. See Form 4798 instead.

For Paperwork Reduction Act Notice, see Form 1040 instructions

343-061-1

Schedule D (Form 1040) 1981 Page **2**

Part III — Summary of Parts I and II

19 Combine lines 7 and 18, and enter the net gain or (loss) here . . . .
  NOTE: *If line 19 is a gain complete lines 20 through 22. If line 19 is a loss complete lines 23 and 24.*
20 If line 19 shows a gain, enter the smaller of line 18 or line 19. Enter zero if there is a loss or no entry on line 18 . . . .
21 Enter 60% of line 20 . . . .
  If line 21 is more than zero, you may be liable for the alternative minimum tax. See Form 6251.
22 Subtract line 21 from line 19. Enter here and on Form 1040, line 12 . . . .
23 If line 19 shows a loss, enter one of the following amounts:
  (i) If line 7 is zero or a net gain, enter 50% of line 19;
  (ii) If line 18 is zero or a net gain, enter line 19; or,
  (iii) If line 7 and line 18 are net losses, enter amount on line 7 added to 50% of the amount on line 18 . .
24 Enter here and as a loss on Form 1040, line 12, the smallest of:
  (i) The amount on line 23;
  (ii) $3,000 ($1,500 if married and filing a separate return); or,
  (iii) Taxable income, as adjusted . . . .

Part IV — Computation of Alternative Tax
(Complete this part if line 20 (or Form 4798, line 8) shows a gain and your tax rate is above 50%. See instructions page 23.)

25 Net short-term gain or (loss) from line 5, from sales or exchanges after June 9, 1981 . . . .
26 Net long-term gain or (loss) from line 16, from sales or exchanges after June 9, 1981 . . . .
27 If line 26 shows a gain, combine line 25 and line 26. If line 26 or this line shows a loss or zero, enter zero and do not complete rest of this part . . . .
28 Enter the smaller of line 26 or line 27 . . . .
29 Enter the smaller of line 20 (or Form 4798, line 8) or line 28 . . . . . .
30 Enter your Taxable Income from Form 1040, line 34 . . . .
31 Enter 40% of line 29 . . . .
32 Subtract line 31 from line 30. If line 31 is more than line 30, enter zero . . . .
33 Tax on amount on line 32. ☐ Tax Rate Schedule X, Y, or Z; ☐ Schedule G. (See instructions page 23) . .
34 Enter 20% of line 29 . . . .
35 Add lines 33 and 34. If the result is less than your tax using other methods, enter this amount on Form 1040, line 35 and check Schedule D box . . . .

Part V — Computation of Post-1969 Capital Loss Carryovers from 1981 to 1982
(Complete this part if the loss on line 23 is more than the loss on line 24)

Section A.—Short-term Capital Loss Carryover

36 Enter loss shown on line 7; if none, enter zero and skip lines 37 through 41—then go to line 42 . . . .
37 Enter gain shown on line 18. If that line is blank or shows a loss, enter zero . . . .
38 Reduce any loss on line 36 to the extent of any gain on line 37 . . . .
39 Enter amount shown on line 24 . . . .
40 Enter smaller of line 38 or 39 . . . .
41 Subtract line 40 from line 38. This is your short-term capital loss carryover from 1981 to 1982 . . . .

Section B.—Long-term Capital Loss Carryover

42 Subtract line 40 from line 39 (Note: *If you skipped lines 37 through 41, enter amount from line 24*) . . .
43 Enter loss from line 18; if none, enter zero and skip lines 44 through 47 . . . .
44 Enter gain shown on line 7. If that line is blank or shows a loss, enter zero . . . .
45 Reduce any loss on line 43 to the extent of any gain on line 44 . . . .
46 Multiply amount on line 42 by 2 . . . .
47 Subtract line 46 from line 45. This is your long-term capital loss carryover from 1981 to 1982 . . . . .

Part VI — Complete this Part Only if You are Electing Out of the Installment Method And are Reporting a Note or Other Obligation at Less Than Full Face Value

☐ Check here if you elect out of the installment method.
  Enter the face amount of the note or other obligation ▶ ....
  Enter the percentage of valuation of the note or other obligation ▶

343-061-1

share of net long-term gains.

On *line 16*, add the amounts on lines 12 through 15 and put the total onto line 16.

Line 17 asks for long-term capital loss carryovers. As with short-term capital losses, the amount of this carryover should have been calculated on the previous year's tax return.

On *line 18*, combine the amounts on lines 16 and 17 to arrive at the net long-term gain or loss.

CALCULATING AMOUNT OF CAPITAL GAIN OR LOSS

On *lines 19 through 24* on page 2 of Schedule D, you will calculate the year's net capital gain or loss. Remember, you will pay taxes on 100% of a *short*-term capital gain, but on only 40% of a *long*-term capital gain. Similarly, you can deduct 100% of short-term capital losses, but only 50% of long-term capital losses, up to a total of $3,000, or $1,500 for married couples filing separate returns. If the amount on line 23 is greater than the $3,000 or $1,500 limitation, then you should complete Part V of Schedule D.

COMPUTATION OF ALTERNATIVE TAX

The alternative tax is another method of computing your tax when you have large capital gains and your tax rate is above 50%. Fill out *lines 25 through 35* of Schedule D to determine your tax liability by this method.

I suggest that you compare the amount of tax you would owe under the alternative tax method with the amount you would owe if you were to use the maximum tax method (see Form 4726, discussed in Chapter 14) or income averaging (see Schedule G, also discussed in Chapter 14). Compute your tax using all these methods, if applicable, in order to determine which method will enable you to pay the lowest amount of tax.

COMPUTATION OF CAPITAL LOSS CARRYOVERS

On *lines 36 through 41* of Schedule D, compute your short-term loss carryover, and on *lines 42 through 47*, compute your long-term capital loss carryover. The amounts on either line 41 or line 47 will be used on next year's tax return.

ELECTING OUT OF INSTALLMENT METHOD

Part VI of Schedule D is used by taxpayers who have sold property and have received a promissory note instead of cash, but who choose not to use the installment method of reporting the gain on the sale. The installment method is now automatic in a deferred payment sale, but a taxpayer may "elect out" of the installment method and report the promissory note as though it were cash received. However, a promissory note is not worth the amount of its face value until it is due and payable. Therefore, it is reported at the discounted value, less than full face value, of what it is worth at the time of sale. In such a situation, you must answer the questions in Part VI of Schedule D. Income tax aspects of real estate installment sales are discussed in Chapter 9.

USING SCHEDULE D EFFECTIVELY

Understanding the provisions of tax laws for capital gains and losses can save you a great deal of money each year in income tax. First, be able to find the exact date on which you purchased each of your investments, for example, the exact month, day, and year you purchased every one of your stocks. Second, always remember the difference between short- and long-term capital gains and losses. If you have an investment that is doing well, whether it is a stock, an investment-quality precious stone, an antique, or a collectible, you ordinarily should keep it for at least a year and a day before you sell it. On the other hand, if you have an investment that is doing poorly, you will probably save tax money if you sell it before one year has passed.

If you've inherited an investment, find out exactly what it was worth on the day you inherited it. Be aware of the type of capital gain or loss you'll have on each of your investments, particularly in dealing with property that you have inherited. Before you sell investment property, be sure that you know what kind of capital gains tax you'd have to pay.

Again, always take into account the fact that the tax rates are progressive. You will always include capital gains and deduct the capital losses in the taxable year in which the investment is sold, except where you can defer a capital gain by trading up in a tax-free exchange. You may want to sell capital investments that have large gains in the year that your other taxable income is relatively low. For example, if you are planning to retire during the taxable year and you have some stocks that have large capital gains, you may want to sell them next year. The reason is that after you have retired, your taxable income will probably be lower, and the amount of tax you will pay on any capital gains will also be lower. Plan ahead to take capital gains in a year that you've been out of work for a long period of time or on strike, or a year where your spouse did not work, or a year where your business was slow.

On the other hand, in a year where your other taxable income is relatively high, you may want to sell stocks or other investments that are doing poorly. If you can take a capital loss, especially a *short-term* loss, on investments, you will be able to lower your taxable income. For example, it may be more advantageous to sell stocks that have declined in value this taxable year than to hold on to them, waiting for them to go back up in value. You may be able to accomplish two things: one, by selling the stocks you'll have some more capital to invest in other things; and two, you'll have a capital loss that will reduce your taxable income.

In the next chapter, let's look at the provisions of tax law that apply specifically to capital gains and losses from the sale or exchange of real estate investments.

CHAPTER NINE

☆

Sale or Exchange of Real Estate

This chapter discusses the supplemental schedules on Forms 2119, 4797, and 6252. Form 2119 is used when you sell your personal residence. Form 4797 is for reporting the sale of rental property, businesses, and farms, and is also used to report casualty losses and thefts relating to business or rental property. Form 6252 is used to compute the amount of capital gain for each year in an installment sale.

SALE OR EXCHANGE OF A PRINCIPAL RESIDENCE—FORM 2119

Form 2119 is used only to report the gain on the sale of a personal residence. You are not able to deduct any losses that arise from the sale of a personal residence.

One of the main purposes in filling out Form 2119 is to defer the capital gains on the sale of your personal residence. A personal residence is defined as the principal or primary dwelling in which you live. At the time of the sale, this must be the place in which you are residing. In the case of a multiple-unit building, such as a triplex, you can defer only the gain on the portion of the building that was used as your personal residence. For example, if you own a triplex and you live in one of the units, when you sell the triplex, you'd be able to defer only one-third of the capital gain. The unit that you occupied would be considered your personal residence, and you would be able to defer the gain attributable to that unit. The gain attributable to the portion of your property that is used to earn rental income cannot be deferred unless there is a tax-free exchange.

Under the 1981 changes in the tax law, you can defer the capital gain on the sale of a personal residence if, within two years, you purchase another personal residence that costs more than the amount you realized from the sale of the first residence, if it was sold after July 20, 1981. The old law, which applies to residences sold before July 20, 1981, allowed a period of only eighteen months in which to purchase a replacement residence. However, if you, as an individual, sold your principal residence before July 21, 1981 and the previous eighteen-month period had not expired at the time, you are given the benefit of the new, two-year period. If you are constructing a new house, then even under the old law, you still have a two-year period in which to defer the capital gain. Deferring the capital gain is not the same as excluding it. *Deferring* the tax on a gain means putting it off for now, to pay it in a future year. *Excluding* an item of income means that it is nontaxable, and that means that tax on it never has to be paid. When you defer a capital gain, you're only putting off paying tax on it for this year. You can defer capital gains again and again, so long as you buy a new residence each time within the replacement period, and so long as the new one costs more than whatever the old one sold for. If you eventually sell a house and do not buy another personal residence within the replacement period, you would then have to pay capital gains tax on all of the amounts that have been previously deferred. You can plan to continually defer capital gains until you and your spouse reach age fifty-five, and then you are able to exclude the first $125,000 of capital gains. This exclusion limit was raised from $100,000 by the new tax law and applies only to sales that were made after July 20, 1981.

Form **2119**	**Sale or Exchange of Principal Residence**	OMB No. 1545-0072
Department of the Treasury Internal Revenue Service	▶ See instructions on back. ▶ Attach to Form 1040 for year of sale (see instruction C).	**1981** 24

Note: *Do not include expenses you are deducting as moving expenses.*

Name(s) as shown on Form 1040	Your social security number

		Yes	No
1 (a)	Date former residence sold ▶		
(b)	Enter the face amount of any mortgage, note (for example second trust), or other financial instrument on which you will receive periodic payments of principal or interest from this sale ▶		
(c)	Have you ever postponed any gain on the sale or exchange of a principal residence?		
(d)	If you were on active duty in the U.S. Armed Forces or outside of the U.S. after the date of sale of former residence, enter dates. From to		
2 (a)	Date you bought new residence. (If none bought, so state). ▶		
(b)	If you constructed new residence, date construction began ▶ date occupied ▶		
(c)	Did you use both the old and new properties as your principal residence?		
(d)	Are any rooms in either residence rented out or used for business for which a deduction is allowed? . . . . (If "Yes" do not include gain on the rented or business portion in line 7; instead include in income on Form 4797.)		

Part I — Computation of Gain and Adjusted Sales Price

3	Selling price of residence. (Do not include selling price of personal property items.)	3
4	Commissions and other expenses of sale not deducted as moving expenses	4
5	Amount realized (subtract line 4 from line 3)	5
6	Basis of residence sold 6	
7	Gain on sale (subtract line 6 from line 5). (If line 6 is more than line 5, enter zero and do not complete the rest of form.) If you bought another principal residence during the allowed replacement period or you elect the one time exclusion in Part III, continue with this form. Otherwise, enter the gain on Schedule D (Form 1040), line 2a or 9a	7
	If you haven't replaced your residence, do you plan to do so within the replacement period? ☐ Yes ☐ No (If "Yes" see instruction C.)	
8	Fixing-up expenses (see instructions for time limitations.)	8
9	Adjusted sales price (subtract line 8 from line 5)	9

Part II — Computation of Gain to be Postponed and Adjusted Basis of New Residence

10	Cost of new residence	10
11	Gain taxable this year (Subtract line 10 from line 9. Do not enter more than line 7.) If line 10 is more than line 9, enter zero. Enter any taxable gain on Schedule D (Form 1040), line 2a or 9a. If you were 55 or over on the date of sale, see Part III	11
12	Gain to be postponed (subtract line 11 from line 7)	12
13	Adjusted basis of new residence (subtract line 12 from line 10)	13

Part III — Computation of Exclusion, Gain to be Reported, and Adjusted Basis of New Residence

		Yes	No
14 (a)	Were you 55 or over on date of sale?		
(b)	Was your spouse 55 or over on date of sale? . . . . (If you answered "No" to 14(a) and 14(b), do not complete the rest of form.)		
(c)	If you answered "Yes" to 14(a) or 14(b) did you own and use the property sold as your principal residence for a total of at least 3 years (except for short temporary absences) of the 5-year period before the sale? . . . . (If you are 65 or over and 1(a) is before 7/26/81, see instruction D.)		
(d)	If you answered "Yes" to 14(c), do you elect to take the once in a lifetime exclusion of the gain on the sale? . . (If "Yes," check yes box and complete the rest of Part III. If "No", return to Part II, line 12 above.)		
(e)	At time of sale, was the residence owned by: ☐ you, ☐ your spouse, ☐ both of you?		
(f)	Social security number of spouse, at time of sale, if different from number on Form 1040 ▶ .... (Enter "none" if you were not married at time of sale.)		

15 (a)	If line 1(a) is before 7/21/81, enter the smaller of line 7 or $100,000 ($50,000, if married filing separate return) . .	15(a)
(b)	If line 1(a) is after 7/20/81, enter the smaller of line 7 or $125,000 ($62,500, if married filing separate return) . . .	15(b)
16	Part of gain included (subtract line 15a or 15b from line 7)	16
17	Cost of new residence. If you did not buy a new principal residence, enter "None." Then enter the gain from line 16 on Schedule D (Form 1040), line 9a, and do not complete the rest of Form 2119	17
18	Gain taxable this year. (Subtract the sum of lines 15 and 17 from line 9. The result cannot be more than line 16.) If line 17 plus line 15 is more than line 9, enter zero. Enter any taxable gain on Schedule D (Form 1040), line 9a	18
19	Gain to be postponed (subtract line 18 from line 16)	19
20	Adjusted basis of new residence (subtract line 19 from line 17)	20

For Paperwork Reduction Act Notice, see back of form.   343-143-1   Form **2119** (1981)

The first thing you see on Form 2119 is the note: "Do not include expenses you are deducting as moving expenses on Form 3903." Always remember that you cannot deduct the same item more than once. A note to the IRS' note: if you are able to defer capital gains tax using Form 2119, it is always better to take the deductions for moving expenses separately, on Form 3903, rather than on Form 2119. The reason is that, since you will not be paying tax on capital gains because you are able to defer them, you should claim moving expenses on Form 3903 because they will then be deductible from your gross income. If you use Form 2119, that deduction would be deferred along with the capital gain. Now let's go through the form line by line.

Line 1(a). Put in the month, day and year that the former residence was sold.

Line 1(b) asks you to enter the face amount of any mortgage, note, or other financial instrument that you have taken back from the buyer and under which you are to receive interest payments. Apparently the IRS is suspicious that taxpayers who are forced to accept "paper" from buyers in the recent tight market are not reporting interest income as they should be.

Line 1(c). If this is the first time that you have ever postponed or deferred gain on the sale of a principal residence, the answer here is "no." If you have deferred such gain before, then check "yes." If the answer is yes, locate a copy of all Forms 2119 that were submitted along with the previous tax returns on which you deferred the gain. Look for the amounts that you deferred on your previous sales. This amount would have been subtracted from your cost basis for the "new residence" on the previous Forms 2119. This amount is called the "adjusted basis of new residence." You need that amount for line 6 on Form 2119. That amount is used to determine the amount of capital gain you have made on the most recent sale of your personal residence.

Line 1(d). If you were on active duty in the armed services for more than ninety days during the year, or were outside U.S. after the sale of the former residence, fill in the appropriate dates. The time you are on active duty or working outside the country is not counted in calculating the eighteen-month or two-year replacement period described above.

Line 2(a). Write in the date that you purchased your new residence. To be able to defer the capital gain, you must have purchased the new residence either eighteen months before or eighteen months after you sold the old residence, if it was sold before July 20, 1981. If it was sold after July 20, 1981, the applicable period is two years. If you are on active duty or working abroad, you must purchase another residence no later than four years after you sell your home.

Line 2(b). If you are building a new house, write in the date construction began, and the date you moved into it.

Line 2(c) Were both the old and new properties used as your principal residence? Check "yes" or "no." Again, remember that you can only defer the capital gain for the sale of one principal residence by buying another principal residence. If you sell a multiple unit building, you can defer only that portion of the capital gain that corresponds to the portion of the building that was used as your personal residence. Conversely, if you sell a single family house and buy a multiple-unit building, you can use only that portion of the cost of the new building that corresponds to the portion of the building that will be your personal residence. For example, say you sold a single family house and purchased a triplex. You are going to live in one of the units of the triplex. The total cost of it was $300,000. You can use only one-third of the cost, or $100,000, to determine whether you can defer all or part of the capital gain from the sale of the old residence.

Line 2(d). If any rooms in either the old or the new residence were rented out or used for business purposes at any time, you have to attach a computation. Any amounts that were deducted for depreciation on previous tax returns cannot be deferred, and you will have to fill out Form 4797. Likewise, if you've claimed home office expenses, a portion of the gain on the house, corresponding to the portion of the house that was used for business purposes, cannot be deferred. You will have to pay capital gains tax on that portion. If, in the new residence, you will be using part of it for business, or renting out part of it, you cannot use that portion in order to defer the capital gains. Take a separate sheet of paper and show the IRS your computations in prorating these amounts.

COMPUTATION OF GAIN AND THE ADJUSTED SALES PRICE— PART I—FORM 2119

Line 3 asks for the selling price of the personal residence, which is the total price you sold it for. Again, if the residence is a duplex and half of it was used as rental property, then you put half of the total selling price on line 3 and the other half would go onto Form 4797, which is explained later in this chapter.

It's very helpful to refer to copies of the escrow papers or other closing documents for both the old house that you sold and the new house that you bought. From the escrow papers you will get the exact numbers that you need to fill out Form 2119.

Line 4. On line 4 put in the total amount of commissions and other expenses of sale that will be subtracted from the total selling price of the old residence. These amounts may include a 6% real estate commission, attorney fees, inspection fees, engineering reports, telephone costs, or even transportation costs. List all of the various expenses you had in order to make the sale.

Line 5, the amount realized, is determined by subtracting line 4 from line 3.

Line 6 is for a very important amount, the basis of the residence sold. If this is the first time you are deferring a capital gain on a personal residence, then the basis of the residence sold should be the original cost of the property, plus all the major improvements that you've made on it since you've owned it. It's quite important to have records of all the improvements that you have made throughout the years, including new or remodeled kitchens, new or remodeled bathrooms, a new roof, a new fence, concrete work, landscaping, painting, major redecorating, wall-to-wall carpeting, major electrical work, plumbing work, etc. If you have done some or all of this work yourself, you cannot include the value of your own labor in the amount of improvements. But, if you've paid anyone for such work, including friends or relatives, you can deduct the amount that you have paid them. You should carefully go back through the years and recall all of the improvements that you have made to your residence.

On *line 7*, you will determine the gain on the sale. That gain is determined by subtracting line 6 from line 5. If the amount on line 6 is greater than that on line 5 then you will put "0" on line 7. That means that you lost money on the sale of the property, but, unfortunately, you cannot deduct capital losses resulting from the sale of a personal residence.

If there is a gain on line 7, and you do not plan to buy another personal residence, or do not choose to take the $100,000 or $125,000 exclusion for taxpayers over fifty-five years of age, then the amount on line 7 will be taxed. Take that amount and put it onto line 2 or line 9 of Schedule D—line 2 in case of a short-term capital gain, and line 9 in case of a long-term capital gain.

If, at the time you file your tax return, you have not yet purchased another principal residence, you can still defer the capital gain. Simply write in "will purchase" in large letters on line 10 of Form 2119, where it asks for the cost of the new residence. When you purchase a new residence that costs more than the amount realized on the old one, and that is purchased within the eighteen-month or two-year time period, you then fill out the remainder of Part II on another Form 2119. If, on the other hand, you say that you will purchase another residence but actually do not within two years, you will have to file an amended return for this year, on Form

SALE OR EXCHANGE OF REAL ESTATE

1040X, and pay a capital gains tax.

Line 8 asks for "fixing-up expenses." These expenses include only decorating and repair expenses that were incurred to help you sell the property. The work must have been done no more than ninety days before you sold the property, or thirty days after the sale. Such expenses are used only in determining the adjusted sales price. Fixing-up expenses are not deductible in determining the actual profit on the sale of your old residence.

Line 9 gives you the adjusted sales price of the old residence. You determine this by subtracting line 8 from line 5. In order to defer the entire capital gain on the sale of the old residence, the cost of the new residence must exceed the adjusted sales price of the old one. You should be very conscious of the adjusted sales price of your old house when you go out to buy another one.

COMPUTATION OF GAIN TO BE POSTPONED AND THE ADJUSTED BASIS OF THE NEW RESIDENCE—PART II—FORM 2119

Line 10 simply asks for the cost of the new residence. If you have not yet purchased the new residence, but plan to, write in "will purchase" as explained above. If you have purchased a new residence, the cost is shown on the escrow papers or other closing documents as the purchase price.

Line 11 asks for the gain that will be taxable this year. If the amount on line 10 is greater than that on line 9, then you have deferred the entire capital gain. The amount on line 11 will therefore be "0."

If the amount on line 9 is greater than the amount on line 10, enter the difference, but do not enter more than the amount that was on line 7 above. For example, if the gain on the sale from line 7 is $25,000 and the cost of your new residence from line 10 is $90,000, and the adjusted sales price on line 9 is $100,000, then you would subtract line 10 ($90,000) from line 9 ($100,000), and get $10,000. Since the $10,000 amount is smaller than the $25,000 amount on line 7, $10,000 would be the amount of gain taxable this year.

If for example, the difference between line 10 and line 9 was $50,000, then you would only have to put $25,000, the amount from line 7, on line 11. In other words, you are only subject to tax on the actual gain from the sale (the amount that appears on line 7), even if the difference between line 10 and line 9 is greater than that amount. Also, if you or your spouse are fifty-five years of age or over on the date of the sale, you can exclude up to $100,000 or $125,000 of gain from the amount on line 11. This exclusion is discussed later in this chapter.

Line 12 asks for the amount of gain that is to be deferred. Subtract the amount on line 11 from the amount on line 7. If the amount on line 11 is "0," all of the capital gain is being deferred, and the total amount of gain on line 7 would go onto line 12.

Line 13 is the adjusted basis of your new residence, and is determined by subtracting line 12 from line 10.

Let's look at an example. You sell your old house, and have a gain on the sale, the amount on line 7, of $50,000. The adjusted sales price on line 9 is $100,000. The cost of the new residence, line 10, is $125,000. Therefore the amount on line 11 would be "0," and you are able to defer all of the capital gain to future years. The amount on line 12 would then be $50,000, the amount on line 7 minus "0," the amount on line 11. The adjusted basis of your new residence would then be $75,000 (the amount on line 10, $125,000, minus the amount on line 12, $50,000).

If, five years from now, you then sell the new residence for $150,000, this is what would happen. If you did not buy another residence, or if you or your spouse were not fifty-five or over at that time, then you would have to pay tax on a capital gain of $75,000, computed as follows: You sell the new residence for $150,000, and its adjusted basis was $75,000 ($150,000 minus $75,000 = $75,000). You would, in fact, pay tax on the gain from the sale of the new residence plus the $50,000 gain on the sale of the old residence that you had deferred on this year's tax return. It is important for all of us to realize that we are just *deferring* the capital gains tax, not excluding it, except in the case of taxpayers fifty-five years of age or older. You may continually defer capital gain by purchasing more and more expensive houses, but the first time you don't qualify for deferral, you'll be subject to tax on all of the capital gains that have been deferred throughout the years. In a way, it's like having a tiger by the tail—if you let go, you'll be eaten alive. The same principle applies to tax-free exchanges of property, which are discussed later in this chapter.

COMPUTATION OF EXCLUSION, GAIN TO BE REPORTED, AND ADJUSTED BASIS OF NEW RESIDENCE PART III—FORM 2119

In order to qualify for the exclusion of gain, you or your spouse must be age fifty-five or older on the date of the sale. You must have owned the property for at least five years before the date of the sale, and, for at least three of those years, it must have been used as your principal residence. If you are sixty-five or older on the date of the sale, you may substitute five of the last eight years for three of the last five years. This exclusion can be taken only once in a taxpayer's lifetime.

If you live in a community property state, or if the property is owned jointly by you and your spouse, and you file a joint tax return, only one of you needs to meet the age, ownership, and use requirements.

If you do not live in a community property state, and the property is not jointly owned, only the spouse who owns the property must meet the requirements in order to qualify for the exclusion.

Since it is a once-in-a-lifetime exclusion, you should use it wisely. If you have purchased another home, or plan to purchase another one, and you can defer all of the capital gain, do not take the exclusion in that year. If you take the exclusion, and later buy another home which would allow you to defer the gain on the old residence, then amend your tax return on Form 1040X to revoke this exclusion. Remember, you have three years after the date of filing a tax return in which to file an amended return.

Under the 1981 tax changes, the exclusion limit has now been raised to $125,000 for sales of houses occurring after July 20, 1981. Always keep these effective dates in mind when you are deciding whether or not to sell your house, or when to buy another one. By knowing the law you can save thousands of dollars in taxes.

EXCHANGING PERSONAL RESIDENCES

Instead of selling, if you trade or exchange one personal residence for another personal residence, you also may be able to defer the capital gain if the new residence has a value that is equal to or greater than the value of your old residence. For example, you exchange a house that is worth $75,000 for a house that is worth $100,000. In such a trade, you most likely will be paying out money rather than receiving any. This allows you to defer the capital gain on your old residence. An exchange is handled basically the same way as a purchase, but instead of paying entirely in cash and notes, you pay part of the price of the new house with your actual, old house.

On the other hand, where you trade down, or exchange personal residences and receive money from the transaction, you may be subject to a capital gains tax. For example, if your old house is valued at $75,000 and the new one at $50,000, and you received $25,000 in cash, that amount, or the amount that you have already determined to be the gain on the exchange of the old residence, whichever is smaller, would be subject to capital gains tax.

SELLING RENTAL PROPERTY— FORM 4797

When rental property is sold or exchanged, Form 4797 must be filled out. This form is also used to report the sale of a business, a sale or exchange of properties used in a trade or business, and involuntary conversions. For the majority of taxpayers, the only time that they will use this form is when rental property is sold.

SALE OR EXCHANGE OF REAL ESTATE 85

Form **4797**	**Supplemental Schedule of Gains and Losses**	OMB No. 1545-0184
Department of the Treasury Internal Revenue Service	(Includes Gains and Losses From Sales or Exchanges of Assets Used in a Trade or Business and Involuntary Conversions) To be filed with Form 1040, 1041, 1065, 1120, etc.—See Separate Instructions	**1981** 31

Name(s) as shown on return | Identifying number

Part I Sales or Exchanges of Property Used in a Trade or Business, and Involuntary Conversions From Other Than Casualty and Theft—Property Held More Than 1 Year (Except for Certain Livestock)
Note: Use Form 4684 to report involuntary conversions from casualty and theft.
Caution: If you sold property on which you claimed the investment credit, you may be liable for recapture of that credit. See Form 4255 for additional information.

a. Kind of property and description	b. Date acquired (mo., day, yr.)	c. Date sold (mo., day, yr.)	d. Gross sales price minus expense of sale	e. Depreciation allowed (or allowable) since acquisition	f. Cost or other basis, plus improvements	g. LOSS (f minus the sum of d and e)	h. GAIN (d plus e minus f)
1							

2 (a) Gain, if any, from Form 4684, Part II, line 25 . . . .
 (b) Section 1231 gain from installment sales from Form 6252, line 19 or 27 . . . . . .
3 Gain, if any, from line 26, Part III, on back of this form from other than casualty and theft . .
4 Add lines 1 through 3 in column g and column h . . . . ( )
5 Combine line 4, column g and line 4, column h. Enter gain or (loss) here, and on the appropriate line as follows:
 (a) For all except partnership returns:
  (1) If line 5 is a gain, enter the gain as a long-term capital gain on Schedule D (Form 1040, 1120, etc.) that is being filed. See instruction E.
  (2) If line 5 is zero or a loss, enter that amount on line 6.
 (b) For partnership returns: Enter the amount shown on line 5 above, on Schedule K (Form 1065), line 8.

Part II Ordinary Gains and Losses

a. Kind of property and description	b. Date acquired (mo., day, yr.)	c. Date sold (mo., day, yr.)	d. Gross sales price minus expense of sale	e. Depreciation allowed (or allowable) since acquisition	f. Cost or other basis, plus improvements	g. LOSS (f minus the sum of d and e)	h. GAIN (d plus e minus f)

6 Loss, if any, from line 5(a)(2) . . . .
7 Gain, if any, from line 25, Part III on back of this form . . . .
8 (a) Net gain or (loss) from Form 4684, lines 17 and 24a . . . .
 (b) Ordinary gain from installment sales from Form 6252, line 18 or 26 . . . .
9 Other ordinary gains and losses (include property held 1 year or less):

10 Add lines 6 through 9 in column g and column h . . . . ( )
11 Combine line 10, column g and line 10, column h. Enter gain or (loss) here, and on the appropriate line as follows:
 (a) For all except individual returns: Enter the gain or (loss) shown on line 11, on the line provided on the return (Form 1120, etc.) being filed. See instruction F for specific line reference.
 (b) For individual returns:
  (1) If the loss on line 6 includes a loss from Form 4684, Part II, column B(ii), enter that part of the loss here and on line 29 of Schedule A (Form 1040). Identify as from "Form 4797, line 11(b)(1)" . . . . . .
  (2) Redetermine the gain or (loss) on line 11, excluding the loss (if any) entered on line 11(b)(1). Enter here and on Form 1040, line 14 . . . .

Part III Gain From Disposition of Property Under Sections 1245, 1250, 1251, 1252, 1254, 1255
Skip lines 20 and 21 if there are no dispositions of farm property or farmland, or if this form is filed by a partnership.

12 Description of sections 1245, 1250, 1251, 1252, 1254, and 1255 property:	Date acquired (mo., day, yr.)	Date sold (mo., day, yr.)
(A)		
(B)		
(C)		
(D)		

Part III is continued on page 2.

For Paperwork Reduction Act Notice, see page 1 of separate instructions. 343-177-1 Form **4797** (1981)

Form 4797 (1981)   Page 2

Relate lines 12(A) through 12(D) to these columns ▶▶▶	Property (A)	Property (B)	Property (C)	Property (D)
13 Gross sales price minus expense of sale				
14 Cost or other basis				
15 Depreciation (or depletion) allowed (or allowable) . . .				
16 Adjusted basis, subtract line 15 from line 14				
17 Total gain, subtract line 16 from line 13				
18 If section 1245 property: (a) Depreciation allowed (or allowable) after applicable date (see instructions) . . . . (b) Enter smaller of line 17 or 18(a)				
19 If section 1250 property: (If straight line depreciation used, enter zero on line 19(i).) (a) Additional depreciation after 12/31/75 (see instructions) . . . . (b) Applicable percentage times the smaller of line 17 or line 19(a) (see instruction G.4) . . . . (c) Subtract line 19(a) from line 17. If line 17 is not more than line 19(a), skip lines 19(d) through 19(h) . . . (d) Additional depreciation after 12/31/69 and before 1/1/76 . . . . (e) Applicable percentage times the smaller of line 19(c) or 19(d) (see instruction G.4) . . . . (f) Subtract line 19(d) from line 19(c). If line 19(c) is not more than line 19(d), skip lines 19(g) and 19(h) . . (g) Additional depreciation after 12/31/63 and before 1/1/70 . . . . (h) Applicable percentage times the smaller of line 19(f) or 19(g) (see instruction G.4) . . . . (i) Add lines 19(b), 19(e), and 19(h)				
20 If section 1251 property: (a) If farmland, enter soil, water, and land clearing expenses for current year and the four preceding years . (b) If farm property other than land, subtract line 18(b) from line 17; if farmland, enter smaller of line 17 or 20(a) . . . . (c) Excess deductions account (see instruction G.5) . . (d) Enter smaller of line 20(b) or 20(c)				
21 If section 1252 property: (a) Soil, water, and land clearing expenses made after 12/31/69 . . . . (b) Amount from line 20(d), if none enter zero . . . (c) Subtract line 21(b) from line 21(a). If line 21(b) is more than line 21(a), enter zero . . . . (d) Line 21(c) times applicable percentage (see instruction G.5) . . . . (e) Subtract line 21(b) from line 17 . . . . (f) Enter smaller of line 21(d) or 21(e)				
22 If section 1254 property: (a) Intangible drilling and development costs deducted after 12/31/75 (see instruction G.6) . . . . . . (b) Enter smaller of line 17 or 22(a)				
23 If section 1255 property: (a) Applicable percentage of payments excluded from income under section 126 (see instruction G.7) . . . (b) Enter the smaller of line 17 or 23(a)				

Summary of Part III Gains (Complete Property columns (A) through (D) through line 23(b) before going to line 24)

24 Total gains for all properties (add columns (A) through (D), line 17) . . . .
25 Add columns (A) through (D), lines 18(b), 19(i), 20(d), 21(f), 22(b) and 23(b). Enter here and on Part II, line 7 .
26 Subtract line 25 from line 24. Enter the portion from casualty and theft on Form 4684, line 19; enter the portion from other than casualty and theft on Form 4797, Part I, line 3 . . . .

Part IV   Complete this Part Only if You are Electing Out of the Installment Method And are Reporting a Note or Other Obligation at Less Than Full Face Value

☐ Check here if you elect out of the installment method.
    Enter the face amount of the note or other obligation ▶ ....
    Enter the percentage of valuation of the note or other obligation ▶

343-177-1

SALE OR EXCHANGE OF REAL ESTATE

In Part I of Form 4797, you determine the capital gain or loss on the sale of rental property held more than one year.

Column a. Write in the kind of property and its location. For example, "two-unit building, San Francisco, California."

In *Column b* put in the date, day, month, and year on which the property was acquired. If it was inherited, put in the exact date on which you became the owner.

Column c. Put in the exact day, month, and year that the property was sold.

In *column d* put in the total sales price minus all the expenses of the sale. Expenses include commissions, real estate brokers' fees, attorneys' fees, fixing-up expenses, transportation costs, telephone costs, etc.

In *column e* put in the total amount of depreciation that you have taken on the property since you've owned it, including the current year. That amount would be found on this year's, or previous years', Schedule E. Include also the amounts of depreciation you have taken on major improvements that you have made on the property since you've owned it.

In *column f* put in the total cost of the property plus all of the improvements you have made on it. These improvements would include additions, new kitchens, baths, air conditioning systems, electrical systems, etc.

In *columns g* or *h* there will appear either a loss or a gain. If it is a gain, take the amount from line 5 and put it on line 14 of Schedule D as a long-term capital gain.

If the amount on line 5 is a loss, then go down to Part II, under "ordinary gains and losses," and put that amount onto line 6.

Part II of Form 4797 is used in relation to sales of rental property in two ways. One is to report a capital loss on the sale of rental property, and the other is to report gain or loss on property that is owned for less than one year, or short-term capital gain or loss. Fill in all the information asked for in columns a through h and determine the capital gain or loss. The amount from this line is not transferred to Schedule D but, instead, goes right onto line 14 of Form 1040, "supplemental gains or losses."

DEFERRING CAPITAL GAINS ON RENTAL PROPERTY

You can defer capital gains on rental property sales through a "like kind" exchange for property of equal or greater value. That means you trade your rental property for another rental property that is worth at least as much as yours. By doing this, you can defer the entire capital gain. Do not exchange property, however, if there is a capital loss, because you will lose the benefit of a deduction from gross income. When you fill out Form 4797, in column d write in the term "like-kind exchange." Again, remember that you are only *deferring* the capital gain. When you later sell the new property, you will be subject to tax on the capital gain on the new property as well as on the amount that you have deferred from the sale of the old property. You can continue to trade up, and therefore defer paying capital gains tax. However, your depreciation deductions will be lower than if you had paid cash for each new property.

You can also defer capital gains on rental property if you sell one property and buy another on the same day. Many real estate firms in California, in the last few years, have been setting up exchanges by holding the money in escrow until the transfer of the new property closed. This method, called the "Starker exchange," has come under some criticism from the IRS. According to many real estate agents, if the money is held in escrow, even though the new property is not purchased for many months after the first one was sold, it can still qualify as a tax-free exchange. So far, the IRS has not specifically disallowed this procedure, but they may do so in the future.

INSTALLMENT SALES— FORM 6252

When you sell your personal residence, rental property, or business, and do not receive all of the purchase price in cash at the closing, there is a deferred-payment sale which is reported on the *installment method*. For example, you sell your house for $100,000. The person who buys it gives you a $20,000 cash down payment along with a promissory note for $80,000 payable in ten years. Instead of receiving all of the selling price in cash, you are going to hold a note or mortgage and collect payments on it. Instead of paying tax on the entire profit or capital gain on the sale, you only have to pay tax on a certain portion of each payment that you actually receive during each taxable year.

By spreading out, over a period of years, the amount of capital gain that will be added to your gross income, you will save tax money. For example, you sell a rental property for cash in 1981 and have a long-term capital gain of $100,000. Therefore, $40,000 would be added to your income for 1981, and, if the extra income forces you up into the 50% tax bracket, you would pay approximately $20,000 in additional taxes for that year. However, instead of receiving the entire $100,000, you hold a note and receive payments on it each year, you'll pay tax only on a percentage of the amount that you receive each year. Since the tax rates are progressive, you will be in a lower tax bracket, and the percentage of your income that is taxed will be lower. You will thus keep more of the profit you made on the sale.

On Form 6252 you calculate the "percentage of profit" that you make on a deferred-payments sale. You then multiply the amount of any payments that you receive for each year by that percentage of profit. If there is a long-term capital gain, you put the amount of the product under Part II of Schedule D. Only 40% of the gain is then taxed. For each succeeding year, you multiply the amount of payments received by that same percentage and, again, put the product onto Schedule D.

Using the example above, if you make $100,000 in long-term capital gain and receive payments totalling $10,000 in 1981, you first determine the percentage of profit by dividing the *contract price* into the total net profit to be realized. Let's say that the percentage of profit is 50%. You multiply the amount that you actually received in 1981, $10,000, by 50% and then put that total, $5,000, under Part II, long-term capital gains, on Schedule D. Forty per cent, or $2,000, of the $5,000 gain is taxable, so, if you are in the 40% tax bracket, you would wind up paying only $800 in additional taxes for 1981. Each year you would continue to use the same 50% figure, and to pay tax on only 40% of the long-term capital gain. In this way, you will pay less in taxes overall by using the installment method of reporting gain on the sale.

WHICH METHOD IS BEST?

My clients frequently ask whether they should sell, exchange, trade up, or set up an installment sale. For personal residences, I think it is usually best to buy a more expensive house and defer the capital gain. Try to delay using up the $125,000 exclusion, because it can be taken only once, and the Congress might raise the limit again.

For rental property, trading up is a very good way of increasing your net worth without having to pay income tax. However, you have to consider your overall tax position for each year. If you have large deductions or losses in one year, you may want to sell property outright in that year because your tax bracket will be lower and you can absorb relatively large gains without paying more tax. If you are going to have higher taxable income in one year, then you may want to structure a tax-free exchange of properties in order to defer the gain and pay no additional tax that year.

I personally do not like installment sales. In times of inflation, you do not want to be a lender, you want to be a borrower. Even if you are holding a note bearing a high interest rate, I feel that it is still better to have the capital, in cash, so that you can invest it and make even more money. The name of the game is capital, and the people with the cash make the most money. I've seen many people who were holding notes and needed cash, and they ended up having to sell the notes at a discount. When you discount a note you are going to suffer a substantial loss. I'd rather sell the property for less money, for all cash, than hold a second or third mortgage.

SALE OR EXCHANGE OF REAL ESTATE

Form **6252**
Department of the Treasury
Internal Revenue Service

Computation of Installment Sale Income
▶ See instructions on back. ▶ Attach to your tax return.
Use a separate form for each sale or other disposition of property on the installment method.

OMB No. 1545-0228

1981

Name(s) as shown on tax return

Identifying number

A Kind of property and description ▶
B Date acquired (month, day, and year) ▶   **C** Date sold (month, day, and year) ▶
D Was property sold to a related party after May 14, 1980? (See instruction C) . . . . ☐ Yes ☐ No
If you checked "Yes," you must complete Part III.

Part I   Computation of Gross Profit and Contract Price *(Complete this part for year of sale only.)*

1 Selling price including mortgages and other indebtedness (Do not include interest.)	1	
2 Mortgages and other indebtedness purchaser assumes or takes property subject to (see instructions)	2	
3 Subtract line 2 from line 1	3	
4 Cost or other basis of property sold	4	
5 Depreciation allowed or allowable	5	
6 Adjusted basis (subtract line 5 from line 4)	6	
7 Commissions and other expenses of sale	7	
8 Add line 6 and line 7	8	
9 Gross profit (subtract line 8 from line 1). If result is zero or less, do not complete rest of form . .	9	
10 Subtract line 8 from line 2. If line 8 is more than line 2, enter zero	10	
11 Contract price (add line 3 and line 10)	11	

Part II   Computation of Taxable Part of Installment Sale
(Complete this part for year of sale and any year a payment is received.)

12 Gross profit ratio (divide line 9 by line 11) (for years after the year of sale, see instructions)	12	
13 For year of sale only—enter amount from line 10 above; otherwise enter zero	13	
14 Payments received during year	14	
15 Add lines 13 and 14	15	
16 Payments received in prior years	16	
17 Taxable part of installment sale (multiply line 15 by line 12)	17	
18 Part of line 17 that is ordinary income under recapture rules (see instructions)	18	
19 Subtract line 18 from line 17. Enter on Schedule D or Form 4797 (see instructions)	19	

Part III   Information and Computation for Related Party Installment Sale
(Complete this part only if you answered "Yes" to question D and did not receive the final installment payment in 1981.)

E Name, address, and taxpayer identifying number of related party
----

F Did the related party resell or dispose of this property, acquired from you after May 14, 1980, during 1981? . . ☐ Yes ☐ No
G If the answer to question F is "Yes," complete lines 20 through 27 below unless one of the following conditions is met (check only the box that applies).
☐ The first disposition was a sale or exchange of stock to the issuing corporation.
☐ The second disposition was an involuntary conversion where the threat of conversion occurred after the first disposition.
☐ The second disposition occurred after the death of the original seller or purchaser.
☐ It can be established to the satisfaction of the Internal Revenue Service that tax avoidance was not a principal purpose for either of the dispositions. If this box is checked, attach an explanation. (See instruction C.)

20 Selling price of property sold by related party	20	
21 Enter contract price from line 11 for year of first sale	21	
22 Enter the smaller of line 20 or line 21	22	
23 Total payments received by the end of tax year. Add lines 15 and 16	23	
24 Subtract line 23 from line 22. If line 23 is more than line 22, enter zero	24	
25 Multiply line 24 by line 12 for year of first sale	25	
26 Part of line 25 that is ordinary income under recapture rules (see instructions)	26	
27 Subtract line 26 from line 25. Enter on Schedule D or Form 4797 (see instructions)	27	

For Paperwork Reduction Act Notice, see back of form.   343-230-1   Form **6252** (1981)

CHAPTER TEN

☆

Lines 13—17 of Form 1040

CAPITAL GAIN DISTRIBUTIONS

As discussed in the previous chapter, capital gain distributions are a type of income received from corporations. They are only 40% taxable. If you have no other capital gains to report, and, thus, do not need to use Schedule D, you should report capital gains distributions on line 13 of Form 1040 rather than on line 12. Calculate 40% of the total capital gains distributions and put that amount on line 13.

SUPPLEMENTAL GAINS OR LOSSES FROM FORM 4797

Line 14 on Form 1040 is rarely used. The amount that is to be put here is calculated by filling out Part II of Form 4797, which is used to report short-term capital gains and losses on sales of rental property, businesses, or property and equipment used in a trade or business. For example, you buy and then sell a rental property within one year. Fill out Form 4797, Part II, ordinary gains and losses, and calculate the short-term capital gain or loss. That amount would then go onto line 14 of Form 1040.

CAPITAL GAINS AND INVESTMENTS

Each year, millions of Americans invest billions of dollars. Let's look at some of the more common investments and how they relate to your income taxes.

First of all, money that is used for investment should never be money that is necessary for you to live on. It is a tragic mistake, almost certain to guarantee financial difficulties, to tie up the money that you need for month-to-month living expenses. Before thinking about making any type of investment, you should sit down and plan a budget. Calculate accurately how much money you need to live on, your projected expenses, and how much money will be left over for you to invest. With investments, there is always a time factor, whether it is six months, six years, or two days. You have to be able to leave investment money tied up for a certain period of time, and it cannot be touched during that time to be spent on other needs. Make sure you do not overextend yourself, i.e., incur debts that are greater than your income. If you do this, you will surely lose on your investments.

For tax purposes, some investments are better than others. Money that you receive in the form of interest income, as from money market funds, treasury bills, savings certificates, etc., and money from dividends on corporate stocks is considered *ordinary income*. While portions of this income may be tax exempt, for example the first $200 or $400 of dividend income, the rest of it is still 100% taxable. If you are in a fairly high tax bracket, then a large part of your income from such sources is simply going to go to the government in taxes.

For tax purposes, investments in growth stocks, precious metals, precious stones, antiques, oriental rugs, ceramics, etc. often are much better. These are considered capital investments, and, if you hold them for more than a year, you have to pay tax on only 40% of the gain. Of course, risk is involved in these investments.

For tax purposes, probably the best investment is in real estate. With real estate there are many tax write-offs—for example, deductions for all of the interest expenses and property taxes that are paid, as well as many tax advantages when the property is sold. In the case of personal residences, you can defer the capital gain when you sell one if you buy another home at a higher cost. You can even exclude the first $125,000 of net profit on the sale of a personal residence if you are age fifty-five or over at the time of the sale. Also, you are not subject to the minimum tax on the gain from the sale of a personal residence. The minimum tax is an additional tax imposed when there is more than $10,000 of long-term capital gain in one taxable year. See the section on the Minimum Tax and Form 4625 below.

Another advantage of real estate as an investment is *leverage*. Leverage has to do with the amount of cash you actually put into property, and the percentage of your return on the investment. For example, if you purchase a house for $80,000, you probably would not put down $80,000 in cash. Let's say you put down $8,000 as a down payment. If the house appreciates, or goes up in value, only 10% in one year, it would then be worth $88,000. If you then sell it for $88,000, you would get $16,000, your $8,000 that you put down and the $8,000 of appreciation in value. Disregarding mortgage payments and deductible interest payments for purposes of this example, your return on that investment would be 100%. The amount that would be taxed if you had owned it for more than one year would only be 40% of the $8,000 profit, or $3,200. In other words, you've doubled your money and are paying taxes on only 40% of the gain! That's quite different from investing in a money market fund that may pay about 16% interest, but which is fully taxable. In fact, if the house in the example above was your personal residence, and you bought another house for more than $88,000 within a two-year period, you would not have to pay any tax at all on the gain!

In some cases, the best investment you can make is simply to upgrade the property you already own. If, by adding a room, fixing the roof, or making any other type of improvement, you can greatly increase the value of your property, that may be in itself a terrific investment.

Rental property is considered one of the best tax shelters, and is otherwise usually a good investment. *Tax shelter* means that you get a lot of tax write-offs by investing in a particular thing. As we will see later in this chapter when we discuss Schedule E, rental property is a source of many write-offs, including all the expenses of the property, as well as depreciation of the building and all of its major improvements. Then, later on, you can exchange rental properties or set up an installment sale in order to avoid the capital gains tax, or at least lower it.

The specific investment you should make is up to you. You should be comfortable with it, feel confident that it will work, and be able to sleep at night. Perhaps the first step you should take is to seek the advice of a financial advisor or planner. Look at the fee as an investment. If professional advice can make you some money and show you some ways to save on taxes, then the fee will be well worth it.

FULLY TAXABLE PENSIONS AND ANNUITIES

If you or your spouse receive any pension or annuity payments that are fully taxable, simply put the total amount received in 1981 on line 15 of Form 1040. Some pensions or annuities are not fully taxable but only partially taxable, and are reported on line 16a of Form 1040.

If your pension or annuity plan is funded entirely by your employer's contributions, or, if you also contribute to the fund during your employment, and such amounts are not taxed at the time, the benefits you receive upon retirement will probably be fully taxable. If you have amounts deducted from your salary that are contributed to a pension or annuity plan, the benefits would be non-taxable as they come back to you in pension or annuity payments, because you pay income taxes on your salary, part of which went into the fund as contributions. Theoretically, in our tax system you don't pay taxes twice on the same item of income.

If the pension or annuity is fully taxable, simply put in the total amount of payments you received from it during the year on line 15. You do not have to fill out any other form. Also, if you or your spouse are retired, check to see if you qualify for the retirement income credit, Schedules R and RP, which are discussed in Chapter 15.

PARTIALLY TAXABLE PENSIONS AND ANNUITIES

Before you fill in *line 16a and b* of Form 1040, you need to have all the necessary information about your pension or annuity plan. Generally, the best places to get that information are from your employer or from the administrator of the pension or annuity plan. Most importantly, find out whether or not the pension or annuity is fully taxable. If not, find out how much of it is non-taxable, or what percentage of the payments you received is non-taxable. Certain pensions or annuities are set up so that you will get back the total amount of your contributions within three years of the date of your first payment. None of the amount of your contributions will be taxable.

On *line 16a* you put in the total amounts you received of pension and annuity payments that are not fully taxable. On page 10 of the instruction booklet for Form 1040 you will find a worksheet on which to figure the taxable portion of this total amount. Transfer the result of your computations to *line 16b* of Form 1040.

SUPPLEMENTAL INCOME— SCHEDULE E

Line 17 of Form 1040 requires you to attach Schedule E if you have certain types of income. Schedule E is used to report rent and royalty income or loss, and income or losses from partnerships, estates, trusts, small business corporations, and windfall profit tax credits and refunds. It is divided into several parts, some of which have nothing to do with the other parts. The form is sort of the IRS' version of the fisherman with the big net who is trying to catch all of the other fish that are getting away. In other words, this form is a catch-all for other types of income. Let's go through it step by step.

Royalty Income or Loss—Part I. Some taxpayers receive royalty income from investments such as oil, natural gas, or oil well drilling companies. If you have such investments, you'll get a yearly statement from the company showing you the total amount of royalty income you received. The statement may also include a depletion-allowance figure, which means you have a tax deduction. The royalty income will go on line 3b and the depletion allowance on line 18 of Part I of Schedule E. The depletion allowance is a tax deduction based on investing in certain natural resources, such as oil, natural gas, timber, etc. The depletion allowance is a percentage of the gross amount of the royalty, and it varies according to the particular natural resource involved. The depletion allowance is then subtracted from the royalty income and the difference is your net income from the investment for the year.

If you have expenses in relation to your royalty income, you should put them onto *lines 4 through 16* of Schedule E. The most common royalty expenses are for transportation and telephone.

Royalty income that is derived from writing or other artistic endeavors does *not* go under Part I of Schedule E. This type of royalty income is considered self-employment income, and would therefore go on Schedule C. Be certain to report each source of income correctly or you may lose the various deductions allowed for each type of income.

Rental Income or Loss—Part I. For most taxpayers, Part I of Schedule E is used for reporting the income and expenses of rental property.

Each rental property is listed separately on Schedule E, and your records also should be kept in a similar fashion. In a sense, each rental property is a separate business, and income, expenses, and depreciation for each property must be kept separate. You may have gains on some properties and losses on others. There is room on Schedule E, under Part I, for three properties. If you own more than that, you can use additional Schedules E. A good technique to follow when you use

SCHEDULE E (Form 1040) Department of the Treasury Internal Revenue Service	**Supplemental Income Schedule** (From rents and royalties, partnerships, estates and trusts, etc.) ▶ Attach to Form 1040. ▶ See Instructions for Schedule E (Form 1040).	OMB No. 1545-0074 **1981** 15

Name(s) as shown on Form 1040 — Your social security number

Part I Rent and Royalty Income or Loss.
1 Are any of the expenses listed below for a vacation home or similar dwelling rented to others (see Instructions)? . ☐ Yes ☐ No
2 If you checked "Yes" to question 1, did you or a member of your family occupy the vacation home or similar dwelling for more than 14 days during the tax year? . . . . ☐ Yes ☐ No

Rental and Royalty Income (describe property in Part V)		Properties			Totals
		A	B	C	
3 a Rents received					3
b Royalties received					

Rental and Royalty Expenses

4 Advertising	4					
5 Auto and travel	5					
6 Cleaning and maintenance . . .	6					
7 Commissions	7					
8 Insurance	8					
9 Interest	9					
10 Legal and other professional fees . .	10					
11 Repairs	11					
12 Supplies	12					
13 Taxes (do NOT include Windfall Profit Tax, see Part III, line 35)	13					
14 Utilities	14					
15 Wages and salaries	15					
16 Other (list) ▶						
17 Total deductions (add lines 4 through 16)	17					17
18 Depreciation expense (see Instructions), or Depletion (attach computation)	18					18
19 Total (add lines 17 and 18)	19					
20 Income or (loss) from rental or royalty properties (subtract line 19 from line 3a (rents) or 3b (royalties))	20					

21 Add properties with profits on line 20, and enter total profits here 21
22 Add properties with losses on line 20, and enter total (losses) here . . . . 22 ( )
23 Combine amounts on lines 21 and 22, and enter net profit or (loss) here 23
24 Net farm rental profit or (loss) from Form 4835, line 50 24
25 Total rental or royalty income or (loss). Combine amounts on lines 23 and 24. Enter here and include in line 37 on page 2 25

For Paperwork Reduction Act Notice, see Form 1040 Instructions. 343-062-1

LINES 13—17 OF FORM 1040
95

Schedule E (Form 1040) 1981 Page **2**

Part II — Income or Losses from Partnerships, Estates or Trusts, or Small Business Corporations

If you report a loss below, do you have amounts invested in that activity for which you are not "at risk" (see Instructions)? ☐ Yes ☐ No
If "Yes," and your loss exceeded your amount "at risk," did you limit your loss to your amount "at risk"? . . . . . ☐ Yes ☐ No

	(a) Name	(b) Employer identification number	(c) Net loss (see instructions for "at risk" limitations)	(d) Net income
Partnerships				

26 Add amounts in columns (c) and (d) and enter here . . . . 26 ( )
27 Combine amounts in columns (c) and (d), line 26, and enter net income or (loss) 27
28 Additional first-year depreciation from 1980/1981 fiscal-year partnerships. Enter amount from Form 1065, Schedule K–1, line 2, but not more than $2,000 ($4,000 if a joint return) . . . 28 ( )
29 Total partnership income or (loss). Combine lines 27 and 28. Enter here and include in line 37 . 29

Estates or Trusts

30 Add amounts in columns (c) and (d) and enter here . . . . 30 ( )
31 Total estate or trust income or (loss). Combine amounts in columns (c) and (d), line 30. Enter here and include in line 37 31

Small Business Corporations

32 Add amounts in columns (c) and (d) and enter here . . . . 32 ( )
33 Total small business corporation income or (loss). Combine amounts in columns (c) and (d), line 32. Enter here and include in line 37 33

Part III — Windfall Profit Tax Summary

34 Windfall Profit Tax Credit or Refund received in 1981 (see Instructions) 34
35 Windfall Profit Tax withheld in 1981 (see Instructions) . . . . 35 ( )
36 Combine amounts on lines 34 and 35. Enter here and include in line 37 36

Part IV — Summary

37 TOTAL income or (loss). Combine lines 25, 29, 31, 33, and 36. Enter here and on Form 1040, line 17 . ▶ 37
38 Farmers and fishermen: Enter your share of gross farming and fishing income applicable to Parts I and II 38

Part V — Depreciation Claimed in Part I.

Complete only if property was placed in service before January 1, 1981. For more space, use Form 4562. If you placed any property in service after December 31, 1980, use Form 4562 for all property; do NOT complete Part V.

	(a) Description and location of property	(b) Date acquired	(c) Cost or other basis	(d) Depreciation allowed or allowable in prior years	(e) Depreciation method	(f) Life or rate	(g) Depreciation for this year
Property A							
	Totals (Property A)						
Property B							
	Totals (Property B)						
Property C							
	Totals (Property C)						

343-062-1

more than one Schedule E is to number the forms consecutively. The first one, for example, would be numbered 'E1,' the second, 'E2,' and so on. The gain or loss of all Schedules E combined is put onto line 17 of Form 1040.

Now let's go through the step-by-step procedures in filling out Part I of Schedule E.

Line 1 asks for a "yes" or "no" answer. If the rental property you are reporting on Schedule E is also your vacation home, then you may have to prorate certain amounts by percentages. When you occupy your rental property for personal use for more than fourteen days during the year, you cannot deduct expenses or depreciation during the time you are there. For example, you use the vacation home for six months, and for six months you rent it out. You would be able to depreciate it only for one-half of the year, and to deduct rental expenses only during the time that it was rented.

Line 2. If the answer to line 2 is "yes," and you or your family occupied the home for more than fourteen days during the year, then you will have to prorate expenses and depreciation. If, for example, you lived in it for two months, and rented it out for the rest of the year, then you could deduct 10/12 of the total expenses and depreciation for the year.

In the next section of Part I of Schedule E, we will be setting up a profit and loss statement for each rental property. Rental properties are treated differently than personal residences. Since you collect income from rental property, you can therefore deduct all of the expenses that go into producing that income. Thus, not only can interest and property taxes be deducted, as with personal residences, but you can also deduct insurance, repairs, utility expenses, redecorating expenses, etc. Also, you are able to depreciate the building, but not the land. According to the IRS, land never wears out, and therefore can never be depreciated. Major, or capital, improvements can also be depreciated. These long-lived additions to the value of the property include major renovations, additions, a new roof, appliances, etc.

If a part of your rental property is also used as a personal residence, then you will have to prorate expenses and depreciation. For example, you own a duplex and live in one of the apartments. If there is a 50/50 division between rental space and personal residence, then one-half of all of the expenses and depreciation would go onto Schedule E, and one-half of only the interest expense and property taxes would go onto Schedule A as itemized deductions. It's important to set out your calculations on Schedule E in order to show the IRS that you understand how the tax laws work.

If you are a member of a partnership that owns a rental property, you should indicate that fact on Schedule E. If you are a half-owner, or one-third owner, etc., you should point out your share in the ownership of the property to the IRS. Write that information in Column a of either Part V of Schedule E or form 4562, whichever you use to claim depreciation expense for your rental property. (Depreciation is discussed below.)

Line 3a of Schedule E. The "rents received" is the total amount of money you *collected* from the tenants of each property. If you ordinarily collect $300 a month, but you only received eleven payments for that year, then you would put $3,300 onto line 3a for property A.

If you rent the property out, but do not receive a "fair market rent," the IRS may challenge you. For example, if you rent the property to friends or relatives and do not charge them as much rent as similar properties go for, the IRS may declare that yours is not really a rental property. In that case, you may lose all or part of your deductions for expenses and depreciation. You should be well aware of this limitation, and be sure that you do collect a fair market rent. Obviously, there is some ambiguity as to what is considered a fair market rent.

A similar limitation applies when you remodel a rental property, but do not rent it for some time afterwards. If it remains vacant for only a small part of the year, then you should have no problem claiming it as a rental property for the entire year. A problem arises, however, when the work is extensive but you get very little or no rent from it. You may be challenged by the IRS, so be prepared. In a clear case of this kind, you could probably avoid an audit by prorating the deductions for expenses and depreciation.

Rental Expenses Expenses incurred in generating your rental income are to be reported on *lines 4 through 16* of Schedule E. In addition to the expense categories included on those lines, you may write in additional categories in the "other" category on *line 16*. The following is a list of additional typical expense categories you can write in:

- Advertising
- Appliances
- Carpentry
- Cleaning
- Electrical
- Furniture
- Gardening
- Hauling
- Insurance
- Interest
- Labor
- Licenses
- Maintenance
- Management
- Painting
- Plumbing
- Repairs
- Roofing
- Snow removal
- Supplies
- Taxes
- Telephone
- Travel & auto expense
- Utilities
- Wages & salaries
- Windows

The amounts to be put onto lines 4 through 16 of Schedule E are for expenses incurred during the taxable year for each of three properties. They are expenses for items and repairs that do not qualify as capital improvements to the property, and that have a useful life of less than one year. Capital improvements with a useful life of *more* than one year must be depreciated. In the past few years the IRS has audited a great many Schedules E. One of their main concerns is with the topic of expenses versus depreciation. I feel that it is necessary to list each type of expense and repair according to separate categories. Do not lump amounts together, and remember that lower numbers look much more believable than larger ones. I think it is also a good idea to separate repair expenses in terms of cost of materials and cost of labor. You cannot deduct amounts for labor that you have performed yourself, only for work that you've paid someone else to do. However, it can be anyone else, whether or not he or she is licensed in a trade or craft, even a friend or relative.

Be careful to analyze the nature of repair expenses. For example, if you repair a crack in a wall, that would be put down as an expense. But, if you build a wall, that would be a capital improvement and would have to be depreciated. Thus, you'd only be able to take a percentage of the total cost in each taxable year over its useful life. Spell out each and every repair, including the cost of materials and supplies and the cost of labor. If you have work done to the roof, do not just write in the word "roof," write in "roof repairs." A new roofing job must be depreciated, whereas roof repairs can be deducted as one-time expenses.

If part of the property is used as your personal residence, then you have to prorate the amounts of certain expenses and repairs. For example, you own a duplex and one-half is a rental unit and one-half is your personal residence. Only one-half of the taxes, interest, insurance, utilities, etc. are deductible on Schedule E—the rental half. If you have repairs done to the rental portion, they would be fully deductible, but repairs that are done to your personal portion are not deductible at all on Schedule E. They come into play only when you *sell* the personal residence. If you have a new roof put over the entire duplex, then, again, only one-half the cost could be depreciated.

Another important expense of maintaining rental property is automobile and other travel. You can deduct the expenses involved in going back and forth to your rental property, going to stores to get supplies and materials, etc. Generally you are able to base the deduction on your total mileage at 20 cents a mile.

If you have a rental property in another state, even across the country, and you take a trip to see it, you may be able to deduct the travel expenses related directly to visiting the rental property. Be certain to save your receipts, and keep a diary. You may also be able to deduct long distance phone calls related to rental property. Be careful to document all of these amounts well, because this is an area that the IRS likes to audit.

A word of caution is needed about certain types of expenses related to rental property. You can deduct the cost of seminars or courses dealing with rental property, various types of investment seminars, property-searching trips, etc. as rental property expenses, but a problem comes along with it. Depending on the circumstances, the IRS may challenge you, saying that, in fact, you don't just invest in rental property but that you are *engaged in the business* of owning rental property. If most of your income comes from rental property or from its sale, the IRS may claim that, since you are in the business of owning rental property, when you sell it, the net gain will be considered ordinary income, rather than long-term capital gain. In other words, the IRS could say that property is the inventory of your business, and when you sell it, you have to declare the profit as business income rather than as the return on an investment.

Do not let this happen to you. Don't go overboard in deducting all of the possible types of expenses. Don't let your only source of income in any taxable year be the amount that you receive in rental income, or the amount that you receive from selling rental property. There is a big, big difference between paying taxes on 100% of a gain that is ordinary income, and 40% of a gain that is long-term capital gain.

On *line 17*, total the amounts in lines 4 through 16 and put that amount here.

Depreciation of Rental Property. *Line 18* of Schedule E asks for depreciation expense. First, in Part V on page 2 of Schedule E, you establish a schedule of depreciation for each of your rental properties. If there are not enough spaces here for your needs, or if the property was placed into service after December 31, 1980, use Form 4562, which is especially designed for depreciation schedules.

First, we will describe how you report depreciation of property that was placed in service *before* January 1, 1981. You will use either Part V on page 2 of Schedule E or Part II of Form 4562. These two forms have similar columns for entering information.

The first item to be depreciated for each of your rental properties is the building itself. Remember, the land that the building is on is not to be depreciated. Let's go through Columns a through g of Part V and set up a depreciation schedule.

In *Column a*, write in the location and description of the property (i.e., single family, duplex, etc.). This should be written on the first line. On the second line, write in the word "land," and on the third line the word "building."

In *Column b*, write in the month and the year that the property was acquired. If it was inherited or a gift to you, put in the date that you took title to it.

In Column c, write in the cost of the building, found in the escrow papers, if you have them. If you inherited the building, the amount to write in would be its fair market value on the date that you inherited it. You may have to get that information from a real estate appraisal.

Above the cost of the building in Column c, write in the cost or other basis of the land. The value of a parcel of land may be obtained from the county tax assessor's office. In different neighborhoods and in different parts of the country, the ratio of land value to building value may be different. Ask other owners of nearby rental property what figure they use, and see how their answers apply to your property. A general rule of thumb is that, usually, about 25% of the total value of the property is the value of the land. On the second line, write in the amount for the land and enclose it in in parentheses, because you are going to subtract the value of the land from the total value of the property. On the next line, put in the value of the building. This is the amount that will be used as the basis for depreciation. It is the total cost of the property minus the value of the land. For example, you buy a piece of property for $100,000 and the value of the land is $25,000. $75,000 is therefore the value of the building, and is its basis for depreciation. At the end of the useful life of the building, you will have deducted $75,000 from the income of the property, over the years.

In *Column d*, put in the amount of depreciation that has been taken for the property in prior years. If this is the first time that you have set up a depreciation schedule for a particular property, then the amount here would be "0."

In *Column e*, put in the method of depreciation that you have elected to adopt for the property in question. There are different methods of depreciation for rental property, and each has its own advantages and disadvantages. We will discuss a few of the more common methods.

Most individual taxpayers use the *straight-line* method of depreciation, written "s/l." To calculate your annual deductions under this method, you simply divide the value of the building by the useful life, or rate, in Column f. For example, if the value of the building is $75,000, and the useful life is twenty years, then the amount of the depreciation deduction for this year and each of the remaining twenty years would be $3,750. If you purchased this building in December, for example, then you would be able to depreciate it only for one month of the taxable year. Using the same examples, the amount of the depreciation deduction for this year would be $313, or 1/12 of $3,750.

If half of this property is a rental unit, and half is your personal residence, you would be able to take only one-half of the allowable deduction for the taxable year. If you own this building together with two other people, and are a one-third owner, then, again, you would be able to take only a percentage of the allowable deduction. In this case, it would be one-third of the total amount.

An advantage to using straight-line depreciation appears when you plan to own a property for a long period of time. The amount of annual depreciation deductions remains constant through the years, and deductions are still available up to the end of the useful life of the building.

A disadvantage of straight-line depreciation is that you cannot take larger deductions in the early years of your investment. If your taxable income is expected to be higher now or in the next few years than in the future, then larger deductions now would be of greater benefit.

Accelerated depreciation gives you a greater write-off now, but less in the future. With accelerated depreciation, you can deduct between 125% and 200% of the amount of the depreciation deduction allowed under the straight-line method. For buildings that were built before 1976, you can use the 125% declining balance method of depreciation. For buildings that were built after 1976, you can use the 150% declining balance method. For buildings built in 1981, you can use the 200% declining balance method.

Here is an example of how these methods of accelerated depreciation are calculated. If you adopt the 125% declining balance method, you would write in under Column e "125% db," divide the cost of the building by the life or rate, and then multiply that amount by 125%. If the value of the building is $75,000 and the life twenty years, the result is $3,750. Multiply that amount by 125% to get $4,688. This year you can deduct $4,688 as depreciation on the building. Then, on next year's Schedule E depreciation schedule, you would subtract $4,688 from $75,000, the building's value, divide that amount, $70,312, by 20 years, and then multiply that amount, $3,515.60, by 125%, to reach $4,394.50, the allowable depreciation deduction for the year. As you can see, each year the balance of the *basis* for depreciation declines, leaving a smaller allowable deduction than for the previous year. In the early years of the depreciation schedule, however, the deductions under accelerated depreciation methods are greater than under the straight-line method.

A disadvantage of the accelerated forms of depreciation is encountered when you sell property within a very few years. When you sell, if the amount of depreciation that you have actually deducted is greater than the amount that you would have taken if you had used the straight-line method of depreciation, the actual amount taken is subtracted from the gain on the sale and is considered *ordinary income.* This is known as recapture of excess depreciation. Even if you have owned the property for more than a year, you would have to pay tax on 100% of the excess depreciation. It is not included in the long-term capital gain, only 40% of which is taxed.

In *Column f*, put down the useful life, or rate, the number of years over which depreciation will be spread. Who determines the life or rate? You do.

Under the Reagan administration's new tax bill, for property acquired after January 1, 1981, you can adopt a useful life as short as fifteen years for rental property. That means that you can recover the cost or other basis of the building through depreciation deductions in about fifteen years. Before, for rental property, the life or rate allowed was between twenty and forty years, depending on how old the property actually was. Remember that the shorter the life, the larger the deductions for depreciation each year.

In *Column g*, put down the amount of depreciation for this year. Remember to show the IRS how you arrived at the figure, and whether or not you have prorated that amount for any reason. If you bought the property during the year, the amount in Column g should represent only the months that you've owned it. If you bought it in August, for example, then only 5/12 of the first year's depreciation can be deducted this year. In that case, write in "at 5/12" next to the amount on Column g.

For each of your rental properties, go through the same calculations in Columns a through g. Specifically describe each improvement, such as an air conditioning system, a refrigerator, a new kitchen, etc. Give the date on which it was acquired or the work was completed, the total cost, and adopt the method of depreciation that is best in light of your finances and tax position.

You should carefully determine the useful life, or rate, for each building and improvement, to put into Column f. Within reason, the determination is up to you, but you should be able to back up your claim. The idea behind useful life is that you will have to replace the item in question after a certain period of use. A new appliance may last for only five years, carpeting may last for only three years, but a new roof should last for ten years. It depends upon the quality of the item, how it is used, and your particular needs.

If your rental property also contains your personal residence, then clearly show the IRS that the item to be depreciated is used by the tenants only, or that the amount of depreciation does not include your share. In Column a, next to the description of the property, write in "T" for tenants. If you buy a refrigerator for the tenants, it is fully depreciable. If you buy a refrigerator for yourself, then it is not at all depreciable. Point out to the IRS that you understand this.

Component Depreciation. In the past few years, a new form of real estate depreciation has developed, called *component depreciation.* This method can be used for property that was put into service before January 1, 1981. For property placed into service during 1981 or later, a new method called "Accelerated Cost Recovery System" is used. It is described below.

Under component depreciation, you figure depreciation separately for each of the different parts that make up a building. When you purchase a building, you also purchase its plumbing system, electrical system, roof, and perhaps carpets, refrigerators, stoves, etc. The life expectancy of the basic structure of the building should be much higher than the life expectancy of its components, such as the plumbing system or the refrigerator. Therefore, instead of depreciating the *entire* building over forty years, for example, you can single out the various components within the building and depreciate them over a shorter period of time. The building structure may be depreciated over fifteen years, the roof over ten years, the plumbing system over eight years, etc.

Additional First-Year Depreciation. In *previous* taxable years, when you purchased an item subject to depreciation for your rental property, you were able to take an additional bonus amount of depreciation in the first year. You could take additional first-year depreciation on certain things such as machinery, equipment, and appliances, but not a building, if it had a useful life of six years or longer. The amount of first-year additional depreciation was computed by taking 20% of the cost of the item. Additional first-year depreciation is not allowed for property placed in service in 1981 or later.

Accelerated Cost Recovery System. This new method of depreciation, or cost recovery, is used for property placed in service *after* 1980. Use Part I of Form 4562 to report depreciation calculated under this method.

Under the ACRS method, rental property can be depreciated over a fifteen-year period using the 175% declining balance method of accelerated depreciation *or* by using a modified form of straight-line depreciation. ACRS gives you a larger tax write-off than other forms of depreciation, so don't be disappointed over the elimination of component depreciation and the additional first-year depreciation.

ACRS is discussed in more detail on pages 65-68 in Chapter 7.

Recording Depreciation Expense. Now, take the total amount of depreciation expense for the year for all items in Column g of either Form 4562 or Part V of Schedule E, whichever you used, and transfer the amount to *line 18* of Schedule E.

COMPUTING RENTAL INCOME OR LOSS

On *line 19* of Schedule E, total all the amounts on lines 17 and 18. Then on *line 20*, determine the income or loss for each property by subtracting line 19 from line 3a.

On *line 21*, put in the total amount of properties that show a profit, and on *line 22*, put in the total amount for properties that show a loss. Combine the amounts from lines 21 and 22, and put the result, either a profit or a loss, on *line 23*.

If you have farm rental income based on crops or livestock produced by a tenant, if you are the landowner or sub-lessor, fill out Form 4835 to determine the net farm rental profit or loss. That amount, if any, is then put onto *line 24* of Schedule E.

On *line 25*, total lines 23 and 24, and then put that total onto *line 3*, on page 2 of Schedule E. The same figure is also entered on line 17 of Form 1040. Remember to indicate a loss by placing the amount within parentheses.

TAX ADVANTAGES OF RENTAL PROPERTY

Rental property is perhaps the best tax shelter of all. What else can you buy for just a fraction of its total cost and not only write off all of the expenses involved with it, but also depreciate it? And, when you sell it, have to pay taxes on only 40% of the gain? Or trade it and not have to pay any taxes at all until some later date? The tax advantages of rental property are fantastic. There are many taxpayers with high incomes who actually pay little or no taxes because of their investments in rental property.

With rental property you can break even, or receive income exactly equal to expenses, and still have a large tax write-off. The reason for that is that the building is depreciable, along with all of its major improvements. So, even if the building is paying for itself, the deductions for depreciation will result in a net loss on Schedule E, which will lower your gross income. Meanwhile, the *market value* of the building is not "depreciating" at all, but is at least maintaining its value, or even going up. For example, in parts of California in the last few years, real estate has been appreciating at a rate of one or two percent, and more, per month.

The beautiful advantage of rental property is that the expenses are 100% tax deductible, and the gain on sale, if it is held for more than a year, is only 40% taxable. Even with very high interest rates, which, of course, are tax deductible, rental property is still about the best investment in terms of the income tax.

There are two things to keep in mind when purchasing rental property: cash flow and leverage. Cash flow has to do with the relationship between the amount of money coming in—the rental income—and the amount of money going out—expenses. Today, because of high interest rates, there is usually a fairly high negative cash flow in most rental properties, particularly in single family dwellings and small multiple-unit buildings. It's important to calculate the amount of an expected negative cash flow before you buy a rental property.

A negative cash flow means that you will have a substantial net loss on Schedule E each year, and lower total taxes. You can deduct losses from rental property indefinitely, unlike losses from a business or profession. This type of loss, if you are in a high tax bracket, can save you a good deal of money on each year's tax return. Remember, though, this tax deduction is only a percentage of the actual money you will save. For example, if you are in the 40% tax bracket, a $2,000 loss would save you $800 in tax, 40% of $2,000. Don't rush out to spend a dollar in order to save 40 cents, because you are still losing 60 cents.

Aside from tax advantages, another reason for investing in a rental property, even if there is a negative cash flow, is that the property should appreciate, unless you buy a turkey, and some day you will make a lot of money when you sell it. There is no point in putting out money every month, even though you are going to get some of it back in tax savings, unless you can get it *all* back, plus some, when you sell. It's therefore essential that the property you invest in is one that is going to increase in value, or appreciate.

Another warning: Don't become overextended and find yourself in a situation where you can't meet the monthly payments. Before you buy a building, make the necessary income and expense projections, and be sure that you can cover them.

In the past few years, there have been real estate seminars all over the country about buying property with no money down. Buying property without putting any money down usually results in a very high negative cash flow. This will give you a large tax deduction, but you may be getting in over your head. In today's market, it is fairly easy to buy property without putting any money down. The problem in real estate today is not buying property, but selling it for a profit. Because of very high interest rates, many people can't qualify for a loan, and sellers are having great trouble disposing of their property. Seminars, instead of showing you how to buy property without any money down, should be giving advice on how to sell your property and still make a profit. This factor must be kept in mind when you consider buying property. We all hope that interest rates will come down soon and that property will become much easier to sell. Meanwhile, we've got to weather the storm, use tax breaks, and live with a negative cash flow. Before you get into something, know what you'll need in order to get out of it, and how to escape with a profit.

USING YOUR EQUITY

Equity is the amount of money and the appreciation in market value in your property. It is calculated by taking the fair market value of the property minus what you actually owe on it, such as mortgages, deeds of trust, etc. Having a large amount of equity can be helpful, and it can also be harmful. For example, if you have a great deal of equity and are trying to sell your house on today's market, you may have some problems. In order for someone to buy your house, they will either have to come up with a lot of cash, or they will have to qualify for a loan at sky-high interest rates, or you'll have to take back paper (that is, you will have to accept and hold a note or mortgage from the buyers instead of cash).

Lately, many people have made money by using the equity in their property. By refinancing the mortgage loan, or by taking out additional mortgages, they have been able to take money out of their properties and reinvest it in other property. For example, you have a house that is worth $100,000 and owe only $10,000 on it. The $90,000 you have in equity can be used as collateral to get a new loan, or to refinance the old loan. You possibly could get a loan for up to 80% of the market value of the property. That would put approximately $70,000 in your pocket, $80,000 minus the $10,000 you already owe. With $70,000, on which no taxes would have to be paid, you could do some real investing, even if you are paying a 20% interest rate. If you can find a return on your investment that is greater than 20%, you would then be using the bank's money to make more of your own. In other words, you borrow at a 20% interest rate, and if you invest the loan for a 25% or 30% return, then you will be making 5% or 10% on the borrowed money. The kicker, of course, is that it is not easy to find investments that produce a better return than the high cost of interest on the new loan.

You should try to get the right kind of loan. It should be for as long a term as possible and be assumable, meaning that, if you sell the property, the buyers can then take over the loan, or assume it. Also, it should be at the lowest possible interest rate. In this way you will be doing two things: having money to invest, and making it easier to sell your house in today's market. The key, though, is to be able to use the money where you know that you can get a return on the investment that is higher than the cost of the money.

Loan fees, sometimes called "points," are tax-deductible, along with interest expenses. For personal residences, loan fees are totally deductible, in the year they are paid, on Schedule A under itemized deductions. For rental property, loan fees have to be amortized, which is very similar to depreciation, over the life of the loan. So, if you have a good investment prospect and have some equity in your property, you may want to borrow in order to take advantage of the investment opportunity.

INCOME OR LOSSES FROM PARTNERSHIPS, ESTATES, TRUSTS, OR SMALL BUSINESS CORPORATIONS PART II OF SCHEDULE E

Income or losses you receive from partnerships, estates, trusts, or small business corporations are reported under Part II on page 2 of Schedule E. Before you can complete Schedule E to your personal income tax return, the returns of the partnership, estate, trust, or small business corporation must have been completed and filed. After that, there is very little that has to be done in order to report such income on your personal return. Basically, all you need to do is to transfer figures from one form to another.

At the top of Part II of Schedule E, you are asked if, where you have a loss from a partnership, estate, trust, or small business corporation, whether you have amounts invested in that activity for which you are not "at risk." Be sure to answer "no" if all of your investment in the activity is at risk. If part of your investment is not at risk, the loss you can claim is limited to the amount that *is* at risk.

Partnerships. For a partnership, an information return on Form 1065 must be filed with the IRS on behalf of the partnership. The partnership itself pays no taxes—it is not even classified as a taxpayer. Each individual partner reports his or her share of items of income, deductions, credits, and losses on his or her personal return. Each partner is given a copy of the partnership's Form 1065 along with his or her individual schedule K-l. On the Schedule K-l you will find the exact amounts and other information you need to fill in the Partnerships section of Part II, Schedule E, for your personal return. Simply put in the name of the partnership, the partnership identification number, which begins with the numbers 94-, and the amount of net gain or loss. If there is an additional first-year depreciation amount, put that on line 28 of Part II. Do this for each partnership that you are involved in.

I personally feel that if you are involved in a business with others that is doing well, you should consider incorporation. There are two basic reasons to incorporate. One is that you greatly reduce your own personal liabilities when you incorporate. The second is that in a highly profitable business, you will pay less tax as a shareholder in a corporation than you would as a partner or a sole proprietor. For these two reasons, it may be worth the legal and accounting fees involved in organizing a corporation. On the other hand, in the early years of a business when net losses are more likely, a partnership or a Subchapter S corporation, which is discussed later in this chapter, allows you to deduct your share of the losses from your personal gross income. In an ordinary corporation, that is not possible.

Estates or Trusts. If you receive income or losses from an estate or a trust, simply plug in the information and the amounts from the Schedule K-1 that you should have received into Columns a through d on Part II of Schedule E.

Trusts can be very useful in avoiding income taxes. Through trusts, you can lessen your income tax burden by spreading income from certain investments among other people. For example, a prosperous son or daughter could establish a trust and give income-producing assets to provide for the support of his or her aged mother. If the mother is in a much lower tax bracket, the interest income to her from the trust would be taxed at a much lower rate. A type of trust could be set up to last for a period of ten years or the life of the mother, after which the assets of the trust return to the son or daughter. For years, the wealthy in the United States have been using trusts to reduce their income taxes, but everyone can take advantage of these laws. Setting up a trust is a fairly technical process, and you should consult an attorney for assistance in drawing up the documents.

Small Business Corporations. If you are a shareholder of a small business corporation, also called a *Subchapter S corporation* for its place in the tax code, and a *tax option corporation*, the information you need for Schedule E is also found on a Schedule K-1. The Subchapter S corporation must file Form 1120S. Again, you simply plug the information from Schedule K-1 into Columns a through d on Part II of Schedule E.

Small business corporations, like all corporations, limit your personal liability. In most businesses, especially nowadays, that is a major concern. If your business is sued by creditors or by injured parties, many of your personal assets can be taken to pay the claims, unless the business is incorporated or you are only a limited partner. However, unlike normal corporations which are taxed as taxpayers, Subchapter S corporations are taxed like partnerships. This is theoretically the best of two worlds.

Investment Tax Credits. One last point should be made about partnerships, estates, trusts, and small business corporations. All of these entities can distribute investment tax credits. If you receive a share of an investment tax credit, that information will be provided to you on the Schedule K-1 that you receive from the partnership, estate, etc. Do not overlook any investment tax credit that you may receive. If you are entitled to take any, fill out Form 3468. Tax credits are discussed in detail in Chapter 15.

Windfall Profit Tax Summary. If you received a windfall profits tax credit or refund in 1981, put the amount of it onto *line 34*. On *line 35*, put in the amount of windfall profit tax that was withheld during the year, if any. Subtract line 35 from line 34 and put that amount onto *line 36*.

Summary of Information on Schedule E.-
Now you're just about finished filling out Schedule E. Total all the amounts—gains and losses—from lines 25, 29, 31, 33, and 36, and enter the sum on line 37 of Schedule E and also on line 17 of Form 1040.

CHAPTER ELEVEN

☆

Lines 18—21 of Form 1040

**FARM INCOME OR LOSS—
SCHEDULE F**

Farm income and expenses are reported on Schedule F. It is similar to filling out Schedule C for self-employment income. Schedule F is divided into parts according to accounting methods—the *cash method*, where you take in income or deduct expenses only when you receive or make payments, or the *accrual method*, where you take in income when it is *earned* and deduct expenses when they become *payable*, regardless of actual payments.

One major difference between Schedule F and Schedule C involves livestock. If you have purchased livestock, not including poultry, for draft, breeding, sport, or dairy purposes, then these animals can be depreciated. When they are sold, you have to calculate your net profit or loss on the sale on Form 4797. If you've kept the animal for over a year, or two years in the case of cattle and horses, you only have to pay taxes on 40% of the net profit.

Another difference in dealing with livestock, as opposed to business equipment, is that they have the ability to increase your inventory, i.e., reproduce. The offspring of livestock must be handled differently from the parents for tax purposes. When the offspring are sold, the gain is considered to be ordinary income, a part of your other farm income.

Many people own small farms as a secondary source of income. They may be wage earners, or self-employed city folk using the farm as another means of income. Their only actual income from the farm may be from leasing the land to a farmer. Since they do own a farm, and do have income, they are still entitled to deduct all of the expenses involved in earning or trying to earn farm income. Farm expenses include labor hired, feed purchased, transportation to and from the farm, interest on a mortgage, depreciation of a new tractor, digging a new well, etc.

The point is that your expenses may well be greater than your income. In that case you have a net loss and a tax write-off. Don't hesitate to use the tax advantages of Schedule F.

**UNEMPLOYMENT COMPENSATION—
LINES 19A & 19B OF
FORM 1040**

A few years ago, the government began making unemployment compensation, or unemployment insurance, taxable under certain circumstances. If you are single, or married but not filing a joint return and you did not live with your spouse at any time during the year, then if you have over $20,000 of other income, you are subject to income taxes on the unemployment benefits you received. If you are married and filing a joint return, then the figure is over $25,000. If you are married, filing a separate return, and have lived with your spouse at any time during the year, then any amount of unemployment compensation you received is taxable, no matter what your income. In the instructions in the Federal Income Tax Forms booklet, sent to taxpayers by the IRS each year, there is a worksheet to fill out in order to calculate the amount of unemployment compensation that is taxable. You will receive a Form 1099-UC from the unemployment compensation agency, and it will state the total amount of benefits you received during the taxable year. Put that total on *line 19a* of Form 1040. On *line 19b*, put in the amount that is taxable from the worksheet.

OTHER INCOME—
LINE 20 OF FORM 1040

In case you haven't found a slot for every bit of your taxable income yet, the IRS provides *line 20*, "Other Income," on Form 1040. This is a catchall to catch all catchalls. Unfortunately, many taxpayers put down the wrong type of other income here. Usually, the mistake that is made is to put down self-employed income that should go on Schedule C and on line 13 of Form 1040. By putting the gross amount of such income on line 20, and not taking off all of the legitimate, business-related deductions on Schedule C, a taxpayer will lose money.

For example, I have prepared returns for a man who was a teacher earning W-2 income, and also a consultant for the school district. For years, he declared the total amount of consulting income as "other income." He was never able to deduct any business-related expenses and, therefore, greatly overpaid his taxes each year. The IRS eventually picked this up and, seeing that it was self-employed income, wanted him to pay self-employment social security tax on it. Then, not only did he have to pay tax on the gross or total amount, he also had to pay social security taxes on it. I helped him fill out Schedule C. He then deducted all of his legitimate, business-related expenses, and he saved a great deal of money.

The types of income that are most frequently reported on line 20 of Form 1040 are: lump-sum distributions from pension and profit-sharing plans, but only the ordinary-income amounts; tips that have not been included in W-2 income; amounts for meals and lodging not included in your W-2 income; certain sick-pay amounts; and net winnings from gambling.

Lump-Sum Distributions from Pension and Profit-Sharing Plans. You can reduce your income tax on these distributions if you report them properly. Say you have worked for a company for a number of years and have contributed money to the company's pension plan. You leave the job, and are given a distribution of all of the money you contributed, plus the additional amount earned on it through the plan's investments. Because you receive these amounts in one payment, it is called a *lump sum distribution*. You will receive a statement after the end of the year from the company or the pension plan administrator. On it, there will be boxes entitled "ordinary income," and "capital gain part." The amount in the ordinary income box is 100% taxable, and goes on line 20 as "other income." The amount in the capital gain box is only 40% taxable and would go either onto line 13, capital gains distributions, on Form 1040, or with other amounts of capital gain on Schedule D and line 12 of Form 1040.

If you receive a lump-sum distribution of several thousand dollars, you may elect to use a special ten-year income-averaging method. This is a special tax break the government gives you when you receive a large lump-sum distribution. To take advantage of this provision, you must fill out Form 4972. Put the total amount of the lump-sum distribution, including the ordinary income part and the capital gain part, on Form 4972. If you file Form 4972, do not put in any amounts relating to the lump-sum distribution on line 20 of Form 1040. Instead of adding the ordinary income part to your gross income, you will calculate a separate, additional tax on Form 4972. On line 36 of Form 1040, "additional taxes," check the box next to "Form 4972," and enter the amount of tax from line 28 of Form 4972.)

Tip Income. On *line 20*, you can also report tip income that was not included on your W-2's, and was thus not reported on line 7 of Form 1040. This type of income might be received by cab drivers, waiters, and waitresses. If you do report such tip income on line 20, then you must also fill out Form 4137, Computation of Social Security Tax on Unreported Tip Income. In other words, you are required to pay social security tax on tip income that has not been reported to your employer and included on your W-2. In certain occupations, you must be careful as to how you report your tip income. For example, if you put down "waitress" as your occupation in the heading of Form 1040, but you do not declare any tip income on any line, you will have a problem with the IRS. If you do receive tips, you may want to report them to your employer to be included as part of your W-2 income, and thus avoid having to fill out Form 4137.

Reimbursement for Meals and Lodging. With regard to payments received for the cost of meals and lodging, you may be able to offset this income by filling out Form 2106, Employee Business Expenses. Many times when you are given money for meals or lodging money, it is in relation to your job, and thus there may be tax deductions available to you. Fill out Form 2106, show your exact meal and lodging expenses, and then show the amount of the employer's payments if not included on Form W-2. If the payments are less than the actual expenses, then you would have a tax write-off. The net amount would go onto line 23 of Form 1040 as an employee business expense, which is an adjustment to your income. However, if the employer's payments are greater than the actual deductible expenses, then you put that amount on line 20 as "other income." Be sure, though, to read the instructions for employee business expenses and Form 2106. We will discuss Form 2106 in detail in Chapter 12.

Net Gambling Winnings. If you win a large amount of money in gambling at a race track or at a casino, your social security number is recorded and your winnings are reported to the IRS. Really big winners may have amounts withheld from their winnings at a race track or casino. Income from gambling is fully taxable and should go onto line 20 as "other income." There is, however, a tax law that may allow you to offset some or all of your winnings. The law states that you can deduct gambling losses to the extent of gambling winnings. For example, in 1981 you won a $10,000 pay-off at the race track. If you have been keeping records of your winnings and losses, and can prove them, you can deduct all your losses from the $10,000. A few years ago, while losing money at the Belmont Racetrack, I noticed a man going around and picking up discarded betting tickets from the ground. I wondered if he had been a big winner and knew the Internal Revenue Code well.

If you have large gambling winnings as well as gambling losses, write on line 20, "see attached statement of gambling winnings." On a separate sheet of paper, create a statement of gambling winnings, including your name and social security number, and show all of your winnings and all of your losses for the taxable year. The difference of the two amounts would be the amount of net winnings or net losses. Remember, though, gambling losses cannot bring the difference below zero—you cannot deduct the loss from your gross income, but you can bring your winnings down to zero by subtracting losses. If you end up with net winnings, put the total on line 20.

If you gamble a lot and consistently win big, you should set yourself up as a professional gambler and report winnings and losses on Schedule C, but only if this is legal in the state in which you live. You can also deduct all of the expenses involved in earning income as a professional gambler. Instead of reporting your income on line 20 of Form 1040, you would use Schedule C and put the net profit onto line 11 of Form 1040.

TOTAL INCOME

On *line 21* of Form 1040, "total income," simply add all of the amounts on lines 7 through 20, but remember to subtract negative amounts, as in losses. For most taxpayers, there may be only one or two amounts on all of these lines. That's fine. If a line doesn't apply to your income, then just skip it. However, you should understand what each line means, where to put the various items of taxable income, and how to use the tax laws to save money. You should be familiar with the different tax forms, whether or not you will use them this year.

PART IV
DETERMINING YOUR TAXABLE INCOME

CHAPTER TWELVE

☆

Adjustments to Income

Lines 22 to *31* on Form 1040 are for reporting adjustments to income and calculating adjusted gross income. Adjustments to income are like deductions in that they lower your gross income and therefore reduce your income tax. They can play a crucial part in saving you money on your tax return. Many, many people are unaware of them, and therefore lose money each year because they don't claim everything they are entitled to.

It is well worth the effort to become acquainted with the various forms related to the income adjustments on Form 1040. Even if they don't directly apply to this year's tax return, there is always a good possibility that they will be helpful to you in the future. One great advantage of the adjustments is that they can be used without having to itemize deductions on your tax return. Even if you don't have enough itemized deductions to fill out Schedule A, you still can claim the adjustments to income and save money. For example, many non-homeowners who do not have enough itemized deductions to fill out Schedule A may still have employee business expenses, moving expenses, or payments to an Individual Retirement Account. All of these adjustments to income can be claimed without itemizing deductions.

MOVING EXPENSES—
FORM 3903

The government allows you to deduct the expenses you incur in changing your place of residence but only if the move is related to a change in your job or the location of your job. Regardless of whether you are self-employed or a wage earner, if you meet the criteria set by the IRS, you can deduct these expenses. In certain circumstances, Form 3903, the Moving Expense Adjustment, may be the most important form in your tax return in a particular year. If, for example, you have moved across the country and spent thousands of dollars in the process, filling out Form 3903 may save you more in tax than any other deduction. Let's go though the qualifications and the step-by-step procedures in filling out Form 3903.

Line (a). The point of the question here is that you must have moved to a new residence and also have changed jobs, or job location, as well. You don't necessarily need to have changed employers, only the place where your job is located. The move, and the subsequent moving expenses, must be related to a change in your job location. Write in the exact distance in miles from where you used to live to where your new job location is. This applies if you moved around the world, across the country, or just across town.

Line (b) asks for the number of miles from your old place of residence to your old job location.

The difference between the number of miles on line (a) and on line (b) must be thirty-five or more. If the distance is less than thirty-five miles, you are not able to claim the deduction for moving expenses. The thirty-five-mile rule, however, does not apply to members of the armed forces. If the difference is at least thirty-five miles, and you also meet the time test, then fill out the rest of the form.

The time test involved in the qualifications for deducting moving expenses is sometimes called the 39/78 week test. The thirty-nine-

Form **3903**
Department of the Treasury
Internal Revenue Service

Moving Expense Adjustment
▶ Attach to Form 1040.

OMB No. 1545-0062

1981

Name(s) as shown on Form 1040 | Your social security number

(a) What is the distance from your **former** residence to your **new** job location? .... miles

(b) What is the distance from your **former** residence to your **former** job location? .... miles

(c) If the distance in (a) is 35 or more miles farther than the distance in (b), complete the rest of this form. If the distance is less than 35 miles, you cannot take a deduction for moving expenses. This rule does not apply to members of the armed forces.

1 Transportation expenses in moving household goods and personal effects 1

2 Travel, meals, and lodging expenses in moving from former to new residence 2

3 Pre-move travel, meals, and lodging expenses in searching for a new residence after getting your job 3

4 Temporary living expenses in new location or area during any 30 consecutive days after getting your job 4

5 Total. Add lines 3 and 4 5

6 Enter the smaller of line 5 or $1,500 ($750 if married filing a separate return and you lived with your spouse who also started work during the tax year) . . 6

7 Expenses for: (Check only one box)
  (a) ☐ sale or exchange of your former residence; or,
  (b) ☐ if renting, settlement of unexpired lease on your former residence . . 7

8 Expenses for: (Check only one box)
  (a) ☐ buying a new residence; or,
  (b) ☐ if renting, getting a lease on a new residence 8

9 Total. Add lines 6, 7, and 8 9

Note: Amounts on lines 7(a) and 8(a) not deducted because of the $3,000 (or $1,500) limit on moving expenses may generally be used either to decrease the gain on the sale of your residence, or to increase the basis of your new residence. See "Double Benefits" in Instructions.

10 Enter the smaller of line 9 or $3,000 ($1,500 if married, filing a separate return, and you lived with your spouse who also started work during the tax year) 10

11 Total moving expenses. Add lines 1, 2, and 10 11

12 Reimbursements and allowances received for this move. Do not report amounts included on your Form W–2 12

13 If line 12 is less than line 11, enter the difference here and on Form 1040, line 22 13

14 If line 12 is larger than line 11, enter the difference here and on Form 1040, line 20, as "Excess moving reimbursement" 14

General Instructions

Paperwork Reduction Act Notice.—The Paperwork Reduction Act of 1980 says we must tell you why we are collecting this information, how we will use it, and whether you have to give it to us. We ask for the information to carry out the Internal Revenue laws of the United States. We need it to ensure that you are complying with these laws and to allow us to figure and collect the right amount of tax. You are required to give us this information.

A. Who May Deduct Moving Expenses.—If you moved your residence because of a change in the location of your job, you may be able to deduct your moving expenses. You may qualify for a deduction whether you are self-employed or an employee. But you must meet certain tests of distance and time, explained below. If you need more information, please get **Publication 521**, Moving Expenses.

Note: If you are a U.S. citizen or resident who moved to a new principal work place outside the United States or its possessions, get Form 3903F, Foreign Moving Expense Adjustment.

(1) *Distance Test.*—Your new job location must be at least 35 miles farther from your former residence than your old job location was. For example, if your former job was 3 miles from your former residence, your new job must be at least 38 miles from that residence. If you did not have an old job location, your new job must be at least 35 miles from your former residence. (The distance between the two points is the shortest of the commonly traveled routes between the points.)

(2) *Time Test.*—If you are an employee, you must work full time for at least 39 weeks during the 12 months right after you move. If you are self-employed, you must work for at least 39 weeks during the first 12 months and a total of 78 weeks during the 24 months right after you move.

You may deduct your moving expenses for 1981 even if you have not met the "time" test before your 1981 return is due. You may do this if you expect to meet the 39-week test by the end of 1982 or the 78-week test by the end of 1983. If you have not met the test by then, you will have to do one of the following:

● Amend your 1981 tax return on which you deducted moving expenses. To do this, use Form 1040X, Amended U.S. Individual Income Tax Return.

● Report as income on your tax return for the year you cannot meet the test the amount you deducted on your 1981 return.

(Continued on back)

343-162-1

Form **3903** (1981)

week test applies to wage earners, and the seventy-eight-week test to self-employed people. For married couples filing a joint return, these tests can apply to either or both spouses.

If you are an employee, after you settle into your new location, you must work full-time for thirty-nine weeks during the next full year, that is, a minimum of thirty-nine weeks out of the following fifty-two weeks at a full-time, W-2 position.

For self-employed people, the requirement is seventy-eight weeks within the next two full years after settling in after the move.

In many cases you may not meet the thirty-nine- or seventy-eight-week test by the time you must file a tax return for the previous year. If you expect that you will be able to meet the test, then fill out Form 3903 and deduct all of your legitimate expenses. If, later on, circumstances change and you cannot meet this test, then you are required to file an amended tax return on Form 1040X and to report as income the amount you previously claimed as a moving expense adjustment.

Line 1 of Form 3903 asks for the total amount of expenses in moving all of your household goods such as furniture, books, appliances, etc. and all of your personal effects such as clothing, papers, medication, etc. You may have rented a van or a truck, or paid a professional moving firm. All of these costs are tax-deductible on line 1.

Line 2. Put down the amount you spent for travel, meals, and lodging while moving from your old residence to your new residence. If, for example, you moved across country, that would include airfare, meals, and lodging expenses. If you drove a car in moving from your former residence to your new one, then you can deduct your actual out-of-pocket expenses for gasoline, oil, and repairs, or you can take the number of miles you drove and multiply it by nine cents per mile. It is a good idea to keep a diary for these expenses. If you are driving from one state to another, keep an actual record of all expenses, and keep all of your receipts. If you are audited, the diary and the receipts will be very helpful.

Line 3. This is where filling out Form 3903 becomes a little trickier. This line asks for pre-move travel, meals, and lodging expenses that were incurred while searching for a new place to live *after* you have accepted a new job. The key term here is "after obtaining employment." You may include all of the expenses of travelling to the new job location, before you move, in order to look for a new residence. You can deduct these costs only if you began the house-hunting trip after you got the job. You may also include the expenses involved in going back to your old residence after getting the job, and travelling to the general location of the new work place specifically to look for a new residence.

For example, you live in New York and go to Los Angeles to look for a job. After receiving an offer and accepting it, you then fly back to New York. The expenses of the flight back are deductible on line 3. Then, you make another trip to the Los Angeles area to look for a place to live. That flight is also a deductible expense. If you had agreed to take the job before your first trip to Los Angeles, you would also be able to deduct the cost of the first flight from New York to Los Angeles. Otherwise, that flight would not be deductible on line 3. However, it may be deductible as an employee business expense on Form 2106, which is discussed later in this chapter. Keep these tax provisions in mind when you think about changing jobs and moving, and plan ahead in order to save money at tax time.

You can also deduct the expenses of all pre-move travel for the purpose of finding a new place of residence, including costs incurred by you or by any member of your household. Your house-hunting does not have to be successful in order to qualify for this deduction. If you drive your car, deduct the actual costs, or multiply the number of miles traveled by nine cents a mile.

If you are self-employed, you may also claim the moving expense adjustment, but only if you had made substantial arrangements to begin your business in the new location before you move.

Line 4. You can deduct temporary living expenses near the new job location for a period of thirty consecutive days after you take the new job. In other words, you obtain employment, move to the new location, and then are hit with a lot of expenses while you get settled in the new place. You may have to stay in a motel for three weeks or so until you can move into an apartment. You may have to eat every meal in a restaurant, because you have no kitchen. You can include these costs for any period of thirty consecutive days after you get the job.

If you are self-employed, you can deduct temporary living expenses only if you had already made substantial arrangements to begin work or to start your business in the new location. If you move first, before getting a new job or setting up a new business, then these expenses cannot be claimed on Form 3903.

On *line 5*, simply add up the amounts on lines 3 and 4.

Line 6. The maximum deduction allowed for pre-move travel, meals, lodging, and temporary living expenses is $1,500, or $750 if you are married and filing separate returns, and you lived with your spouse who also started work during the taxable year. On line 6, therefore, put in the total of line 5 up to the amount of $1,500, or $750, as the case may be.

Line 7 asks about various expenses related to moving out of your old residence.

Line 7(a). If you incurred expenses in selling or exchanging your former residence, check box 7(a). These expenses include closing costs, legal fees, telephone calls, travel and transportation expenses, etc. Any expenses that are deducted on Form 3903 cannot also be deducted on Form 2119, Sale or Exchange of Principal Residence. If you have the choice, it is better to put these expenses here because the expenses on Form 3903 are 100% tax-deductible. If you owned your personal residence for more than one year, then these expenses would offset only the capital gain on the sale of the residence, which is only 40% taxable. Also, if you purchased a new residence for more money than the old one sold for, you are able to defer the capital gain and not have to pay any taxes on it until later. Therefore, when you have a choice, put these expenses on Form 3903 and claim them as moving expenses.

Line 7(b). If your former residence was leased and you had to pay the landlord to terminate the lease, check box 7(b). The amount of a settlement on an unexpired lease is treated as a moving expense.

Line 8. The expenses involved in buying a new residence or in getting a lease on a new residence are also treated as moving expenses.

Line 8(a) asks for expenses involved in buying a new residence in relation to your move. These expenses would include closing costs, various fees and charges, attorney fees, termite inspections, etc. Do not include any property taxes or interest that you have paid at closing, because those amounts should be reported on Schedule A, Itemized Deductions. Again, any amounts that are included on Form 3903 cannot also be included on Form 2119.

Line 8(b). If you are going to rent a new residence, the expenses involved in getting a lease are reported here. You may be charged a fee to get a new lease, or have to pay a commission to a landlord or a realtor. A security deposit cannot be claimed, as it should be returned to you in the future, and is not an expense.

On *line 9*, total the amounts on lines 6, 7 and 8. Also, observe the Note under line 9: Any amounts included on lines 7(a) and 8(a) that were not deducted because of the $3,000 (or $1,500) limitation on moving expenses should be reported on Form 2119, to decrease the capital gain on the selling of the residence, or to increase the basis of your new residence, if applicable.

Line 10. The maximum deduction allowed for lines 6, 7, and 8 is $3,000, or $1,500 for a married couple filing separate returns where both spouses are involved in the move. Therefore, enter the amount from line 9 up to the amount of $3,000, or $1,500, as the case may be.

Line 11 is the total amount of your moving expenses. Add lines 1, 2 and 10.

Line 12. "Reimbursements and allowances received" means money you were given, most likely by your employer, to cover expenses of a move. If you did not receive any allowance or reimbursement for moving expenses, or if you did receive an amount but it is included on your W-2 statements, put in "0" on line 12.

If you have been reimbursed for all or part of the moving expenses, and that amount has not been included on your W-2 statement, in other words, tax has not been withheld on it, then put that amount on line 12. Since moving expenses are deductible, any amount paid to you by your employer that has already been included on your W-2 should be subtracted from your gross income. Therefore, do not put in amounts from your W-2 that, in effect, have already been taxed, as reimbursements on line 12.

Sometimes employers pay all of the expenses of a move, but fail to include the amount on the employee's W-2. Some taxpayers make the mistake of not including a Form 3903, which would show the IRS that the moving expenses cost a certain amount and that they were reimbursed a certain amount. The IRS may get information about the reimbursement, and if they don't see Form 3903 as part of your tax return, they may then question you about it. They may even assume that this was additional income and that now you should be paying additional tax on it. So, therefore, fill out Form 3903, even if your employer paid for the move and you wind up with a zero net moving expense adjustment.

Line 13. Subtract the amount in line 12 from line 11 to arrive at your net moving expense adjustment. Then take the amount on line 13, and enter it onto line 22 of Form 1040.

Line 14. If the amount on line 12 is greater than the amount on line 11, then you have "excess moving reimbursement." In other words, you received more money for the move than you actually spent on it. You made a profit on the move, and that additional income is taxable. Report it on line 20 of Form 1040, under "other income." However, in all my years of doing taxes, I have never seen an amount on line 14.

The total amount of your moving expense adjustment should reflect the extent of the move. By extent, I mean the distances involved, the numbers of people moving, and quantity of your belongings. For moves that cover short distances and involve single people with no dependents, the total amount would naturally be lower.

But when a large family moves across the country, and houses must be sold and bought, the total expenses can be very high. Be sure to keep all of your receipts and to keep a moving expense diary, so you can take full advantage of the moving expense adjustment to income.

FOREIGN MOVING EXPENSES— FORM 3903F

There is a new form, Form 3903F, for taxpayers who move their residences outside the United States because of a job location change. The same thirty-five mile and thirty-nine/seventy-eight week test requirements apply as for moves within the United States, but there are larger limits on certain deductions. For example, you can deduct temporary living expenses in a new location or area for any ninety consecutive days after getting your job. Also, the limit for pre-move travel, meals, and lodging expenses, and the temporary living expenses is $4,500, or $2,500 if you are married and filing separate returns and you lived with your spouse who also started work during the year.

If you moved to a new job location in a foreign country during 1981, be sure to use Form 3903F and take full advantage of it.

EMPLOYEE BUSINESS EXPENSES— FORM 2106

When to Claim Employee Business Expenses. Employee business expenses are to

Form **3903F**	**Foreign Moving Expense Adjustment**	OMB No. 1545-0062
Department of the Treasury Internal Revenue Service	▶ Attach to Form 1040.	**1981**

Name(s) as shown on Form 1040 | Social security number

(a) City and country in which your former place of work was located ▶ ....
(b) City and country in which your new place of work is located ▶

1	Transportation and storage expenses for household goods and personal effects	1
2	Travel, meals, and lodging expenses in moving from former to new residence	2
3	Pre-move travel, meals, and lodging expenses in searching for a new residence after getting your job	3
4	Temporary living expenses in new location or area during any 90 consecutive days after getting your job . . .	4
5	Total (Add lines 3 and 4)	5
6	Enter the smaller of line 5 or $4,500 ($2,250 if married filing a separate return and you lived with your spouse who also started work during the tax year) . .	6
7	Expenses for: (Check one.) (a) ☐ sale or exchange of your former residence; or, (b) ☐ if renting, settlement of unexpired lease on your former residence . .	7
8	Expenses for: (Check one.) (a) ☐ buying a new residence; or, (b) ☐ if renting, getting a lease on a new residence	8
9	Total (Add lines 6, 7, and 8.)	9
10	Enter the smaller of line 9 or $6,000 ($3,000 if married filing a separate return and you lived with your spouse who also started work during the tax year)	10
	Note: Amounts on lines 7(a) and 8(a) not deducted because of the $6,000 (or $3,000) limitation may generally be used either to decrease the gain on the sale of your residence, or to increase the basis of your new residence. See "Double Benefits" in Instructions.	
11	Total moving expenses (Add lines 1, 2, and 10.)	11
12	Reimbursements and allowances received for this move (other than amounts included on Form W–2) .	12
13	If line 12 is less than line 11, enter the difference here and on Form 1040, line 22	13
14	If line 12 is more than line 11, enter the difference here and on Form 1040, line 20, as "Excess moving reimbursement"	14

General Instructions

Paperwork Reduction Act Notice.—The Paperwork Reduction Act of 1980 says we must tell you why we are collecting this information, how we will use it, and whether you have to give it to us. We ask for the information to carry out the Internal Revenue laws of the United States. We need it to ensure that you are complying with these laws and to allow us to figure and collect the right amount of tax. You are required to give us this information.

Use this form only if you are a U.S. citizen or resident moving to a new principal work place outside the United States or its possessions.

Who May Deduct Foreign Moving Expenses.—If you moved your residence outside the United States because of a change in the location of your job, you may be able to deduct your moving expenses. You may qualify for a deduction whether you are self-employed or an employee. But you must meet certain tests of distance and time, explained below. If you need more information, please get **Publication 521,** Moving Expenses, and **Publication 54,** Tax Guide for U.S. Citizens Abroad.

(a) *Distance Test.*—Your new job location must be at least 35 miles farther from your former residence than your old job location was. For example, if your former job was 3 miles from your former residence, your new job must be at least 38 miles from that residence. If you did not have an old job location, your new job must be at least 35 miles from your former residence. (The distance between the two points is the shortest of the commonly traveled routes between the points.)

(b) *Time Test.*—If you are an employee, you must work full time for at least 39 weeks during the 12 months right after you move. If you are self-employed, you must work for at least 39 weeks during the first 12 months and a total of 78 weeks during the 24 months right after you move.

You may deduct your moving expenses for 1981 even if you have not met the "time" test before your 1981 tax return is due. You may do this if you expect to meet the 39-week test by the end of 1982 or the 78-week test by the end of 1983. If you have not met the test by then, you will have to do one of the following:

• Amend your 1981 tax return on which you deducted moving expenses. To do this, use Form 1040X, Amended U.S. Individual Income Tax Return.

• Report as income on your tax return for the year you cannot meet the test the amount you deducted on your 1981 return.

If you do not deduct your moving expenses on your 1981 return, and you later meet the time test, you may file an amended return for 1981, taking the deduction. To do this, use Form 1040X.

Exceptions to the Distance and Time Tests.—

You do not have to meet the time test if your job ends because of death, disability, transfer for the employer's benefit, or layoff or other discharge besides willful misconduct.

You do not have to meet the time test if you meet the requirements for a retired person or survivor outside the United States.

If you are in the armed forces, you do not have to meet the distance and time tests if the move is due to a permanent change of station. A permanent change of station includes a move in connection with and within 1 year of retirement or other

(Continued on back)

343-163-1 | Form **3903F** (1981)

ADJUSTMENTS TO INCOME

be used only for taxpayers who are wage earners, i.e., receive W-2 income. These expenses are considered adjustments to income and will therefore lower your taxable income. Any expenses that are related to self-employed income must be reported on Schedule C, and not on Form 2106. Most wage earners probably do not even know about this form, let alone use it. In fact, many people can qualify to deduct employee business expenses, but are entirely unaware of the possibility. This is a major area in which the large national tax preparation firms do not take advantage of the tax laws for the benefit of their clients. You do not have to itemize deductions on Schedule A in order to be able to take employee business expense deductions on Form 2106.

There are five basic types of employee business expense deductions that are reported on Form 2106. They are:

• Out-of-town trips, overnight or longer, that are related to your job or profession. That can also mean job-hunting trips.

• Any travel, but not overnight, that is done specifically in relation to your job or profession.

• All transportation involved in going from one salaried (W-2) job to another salaried job in the same day.

• All job-related transportation for outside sales people who are paid on a W-2 salaried basis. "Outside sales" refers to working in the field and visiting customers at their places of business.

• All job- or profession-related education expenses reported as itemized deductions on Schedule A, including transportation, tuition, fees, books, and supplies.

Anyone with W-2 wages can deduct any one or more of the above types of expenses on Form 2106. You may want to use more than one Form 2106 if you have many large amounts and different types of deductions. Also, each form is for an individual taxpayer, so, if you are filing a joint return, you have to fill out separate Forms 2106 for each spouse when both husband and wife can claim employee business expenses.

There are specific occupations and certain situations that lend themselves well to this adjustment. Wage earners in professional or technical fields are the most common users of this form. Engineers, teachers, social workers, technicians, resident doctors, etc., use this form to claim expenses when they go to seminars or conferences, both local and out-of-town, or do local travel for their employers. Anyone who takes educational or professional courses for advancement in his or her present job or profession can also use Form 2106.

Blue collar workers also benefit greatly from employee business expense deductions. They can claim deductions for going to union conventions, conferences, seminars, or having to go on out-of-town trips for their employers. For example, railroad conductors, brakemen, firemen, etc. who go out of town as part of their daily job can deduct expenses for meals and lodging on Form 2106, if they are out of town overnight. Truck drivers who travel out of town or overnight can do the same. Of course, you must subtract from these expenses any amounts of reimbursement you receive from your employer. But in most cases, the expenses are greater than the company allowance, and, therefore, you will have a tax deduction.

People who have more than one job may also have a tax write-off on Form 2106. If you have two W-2, salaried income jobs, and travel from one job location to the other in the same day, then you can deduct your transportation expenses. Or, if you are required by your employer to go to different job sites on the same day you can also deduct the expense of going to the other sites. Workers who often go to two or more job sites on the same day should keep accurate records of their mileage expenses so they can deduct the full amount on Form 2106 and be able to back up the claim.

Union officers or representatives can deduct expenses for mileage to union meetings, conferences, conventions, classes, and different job sites, as well as all business expenses involved in their union work and activities.

Form **2106**	**Employee Business Expenses**	OMB No. 1545-0139
Department of the Treasury Internal Revenue Service	(Please use Form 3903 to figure moving expense deduction.) ▶ Attach to Form 1040.	**1981**

Your name	Social security number	Occupation in which expenses were incurred
Employer's name	Employer's address	

Paperwork Reduction Act Notice.—The Paperwork Reduction Act of 1980 says we must tell you why we are collecting this information, how we will use it, and whether you have to give it to us. We ask for the information to carry out the Internal Revenue laws of the United States. We need it to ensure that you are complying with these laws and to allow us to figure and collect the right amount of tax. You are required to give us this information.

Instructions

Use this form to show your business expenses as an employee during 1981. Include amounts:
- You paid as an employee;
- You charged to your employer (such as by credit card);
- You received as an advance, allowance, or repayment.

Several publications available from IRS give more information about business expenses:
Publication 463, *Travel, Entertainment, and Gift Expenses.*
Publication 529, *Miscellaneous Deductions.*
Publication 587, *Business Use of Your Home.*
Publication 508, *Educational Expenses.*

Part I.—You can deduct some business expenses even if you do not itemize your deductions on Schedule A (Form 1040). Examples are expenses for travel (except commuting to and from work), meals, or lodging. List these expenses in Part I and use them in figuring your adjusted gross income on Form 1040, line 31.

Line 2.—You can deduct meals and lodging costs if you were on a business trip away from your main place of work. Do not deduct the cost of meals you ate on one-day trips when you did not need sleep or rest.

Line 3.—If you use a car you own in your work, you can deduct the cost of the business use. Enter the cost here after figuring it in Part IV. You can take either the cost of your actual expenses (such as gas, oil, repairs, depreciation, etc.) or you can use the standard mileage rate.

The mileage rate is 20 cents a mile up to 15,000 miles. After that, or for all business mileage on a fully depreciated car, the rate is 11 cents a mile. If you use the standard mileage rate to figure the cost of business use, the car is considered to have a useful life of 60,000 miles of business use at the maximum standard mileage rate. After 60,000 miles of business use at the maximum rate, the car is considered to be fully depreciated. (For details, see **Publication 463**.)

Caution: You cannot use the mileage rate for a leased vehicle.

Figure your mileage rate amount and add it to the business part of what you spent on the car for parking fees, tolls, interest, and State and local taxes (except gasoline tax).

Line 4.—If you were an outside salesperson with other business expenses, list them on line 4. Examples are selling expenses or expenses for stationery and stamps. An outside salesperson does all selling outside the employer's place of business. A driver-salesperson whose main duties are service and delivery, such as delivering bread or milk, is not an outside salesperson. (For details, see **Publication 463**.)

Line 5.—Show other business expenses on line 5 if your employer repaid you for them. If you were repaid for part of them, show here the amount you were repaid. Show the rest in Part II.

Part II.—You can deduct other business expenses only if (a) your employer did not repay you, and (b) you itemize your deductions on Schedule A (Form 1040). Report these expenses here and under Miscellaneous Deductions on Schedule A. (For details, see **Publication 529**.)

You can deduct expenses for business use of the part of your home that you exclusively and consistently use for your work. If you are not self-employed, your working at home must be for your employer's convenience. (For business use of home, see **Publication 587**.)

If you show education expenses in Part I or Part II, you must fill out Part III.

Part III.—You can deduct the cost of education that helps you keep or improve your skills for the job you have now. This includes education that your employer, the law, or regulations require you to get in order to keep your job or your salary. Do not deduct the cost of study that helps you meet the basic requirements for your job or helps you get a new job. (For education expenses, see **Publication 508**.)

Part IV, line 8—Depreciation
Cars placed in service before 1/1/81:
You must continue to use either the standard mileage rate or the method of depreciation you used in earlier years. You cannot change to either of the new methods available in 1981.

Cars placed in service after 12/31/80:
If you placed a car in service in 1981 and you do not use the standard mileage rate, you must use the new Accelerated Cost Recovery System (ACRS). One method lets you deduct the following percentages of your cost basis regardless of what month you placed the car in service:
1981—25%
1982—38%
1983—37%

Example: You bought a new car, without a trade-in, for $10,000 in September 1981, and used it 60% for business. Your basis for depreciation is $6,000 ($10,000 × 60%). For 1981 your depreciation deduction is $1,500 ($6,000 × 25%). If your percentage of business use changes in 1982, you must refigure your basis for depreciation.

There is also an alternate ACRS method under which you may use a straight-line method over a recovery period of 3, 5, or 12 years.

Note: *If you use the mileage rate, you are considered to have made an election to exclude this vehicle from ACRS.*

You do not have to consider salvage value in either of these methods. Please see **Publication 463** for details on how to figure the deduction under either method.

PART I.—Employee Business Expenses Deductible in Figuring Adjusted Gross Income on Form 1040, Line 31	
1 Fares for airplane, boat, bus, taxicab, train, etc.	
2 Meals and lodging	
3 Car expenses (from Part IV, line 21)	
4 Outside salesperson's expenses (see Part I instructions above) ▶	
5 Other (see Part I instructions above) ▶	
6 Add lines 1 through 5	
7 Employer's payments for these expenses if not included on Form W-2	
8 Deductible business expenses (subtract line 7 from line 6). Enter here and include on Form 1040, line 23	
9 Income from excess business expense payments (subtract line 6 from line 7). Enter here and include on Form 1040, line 20	
PART II.—Employee Business Expenses that are Deductible Only if You Itemize Deductions on Schedule A (Form 1040)	
1 Business expenses not included above (list expense and amount) ▶	
2 Total. Deduct under Miscellaneous Deductions, Schedule A (Form 1040)	

343-142-1   Form **2106** (1981)

ADJUSTMENTS TO INCOME

Form 2106 (1981)   Page **2**

PART III.—Information About Education Expenses Shown in Part I or Part II

1 Name of educational institution or activity ▶ ....
2 Address ▶ ....
3 Did you need this education to meet the basic requirements for your job? . . . . ☐ Yes ☐ No
4 Will this study program qualify you for a new job? . . . . ☐ Yes ☐ No
5 If your answer to question 3 or 4 is Yes, you cannot deduct these expenses. If No, explain (1) why you are getting the education, and (2) what the relationship was between the courses you took and your job. (If you need more space, attach a statement.) ▶ ....
6 List your main subjects, or describe your educational activity ▶ ....

PART IV.—Car Expenses (Use either your actual expenses or the mileage rate.)

	Car 1	Car 2	Car 3
A. Number of months you used car for business during 1981 . .	_____ months	_____ months	_____ months
B. Total mileage for months in line A	_____ miles	_____ miles	_____ miles
C. Business part of line B mileage	_____ miles	_____ miles	_____ miles

Actual Expenses (Include expenses on lines 1–5 for only the months shown in line A, above.)

	Car 1	Car 2	Car 3
1 Gasoline, oil, lubrication, etc.			
2 Repairs			
3 Tires, supplies, etc.			
4 Other: (a) Insurance			
(b) Taxes			
(c) Tags and licenses			
(d) Interest			
(e) Miscellaneous			
5 Total (add lines 1 through 4(e))			
6 Business percentage of car use (divide line C by line B, above)	%	%	%
7 Business part of car expense (multiply line 5 by line 6) . .			
8 Depreciation (see instructions on front) . . . . **Caution:** *If you use ACRS, skip line 9 and enter the amount from line 8 on line 10.*			
9 Divide line 8 by 12 months			
10 Multiply line 9 by line A, above			
11 Total (add line 7 and line 10; then skip to line 19) . . .			

Mileage Rate

12 Enter the smaller of (a) 15,000 miles or (b) the combined mileages from line C, above . . . . _____ miles
13 Multiply line 12 by 20¢ (11¢ if car is fully depreciated) and enter here . . . . _____
14 Enter any combined mileage from line C that is over 15,000 miles . . . . . . _____ miles
15 Multiply line 14 by 11¢ and enter here . . . . _____
16 Total mileage expense (add lines 13 and 15) . . . . _____
17 Business part of car interest and State and local taxes (except gasoline tax) . . . . _____
18 Total (add lines 16 and 17) . . . . _____

Summary

19 Enter amount from line 11 or line 18, whichever you used . . . . _____
20 Parking fees and tolls . . . . _____
21 Total (add lines 19 and 20). Enter here and in Part I, line 3 . . . . _____

343–142–1

People who work outside, or in the field, such as sales people, can deduct their mileage to the extent of any reimbursements. Outside sales people can also deduct many other things here. Items such as materials and supplies, gifts and promotions, business lunches and entertainment, telephone expenses, car rental expenses, car lease payments, professional dues and organizations, etc. can all be deducted here on Form 2106.

The main point here is to be very conscious of employee business expenses and of Form 2106. Understand the form, how to use it, and how it relates to your specific occupation. As stated earlier, most taxpayers have never heard of it, yet many people have had legitimate deductions for years and have never taken them. Whether you are a wage earner who makes $500,000 a year, or one who makes $5,000 a year, you may be able to take advantage of the employee business expenses adjustment to income.

Filling out Form 2106. The heading at the top of the form is an important part of filling out Form 2106. Write in the name and the social security number of the person who is to claim employee business expense deductions. Put in the name and address of the employer related specifically to the expenses. The box entitled "occupations in which expenses were incurred" is the most important part of the heading. Be sure to put in only the occupation to which the deductions specifically apply. If you have more than one occupation and different types of expenses pertain to to each one, then you should complete other Forms 2106. The name of the occupation in this box may be different from the one you list in the heading on Form 1040. For example, you may be a factory worker and a union representative. You may have incurred expenses in attending out-of-town union conventions. Therefore, you would put "union representative" in the box, "occupation in which expenses were incurred." It would be a bad mistake to simply write in "mechanic" and then deduct exepenses related to the acivities of a union representative because you would be asking for a tax audit.

People who have jobs in which they work in the field, or outside an office, may be able to claim deductions for local travel. In this case, it is important to include the word "outside" in the description of the "occupation in which expenses were incurred." For example, if you are an outside carpenter, as opposed to a carpenter who works in a shop, be sure to write in the word "outside" when you claim the deductions for going to different job sites. Sales people, especially, should use the description "outside salesperson" when they are taking travel expense deductions.

Part I of Form 2106 is for reporting employee business expenses that will become adjustments to gross income.

Line 1 of Form 2106 is for the expenses of out-of-town trips in which you stay overnight at least one night. Add the various fares of all airplane, boat, bus, taxi cab, or train travel. Do not put any automobile expenses on line 1. Include any taxi or bus fares paid to get to and from the airport or train station—that may add ten to twenty-five dollars to each fare. For example, you are a history teacher and you go to a history teachers' convention in Honolulu. The plane fare is $575, and cab fares to and from the airport amount to $13. Put down the *total* amount that it cost you to go to and from the convention on line 1.

Line 2. Meals and lodging expenses, again, involve out-of-town, overnight trips. For example, you go to a teachers' convention for four days, you must pay for meals and lodging during the convention, and you are never reimbursed for the total amount. It is very important that you keep a diary and save all of your receipts for these amounts.

On *line 3* you put the total amount of automobile expenses relating to employee business travel for either local or out-of-town trips. In order to determine that amount, fill out Part IV on page 2 of Form 2106.

Part IV of Form 2106—Car Expenses. Line A. There are columns here for listing the expenses for three cars, or for one car used in three different tax situations. You could separate the expenses of a long-distance trip from those of the local use of your car. However, I think it's better to fill out two separate Schedules 2106 instead, and to claim each type of expense separately. For example, you drive your car to a convention across the country and also use another car for travelling around locally in your job. Instead of using columns a and b for car 1 and car 2, I think you should fill out two separate Forms 2106. On one Form 2106 show the total amount of expenses for the trip across the country. On the other Form 2106, show the total amount of expenses for all of your local travel related to your job. This is a better tax procedure than combining the expenses of the two cars on one form.

On *line A* under Part IV on page 2 of Form 2106, put in the total number of months you were engaged in the job or profession in which you used the automobile for business purposes. For example, you are a social worker and you use your car in the field for the entire year. In that case, you would put in "12" on line A. If you are a school teacher and do not work during the summer months, you would put in "10" for the number of months.

Line B asks for the total mileage that you traveled in each car on both business and personal trips during the months you used it at all for business purposes. In other words, the school teacher who used her car for ten months should put down the total number of miles that were driven during that ten-month period, say, 15,000 miles. She does not count the other two months during the summer when she was not engaged in her profession.

Line C is for the number of miles that were driven only on business-related trips. For example, of the 15,000 miles driven by the school teacher during the school year, 7,143 miles were traveled when she was on official business. Obviously, it is essential that you keep records throughout the year of the total number of miles that you drive for purposes related to your job or profession.

Remember, commuting to and from work is not tax-deductible, but trips to different job sites or to a second job in the same day, or to a seminar, convention, or union meeting, or to visit clients, etc. are all tax-deductible. You should keep daily records of such trips, and when you prepare your tax return, you should have the total number of miles traveled for the year. Put the portion of the business-related mileage on line C.

There are two methods that can be used to determine your total tax deduction for auto expenses. The first method is to claim your actual out-of-pocket expenses on *lines 1 through 11* on Part IV of Form 2106. Under this method you put down the actual expenses for such items as gas, oil, repairs, insurance, taxes, etc. plus an amount for depreciation of the automobile. Again, you include only those expenses that relate to the business use of your automobile, and only during those months that the car was used for business purposes. For example, you are an outside sales person and you use your car 90% for business and 10% for personal use. Ninety percent of all your gas costs, repairs, insurance, taxes and licenses, etc. would be tax-deductible and would go onto lines 1 through 11. You would also be able to depreciate the car. Automobiles that were placed in service for business use before January 1, 1981 must continue to be depreciated by the same method and over the same life as on previous tax returns. However, cars that were placed in service after December 31, 1980 can be depreciated by the Accelerated Cost Recovery System. That method is described on page 65. You cannot use ACRS if you elect to use the mileage rate. Depreciation is entered on *line 8* of Form 2106.

In other words, in using the actual expenses method for determining your deduction for car expenses, you take your total expenses plus depreciation and multiply that amount by the percentage of business use of the automobile. Obviously, in order to use this method you must keep all of your receipts and keep very accurate records of all of your car expenses throughout the year.

The other method used to determine your car expense deduction is called the "mileage rate method." Calculating this amount is fairly simple. On *line 12*, enter the amount of miles from line C, up to a maximum of 15,000 miles. Multiply the amount on line 12 by 20 cents per mile, or 11 cents per mile if that automobile has been fully depreciated or has been used for over five years in deducting employee business expenses.

On *lines 14* and *15*, determine the amount of your deduction for mileage over 15,000 miles. Simply multiply the number of miles over 15,000 by 11 cents per mile. Then on line 16 add up the amounts from lines 13 and 15, and you will have your total mileage expense. On *line 17* put in the amount of the business portion of car-related interest payments, and of state and local taxes. On *line 18* total lines 16 and 17, and you will have the total amount of your deduction using the mileage rate method.

On *lines 19* through *21*, put in the amount from line 18 or line 11 depending upon which method you used. Add in the total amount of parking fees and tolls, and then you will have your total amount of automobile expenses. The amount from line 21 is also entered on page 1 of the Form 2106 in Part I, on line 3. Obviously it is easier to use the mileage rate method. But, with today's outrageous automobile expenses, a greater deduction probably will result from using the actual expense method. Therefore, it is very important that you keep all of your receipts and daily records of all of your business-related automobile expenses. Now let's go back to page 1 of Form 2106.

Outside Salespersons' Expenses. Line 4 asks for the amounts of expenses of outside sales people only. If you are an outside salesperson, be sure to write that in at the top of Form 2106 under "occupation in which expenses were incurred." Besides automobile expenses, outside salespeople can also deduct many other business-related expenses. These might include gifts and promotions, professional dues and organization membership fees, telephone expenses, materials and supplies, sales and demonstration kits, business lunches and entertainment, etc. List each and every type of expense and the specific amounts for each type on line 4. Do not lump them together, or use the term "miscellaneous." Write in exactly what they are for and the exact amounts.

Partially Reimbursed Expenses. Line 5 is for "other" business expenses, which means those expenses for which your employer reimbursed you, at least partially. For example, your employer repays you for most of your expenses in attending a convention. Write in the words "convention costs" and the amount that you were repaid. If your out-of-pocket expenses were greater than the amount that you were repaid, the difference would be a tax deduction. Be sure to take full advantage of this opportunity to lower your gross income.

When you have other expenses, such as convention costs or seminar fees, etc., and they are not repaid by your employer, I prefer to put these items and amounts on line 2 under Part I, next to "meals and lodging," instead of on line 5. Write in "conference fees," "seminar costs," "gratuities," "incidentals," "car rental," etc. Describe the specific items on the dotted line on line 2, and then include them in the total of expenses for meals and lodging. In this way, you are showing the IRS exactly the types of employee business expenses that you incurred and that they were not paid by your employer. Since line 5 is meant to include only expenses that were paid for by your employer, it's better to claim unreimbursed expenses on line 2.

On *line 6*, simply total lines 1 through 5.

On *line 7* put in any amounts that you received from your employer to cover any of the expenses you are claiming. Any amount received from your employer that is included on your W-2 forms should *not* be put here. Since employee business expenses are tax-deductible on line 7, put in only the reimbursement you received from your employer that has not already been taxed, and thus has not been included on your Form W-2. For example, your employer pays you seventeen cents per mile for your job-related automobile expenses. Since the IRS allows you to deduct twenty cents per mile, the three-cents-per-mile difference would be deductible. Calculate the total amount of automobile expenses and subtract the amount on line 7 from the amount on line 6. This amount would be your total employee business expense deduction. Put that amount here and again on line 23 of Form 1040.

Line 9. If the amount that you receive from your employer is greater than the actual amount of your expenses, then you will have "excess business expense payments." This amount is entered on line 9 of Form 2106, and then again on Form 1040 on line 20 under "other income." As you can imagine, making money on reimbursements from an employer is a very rare and unusual occurrence.

EDUCATION EXPENSES—
PARTS II AND III OF FORM 2106

Parts II and III of Form 2106 should be used for claiming education expenses related to your job or profession. These expenses, unlike those recorded in Part I of Form 2106, are itemized deductions and go onto Schedule A. These expenses ordinarily would not be considered adjustments to income and may only be deducted if you itemize deductions on Schedule A. Employee business expenses involving travel, or going to conferences or conventions, should go on Part I as an adjustment to your income. Job or profession-related education expenses should go under Parts II and III.

In Part II put in the total amount of your education expenses relating to your job or profession. I think that it is important to break these down into three categories: "tuition and fees," "books and supplies," and "transportation." Write in these three terms on the dotted lines and put in the amounts for each. For example, say you spend $496 on tuition and fees, and $47 on books and supplies, including pens, pencils, notebooks, etc.

In computing the amount of transportation expenses, you have to calculate the number of extra miles traveled in going to classes, apart from the number of miles you regularly travel in going back and forth to your job. You cannot deduct amounts for mileage to and from work, or for going to classes on a non-working day. The *additional* miles that you travel to go to classes are tax-deductible. If you go to work, then come home, and then go to school, those miles are not deductible. When you go to school directly from work, the additional miles in getting to class and back home are tax-deductible at the rate of twenty cents per mile, plus additional parking fees and tolls.

Part III on page 2 of Form 2106 is the key to successfully deducting education expenses. This is where you show the IRS that your expenses are tax-deductible, and that you understand this aspect of the tax system.

Lines 1 and *2*. Write in the name and address of the educational institution you attended during the year. "Educational institution" means colleges, universities, formal training centers, open universities, adult education courses, etc. If you have attended more than one educational institution during the year, fill out a separate Form 2106 for each. Do not combine the amounts spent in attending different educational institutions. For example, if you attended two different colleges during the year, fill out two separate Forms 2106.

Lines 3 and *4*. Contrary to what most taxpayers believe, the answers to both of these questions should be "No." Courses taken in order to qualify for a new trade or business, on line 4, are absolutely *not* deductible. The history teacher who takes courses to become a welder cannot deduct them. If you are a printer, and are taking courses to become a computer operator, then they are not tax-deductible.

The question on line 3 is a little less straightforward. You may be in a job and need to take courses to meet its basic requirements. If you are *already* in this job and are taking such courses, the answer can be "yes," and the courses can still be tax-deductible. But, if you are not already in a particular job and you are taking courses to meet its basic requirements, then the expenses of the courses are not tax-deductible. The key is that these courses must help you in your *present* job. Therefore, they cannot be courses that will help you to get a new job, nor can they necessarily be courses to help you meet the basic requirements of your present position.

On *line 5* write in: "Courses taken to maintain and improve my skills as a _____," and write in your specific job description. The key words here are to maintain or improve the skills required by your *present* position. Courses, books, and materials, and transportation are all tax-deductible if education expenses so qualify.

Line 6 asks for a description of the specific courses you have taken that relate directly to your present position. List each course separately and try to relate course titles to your present position. For example, a history teacher who takes classroom supervision courses may be able to deduct them if he can show these courses improve his skills as a history teacher. The course may have included supervison of teenagers, which would be helpful in his teaching position. Instead of writing in just the word "supervison" for the courses taken, he should write in "supervison of high school students."

In certain fields, such as medical and technical positions, courses with highly technical names are common. Don't hesitate to write them in. If possible, use the most technical title, a title that an IRS agent would not touch with a ten-foot pole.

Many working people can take advantage of the education expense deduction. For example, workers who use mathematics in their jobs, for example, cashiers, carpenters, and engineers, can deduct the expenses of taking classes in mathematics. People whose jobs involve communications skills, including writing and speaking, may be able to deduct the expenses of courses in English and speech, even remedial courses. A person who works in a bilingual occupation may be able to deduct foreign language courses. The key is that the courses must be relevant to your present position.

Using Form 2106 Properly. People are always asking me, "Can I deduct my trip to Hawaii or Chicago, or write off part of my car when I have to go around town for my job?" My answer is that all business-related expenses are tax-deductible, but personal expenses are not.

If you can prove that all or even part of a trip to Hawaii was related to your job or profession, then you can deduct all or part of the expenses of it. That means keeping records, saving receipts, and even, perhaps, asking for a letter from your supervisor or employer stating that the trip was job-related. You may not be able to deduct the entire trip, but you still may be able to deduct a portion of it. For example, you are a history teacher who goes on a trip to Hawaii. If you teach about Hawaii in your classroom, and you bring back materials and information from Hawaii, you probably can deduct a reasonable portion of your trip. In Hawaii, on the days that you visit museums and go on historical tours, you can deduct the expenses of such activities. But on the days you go scuba diving or lie in the sun on the beach, your expenses would not be deductible. Your round-trip air fare would be tax-deductible. The expenses of your spouse, if not also a history teacher, would not be deductible.

When you go on a trip that is part business and part pleasure, you must carefully document the proportion related to business for the IRS. On a separate sheet of paper, prepare a statement showing the IRS all of your expenses, and then divide them into expenses that were business-related and others that were personal. By attaching such a statement, you show the IRS that your trip cost a certain amount of money, some of it was for personal expenses, and, therefore, you did not deduct those from your income.

During an audit, the IRS usually argues that a long trip is not for business only. By itemizing the expenses of a trip and deducting only a portion of the total amount, you concede that the trip was partly for pleasure, but you still deduct the expenses that relate to your business or profession. This method will greatly decrease your chances of being audited.

Employee business expenses are deductible by many working people. You should understand the rules, how they relate to your specific occupation, and how to use Form 2106 properly.

Employee business expenses in Part I of Form 2106 are adjustments to income and go onto line 23 of Form 1040. Employee business expenses, including education expenses, in Parts II and III of Form 2106 are transferred to Schedule A, "Itemized Deductions," on line 31, "Other Miscellaneous Deductions." On line 31 of Schedule A, write in "education expenses—see Form 2106," and put in the amount from line 2 of Part II of Form 2106.

A few years ago I did a tax return for a construction worker. For years he had been doing the short form because he couldn't itemize deductions. Because he had to go to different work sites each day as part of his job, he was able to claim employee business expenses on Form 2106. Even though he couldn't itemize, he still had a substantial tax write-off, which he could claim only by using the "long" form.

Another example is a postal worker who moonlighted as a night watchman. He went from one job to the other in the same day. Again, this was tax deductible on Form 2106, but not on the "short" form.

PAYMENTS TO AN INDIVIDUAL RETIREMENT ACCOUNT

Line 24 of Form 1040. Taxpayers who are able to invest in an individual retirement account can make an adjustment to income on line 24 of Form 1040. To be eligible, a taxpayer cannot have been covered by any other retirement plan, except for social security. Through 1981, the maximum amount of this deduction is $1,500 for an individual working taxpayer, but no more than 15% of the total compensation, i.e., wages, salaries, professional fees, and other amounts received for personal services. This limitation does not include amounts received as interest, dividends, or earnings from property, such as rental income. Each working spouse, if qualified, can deduct 15% of total compensation up to $1,500. Where only one spouse works and qualifies for an IRA account, then the maximum amount of the deduction goes up to $1,750.

Beginning in 1982, every working person can put money in an IRA account, regardless of other retirement plans. Also, the amount of the total deduction will be increased to $2,000, or $2,250 where only one spouse is working.

The tax advantages of putting money into an IRA account are simple. The dollars you earn and put into these accounts are not taxed in the year you earn and deposit them. You must leave the money in the IRA until retirement age, but then, when you take the money out, you will be in a much lower tax bracket. Even though the money will be taxable at that time, you will end up paying much less in tax than you would if it had been taxable in 1981 when you were in a higher tax bracket. For example, in 1982 you make $30,000 a year in compensation, and put $2,000 into an IRA account. You will pay taxes on $28,000 for 1982. If you are in the 40% tax bracket, that will save you $800 in tax. Twenty-five years from now, when you retire and withdraw the money from the IRA, you will be in a lower tax bracket, since your taxable income will be lower after you retire. At that point, you may be in only the 20% tax bracket, and, therefore, when you receive $2,000, you'd only pay $400 in tax. A second, great benefit of an IRA is that the interest on the amounts you deposit each year is not taxable until you retire and withdraw your savings. In an ordinary bank account, you pay tax on the interest every year, even if you never receive any interest payments in cash.

That is the attractiveness of all IRA and Keogh accounts—to put off paying taxes on your income until you are in a lower tax bracket.

If you should withdraw money from an IRA before age 59½, you will be subject to a special tax penalty of a flat 10% of the total amount that you withdraw during the taxable year. You must fill out Form 5329 in order to calculate the amount of this tax penalty.

PAYMENTS TO A KEOGH RETIREMENT PLAN

Line 25. Keogh plans are for self-employed taxpayers who have put money into a special tax-deferred retirement plan. The amount invested in the Keogh plan is considered to be an adjustment to income. Through 1981, self-employed people can put 15% of their self-employed net profit into a Keogh plan, up to a maximum of $7,500 per year. Beginning in 1982, that limit is increased to $15,000 a year. Again, for people who withdraw money prematurely from a Keogh plan, there is a tax penalty. A Keogh plan allows the same benefits as an IRA. Self-employed people can defer some tax now, when their taxable incomes are high, and then pay tax on the money later, when their taxable incomes are lower.

Keogh plans and IRAs are also good investments. Your money will earn more money in the form of interest, dividends, or capital gains. The advantage is that, unlike other investments, you do not have to pay tax on the additional money, until you receive it. Thus, without taxes deducted from interest or dividends each year, your investment grows at a higher rate, particularly during the years you are in a higher tax bracket.

Beginning in 1982, certain other changes have been made regarding Keogh plans and IRAs. For Keogh plans, any partners involved in a plan will be prohibited from borrowing from the plan. Also, IRAs and Keogh plans will not be able to invest in collectibles, such as diamonds, rare coins, antiques, etc.

INTEREST PENALTY ON EARLY WITHDRAWAL OF SAVINGS

Line 26. People who invest in certificates of deposit or other long-term bank accounts and who prematurely withdraw from these accounts are penalized by the bank. In long-term, high-interest bank accounts, it is required that you leave your money in them for a specified period of time. If you withdraw any money before this time period is up, the bank will charge you a penalty. That penalty is the loss of a certain amount of interest. At the end of the year, the bank will send you a statement showing the dollar amount of the penalty. Put the total amount of the penalty on line 26 of Form 1040. It is considered an adjustment to income and is, in effect, a tax deduction. It is necessary to report penalties in this way because on line 8a of Form 1040 you must report the gross amount of interest credited to your account. The place to subtract any penalties for early withdrawal is on line 26.

ALIMONY PAID

Line 27 of Form 1040. Alimony, or spousal support, that you pay to your ex-spouse is tax-deductible as an adjustment to income. *Child support* payments are not tax-deductible—only alimony payments. The distinction between the two types of support payments is discussed above in Chapter 6. Simply put in the total amount of alimony that you paid out during the taxable year on line 27.

DISABILITY INCOME EXCLUSION FORM 2440

Line 28. The disability income exclusion is an adjustment to income for people who are under age sixty-five and who are permanently disabled. That means they are not able to work, nor will they be able to go back to their job in the future. If you are receiving disability income, you may be able to exclude, and, thus, not pay taxes on, up to $5,200 for any given tax year. If you are filing a joint tax return, and both spouses can qualify for the exclusion, you can exclude up to a maximum of $10,400.

In order to claim this exclusion, you must fill out Form 2440. The bottom part of that form contains a Physician's Certificate of Permanent Total Disability. You must ask your physician to complete this section and it must be sent in as an attachment to your tax return.

ADJUSTMENTS TO INCOME 127

Form **2440** Department of the Treasury Internal Revenue Service	**Disability Income Exclusion** (Applies Only to Disabled Retirees Under Age 65) ▶ Attach to Form 1040. ▶ See Instructions on back.	OMB No. 1545-0069 **1981** 25

Name(s) as shown on Form 1040 | Social security number

See Instruction B for Income Limits on Exclusion

Date you retired (if after December 31, 1976, also enter this date in the space after box (2) on physician's statement below).	Employer's name (also give payer's name, if other than employer)
Yourself	
Spouse	

Note: To take the disability income exclusion, you must complete lines 1 through 9.

Joint return filers use column (a) for wife and column (b) for husband. All other filers use column (b) only.

	(a)	(b)
1 Enter total disability pay you got during 1981.		
2 (i) Multiply $100 by the number of weeks for which your disability payments were at least $100. Enter total		
(ii) If you received disability payments of less than $100 for any week, enter the total amount you received for all such weeks		
(iii) If you received disability payments for less than a week, enter the smaller amount of either the amount you received or the highest exclusion allowable for the period (see Instruction D)		
(iv) Add lines (i), (ii), and (iii). Enter total.		
3 Add amounts on line 2(iv). Enter total.		
4 Enter total income from Form 1040, line 21.		
5 Add amounts on Form 1040, lines 22 through 27 and line 29. Enter total.		
6 Subtract line 5 from line 4.		
7 Amount used to figure any exclusion decrease (see Instruction B).		$15,000.00
8 Subtract line 7 from line 6 (if line 7 is more than line 6, enter zero).		
9 Subtract line 8 from line 3. This is your disability income exclusion. Enter here and on Form 1040, line 28.		

10 If you filed a physician's statement for this disability in an earlier year, please check this box. (You do not have to file another statement.) ▶ ☐

For Paperwork Reduction Act Notice, see instructions on back. Form **2440** (1981)

Physician's Statement of Permanent and Total Disability

▶ Please complete and return to taxpayer.

Name of disabled taxpayer | Social security number

I certify that the taxpayer named above was (check only one box—please see instructions below):
(1) ☐ Permanently and totally disabled on January 1, 1976, or January 1, 1977.
(2) ☐ Permanently and totally disabled on the date he or she retired. Date retired ▶

Physician's name

Physician's address

Physician's signature | Date

Instructions for Statement

Taxpayer

Please enter your name and social security number. If you retired after December 31, 1976, enter your retirement date in the space after box (2).

Physician

Box (1) applies to taxpayers who retired before January 1, 1977.
Box (2) applies to taxpayers who retired after December 31, 1976.

What is Permanent and Total Disability?

A person is permanently and totally disabled when—

• He or she is unable to engage in any substantial gainful activity because of a physical or mental condition; and
• A physician determines that the disability (a) has lasted or can be expected to last continuously for at least a year; or (b) can be expected to lead to death.

343-156-1

If your total income is $15,000 or more, you may not be able to receive the disability income exclusion. You must subtract all income in excess of $15,000 from your total income, and then subtract that difference from your allowed disability income exclusion. For example, if you can get the $5,200 exclusion, but your total income (including your spouse's income on a joint return) is $25,000, then you would subtract $15,000 from the $25,000. That $10,000 difference would then be subtracted from the $5,200 exclusion, which would leave you '0' no disability income exclusion. If you do qualify, fill out Form 2440, have it certified by your physician, and take full advantage of the disability income exclusion.

OTHER ADJUSTMENTS— LINE 29 OF FORM 1040

This category included three types of tax write-offs: excess foreign living expenses; forestation/reforestation amortization; and repayment of "sub-pay" under the Trade Act of 1974.

Excess foreign living expenses may be claimed by taxpayers who have lived abroad and have incurred foreign living expenses in excess of employer payments or reimbursements. Fill our Form 2555 to calculate your deduction and put that amount on line 29. Write in "Expenses from Form 2555" and take the deduction adjustment.

Forestation/reforestation amortization (boy, what a mouthfull!) has to do with claiming a deduction for certain forestation-/reforestation expenditures. It is only for taxpayers who qualify for this adjustment to income and who do not claim a deduction for the same amounts on Schedule C or Schedule F. In other words, the IRS is giving you this deduction even if you do not set up your involvement with forestation/reforestation as a business. Write in a description of your deduction and put the amount onto line 29.

Repayment of sub-pay involves taxpayers —for example, auto workers—who have received supplemental unemployment benefits that have been included as income in past tax returns and who repaid any or all of such benefits during 1981. Put in the amount that you repaid during 1981 and write in "sub-pay TRA." The IRS now allows you to reduce your gross income by this amount, since you've already paid taxes on it in past years.

If you have more than one of the allowable adjustments on line 29, write in the left margin each adjustment title and put the total amount onto line 29.

TOTAL ADJUSTMENTS

On *line 30*, simply total all of the amounts on lines 22 through 29 of Form 1040. This will give you the total amount of adjustments to income.

ADJUSTED GROSS INCOME

Line 31. Your adjusted gross income is calculated by subtracting your total adjustments to income on line 30 from your total income on line 21. If the amount on this line is under $10,000, you may be able to qualify for the "Earned Income Credit," which is discussed below in Chapter 17.

After computing your adjusted gross income, turn the Form 1040 over. Copy the amount on line 31 onto line 32a.

CHAPTER THIRTEEN

☆

Itemized Deductions—Schedule A

ITEMIZING OR TAKING THE STANDARD DEDUCTION

Before we go on to the instructions for filling out Schedule A, let's consider the alternatives in calculating taxable income on line 34. There are two possibilities here: to itemize deductions by filling out Schedule A, or to take the "standard deduction." The standard deduction is a minimum amount that the government allows everyone to claim. It is the smallest deduction that anyone can take.

There are three different standard deductions and they are based solely on your filing status. If you file in the status of single by checking box number 1 under "filing status," or unmarried head of household (box number 4), the standard deduction is $2,300.

If your filing status is married filing joint return (box number 2 under filing status), or if you file as a qualifying widow(er) with one or more dependent children (box number 5), then the standard deduction is $3,400.

If you are filing in the status of married filing separate return (box number 3), then the standard deduction is $1,700 for each spouse. Remember also that in the status of married filing separate return, if one spouse chooses to itemize deductions, then the other spouse must also itemize deductions.

It is not difficult to decide whether to itemize deductions or to take the standard deduction. Simply fill in Schedule A, line by line, and see whether or not the total amount of your deductions is greater than the standard deduction. If it is, you should itemize. Be sure to send in Schedule A with your tax return.

Itemizing deductions simply means filling out all the information required on Schedule A and coming up with more deductions than the standard deduction for your particular filing status. In other words, if you are married and filing a joint tax return, in order to be able to itemize deductions, you must have a total of more than $3,400 in itemized deductions on Schedule A. If you fill out Schedule A and do not have deductions totalling more than $3,400, then don't itemize. Simply take the standard deduction. The most important thing is to know what deductions are allowed and how they apply specifically to you. We shall go through every legitimate itemized deduction allowed, and show how each should be treated on Schedule A.

I think it's very important to note here that although we have discussed many tax-saving techniques so far in this book, we still haven't gotten to filling out Schedule A. The point is that there are many considerations in saving tax money besides whether or not to itemize deductions. The forms that we have already discussed, and the ones that are to come, can be just as useful, or in some cases more useful, than itemizing deductions on Schedule A. It is very important to be aware of the existence of the other forms and how to use them properly.

I do many tax returns, particularly for single persons or people who do not own a home, that do not involve itemized deductions. Yet, these people have many other types of tax write-offs, including adjustments to income, Forms 2106, Forms 3903, losses from rental property or self-employed businesses, and capital losses. Even if you are not able to itemize, you still can save a great deal of tax money by knowing about

Schedules A&B (Form 1040)	**Schedule A—Itemized Deductions**	OMB No. 1545-0074
Department of the Treasury Internal Revenue Service	(Schedule B is on back) ▶ Attach to Form 1040. ▶ See Instructions for Schedules A and B (Form 1040).	**1981** 07

Name(s) as shown on Form 1040 | Your social security number

Medical and Dental Expenses (Do not include expenses reimbursed or paid by others.) (See page 17 of Instructions.)

1. One-half (but not more than $150) of insurance premiums you paid for medical care. (Be sure to include in line 10 below.) ▶
2. Medicine and drugs.
3. Enter 1% of Form 1040, line 31
4. Subtract line 3 from line 2. If line 3 is more than line 2, enter zero.
5. Balance of insurance premiums for medical care not entered on line 1.
6. Other medical and dental expenses:
   a. Doctors, dentists, nurses, etc.
   b. Hospitals
   c. Transportation
   d. Other (itemize—include hearing aids, dentures, eyeglasses, etc.) ▶
7. Total (add lines 4 through 6d).
8. Enter 3% of Form 1040, line 31.
9. Subtract line 8 from line 7. If line 8 is more than line 7, enter zero.
10. Total medical and dental expenses (add lines 1 and 9). Enter here and on line 33. ▶

Taxes (See page 18 of Instructions.)

11. State and local income
12. Real estate
13. a General sales (see sales tax tables).
    b General sales on motor vehicles.
14. Personal property
15. Other (itemize) ▶
16. Total taxes (add lines 11 through 15). Enter here and on line 34. ▶

Interest Expense (See page 18 of Instructions.)

17. Home mortgage
18. Credit and charge cards
19. Other (itemize) ▶
20. Total interest expense (add lines 17 through 19). Enter here and on line 35 ▶

Contributions (See page 19 of Instructions.)

21. a Cash contributions (If you gave $3,000 or more to any one organization, report those contributions on line 21b).
    b Cash contributions totaling $3,000 or more to any one organization (show to whom you gave and how much you gave) ▶
22. Other than cash (see page 19 of Instructions for required statement).
23. Carryover from prior years.
24. Total contributions (add lines 21a through 23). Enter here and on line 36 ▶

Casualty or Theft Loss(es) (You must attach Form 4684 if line 29 is $1,000 or more, OR if certain other situations apply.) (See page 19 of Instructions.)

25. Loss before reimbursement.
26. Insurance or other reimbursement you received or expect to receive.
27. Subtract line 26 from line 25. If line 26 is more than line 25, enter zero.
28. Enter $100 or amount from line 27, whichever is smaller.
29. Total casualty or theft loss(es) (subtract line 28 from line 27). Enter here and on line 37 ▶

Miscellaneous Deductions (See page 19 of Instructions.)

30. a Union dues.
    b Tax return preparation fee.
31. Other (itemize) ▶
32. Total miscellaneous deductions (add lines 30a through 31). Enter here and on line 38. ▶

Summary of Itemized Deductions (See page 20 of Instructions.)

33. Total medical and dental—from line 10.
34. Total taxes—from line 16.
35. Total interest—from line 20.
36. Total contributions—from line 24.
37. Total casualty or theft loss(es)—from line 29.
38. Total miscellaneous—from line 32.
39. Add lines 33 through 38.
40. If you checked Form 1040, Filing Status box:
    2 or 5, enter $3,400
    1 or 4, enter $2,300
    3, enter $1,700
41. Subtract line 40 from line 39. Enter here and on Form 1040, line 32b. (If line 40 is more than line 39, see the Instructions for line 41 on page 20.) ▶

For Paperwork Reduction Act Notice, see Form 1040 Instructions.

343-059-1

ITEMIZED DEDUCTIONS—SCHEDULE A

the other types of tax deductions. Of course, as we stressed before, in order to claim all of these different types of tax deductions, you must fill out the "long form" Form 1040. Nobody ever saved money on a Form 1040A.

FILLING OUT SCHEDULE A

Here is a list of the more common itemized deductions you can claim on Schedule A:

Medical and Dental Expenses
- Percent of medical insurance premiums
- Medicine and drugs
- Hospital costs
- Ambulance
- Anesthesia
- Nurses
- Hearing aid and batteries
- Eye glasses and examination
- Artificial teeth
- X-rays
- Blood tests
- Medical appliances
- Surgical clothing
- Elastics and braces
- Orthopedic shoes
- Travel to and from doctor (at 9 cents per mile)
- Doctors' and dentists' fees

Taxes
- State and local taxes paid
- Real estate taxes on your home
- General sales tax
- Personal property tax
- Auto license fees (minus registration fees)
- Excess sales tax on auto, boat, motorcycle, mobile or prefabricated home, airplane, etc.
- Sales tax on materials purchased for a new home

Interest Expense
- Home mortgage interest
- Loan origination fees (points)
- Bank and finance company loan interest
- Personal loan interest
- Interest on charge accounts and credit card charges and advances

Contributions
- Religious organizations
- Charitable organizations (listed), such as March of Dimes, United Way, etc.
- Charitable work—transportation at 9 cents per mile plus expenses for mailings, telephone, etc.
- Value of donations of clothing, furniture, etc.
- Carryover of excess contributions from prior years

Casualty or Theft Losses
- Total amount of loss minus insurance reimbursement less $100 limitation

Miscellaneous Deductions
- Union dues plus initiation and assessments
- Employment agency fees
- Uniforms and protective clothing
- Laundry and cleaning for uniforms and protective clothing
- Safety equipment
- Tools, equipment, and supplies
- Professional organizations (dues, meetings, and conventions)
- Professional and trade publications
- Education expenses (see Form 2106)
- Unreimbursed employee business expenses
- Safe deposit box rental fees
- Investment counseling
- Income tax preparation fees
- Income tax books and guides
- Telephone expenses (if required by employer)
- Depreciation of library
- Depreciation of major tools
- Transportation to second job in same day (deduct here instead of on Form 2106)
- Malpractice insurance premiums
- Physical exam required by employer
- Certain child adoption expenses
- Home office expenses

MEDICAL AND DENTAL EXPENSES

"Medical and Dental Expenses" include all of the money that you spend in a year on doctors, dentists, hospitals, and other medical costs, for yourself, your spouse, your children, and any other dependents. Any amounts of money that you have received as reimbursements or payments from medical insurance must be deducted from these amounts. There are many types of expenses that can be related to medical costs and we shall go through them.

Medical and dental expense deductions, unlike the other types of deductions on Schedule A, have a catch. The catch is that you have to subtract three per cent of your adjusted gross income from the total amount of medical and dental expenses. For many taxpayers, particularly those with high incomes, the three-per-cent figure will wipe out most medical and dental expense deductions. In any case, put down all of your medical and dental expenses on lines 1 through 10 of Schedule A to see what amount of deduction will be left.

On *line 1*, put down one-half of all of your medical insurance premium payments up to an amount of $150. Medical insurance premiums include money that you have spent for coverage by Blue Cross, Blue Shield, hospitalization plans, dental plans, etc., including any amounts that have been deducted from your paychecks for such coverage. The medical coverage portion of your automobile insurance premiums is also deductible, as far as it covers you and your family, but not the portion that covers others who may be injured by your car. If you are filing a joint tax return, put down the total amount of medical insurance premium payments for you and your spouse combined.

The amount on line 1 is very important in that it is not reduced by three per cent of your adjusted gross income. Therefore, you may be able to claim up to $150 for the medical insurance premium deduction, and not be able to claim any other deductions for medical and dental expenses. The other half of your total medical insurance premium payments goes onto line 5. For example, if you have paid a total of $500 for medical insurance premiums, then $150 would go onto line 1 and $350 would go onto line 5. However, if you have paid a total of $200 for medical insurance premiums, then $100 would go onto line 1 and $100 would go onto line 5.

Line 2. All medicines and drugs that are prescribed or recommended by a doctor are tax-deductible. For example, birth control pills and special foods or beverages prescribed or recommended by a doctor solely for the treatment of an illness are tax-deductible. Vitamins, iron supplements, etc. that are prescribed by a doctor are also deductible. The key is that to qualify for deduction, an item must be related to a treatment or a doctor's prescription, and must not be just for your personal desires.

In order to be able to deduct any amount for medicines and drugs, you must have spent a total of more than one per cent of your adjusted gross income. Adjusted gross income is the amount on line 31 of Form 1040. For example, if line 31 is $20,000, you must subtract $200 (1% of $20,000) from the total amount spent for medicine and drugs. For many taxpayers, that may eliminate this deduction. It's very important to save receipts for medicines and drugs throughout the year. Many people lose money because they haven't kept accurate records of all of their medicine and drug expenses. Prescriptions can add up to a lot of money each year. If you haven't been doing it in the past, now is the time to start saving all of your receipts.

If you do have a large deduction for medicines and drugs on line 2, be certain that you can back it up with records. If you or someone in your family has a specific disease which requires a lot of medicines and drugs, write in the name of the disease and claim all of the expenses on line 2. For example, someone with a heart condition may need a variety of expensive medicines and drugs. Write in "heart condition" on Schedule A and send in a letter from your doctor to that effect along with the tax return. Don't hesitate to send in photocopies for large amounts of expenses for medicines and drugs. Write "see attached" near line 2 on Schedule A, and include copies of receipts or letters.

Line 3. Enter one per cent of your adjusted gross income, which, again, is the amount on line 31 of Form 1040.

Line 4. Subtract the amount on line 3

from the amount on line 2. If the difference is a negative number, write in "0."

Line 5. Put in the other half or balance of your medical insurance premiums that has not already been claimed on line 1.

Line 6 is where you enter all of the expenses of doctors, dentists, hospitals, eyeglasses, medical appliances, etc. Look at the list of all of the legitimate medical and dental expense deductions to see which ones apply to you. I feel that it's important to list each doctor, dentist, and hospital separately, and to write in each specialty, such as obstetrician, surgeon, etc. Give the IRS the names of your doctors, dentists, and hospitals, and the amounts you paid to each. Use the dotted lines below line 6d. Remember, many smaller numbers look better than a few large ones. Note that if you have been reimbursed by health insurance companies for any amounts, do not include such amounts in the total amount.

After listing each doctor, dentist, psychologist, or psychiatrist, list all of your other types of medical expenses, such as x-rays, blood tests, medical supplies, etc. You may be able to deduct the cost of a vaporizor, a humidifier, or even a water bed or sauna if it is directly recommended by a physician in order to help you to cure a specific illness. If you do take this type of deduction be sure to write in "see attached" and enclose a letter from your physician certifying that he or she did recommend the item in question. Always send a photcopy, never the original.

Also be sure to claim the expenses of all of your travel to and from medical and dental appointments, including taxi, train, and plane fares, as well as ambulance charges. You can deduct medical travel expense in your own car at nine cents per mile. You can deduct parking fees or tolls incurred in going to and from doctors, hospitals, dentists, etc. It is a good idea to keep a diary of these expenses throughout the year.

Line 7. Total all of the amounts on lines 4 through 6c.

Line 8. Calculate three per cent of your adjusted gross income from line 31 of Form 1040. For example, if your adjusted gross income is $20,000 on line 31, then three percent of that sum, or $600, would go onto line 8.

Line 9. Subtract the amount on line 8 from that on line 7. If line 8 is greater than line 7, then enter "0."

Line 10. Add the amount on line 9 and the amount on line 1. That will be your total medical and dental expense deduction. Even when the amount on line 9 is "0," if there is an amount on line 1, that amount would be transferred to line 10 and would become your total medical and dental expense deduction. For many taxpayers, the amount line 10 is $150, one-half of their medical insurance premium payments.

Lessening the Risk of an Audit. One of the most frequently audited categories on a tax return is the deduction for medical and dental expenses. The IRS seems to feel that most taxpayers have extensive medical coverage, and, therefore, have to pay for very few medical and dental expenses out of their own pockets. If you have incurred unusually large medical and dental expenses, you should claim every dollar, but be prepared for an audit. You may want to take certain precautions when you file a tax return claiming a large medical and dental expense deduction.

The most effective precaution is to send in proof of such expenses along with your tax return. If you have large medical, dental, or hospital bills, write in "see attached" on Schedule A, and attach photocopies of the bills and of your cancelled checks.

Tax returns that claim an amount for medical and dental insurance premium payments and also claim large medical and dental expenses are frequently audited. You may have insurance that does not cover 100% of your expenses, or any portion of certain types of expenses. For example, most health insurance policies do not cover psychiatric care. If you have been seeing a psychologist or psychiatrist and your medical insurance does not cover such treatment, point this out to the IRS. Write in the doctor's name and degree in parentheses next to the name, and then the amount of the bills or fees. You might also include a copy of a notice or letter from your insurance company stating that this type of expense is not covered by your policy. The idea here is to stop a tax audit before it gets started.

TAXES

Taxes paid to state, local, or foreign governments, property taxes, sales taxes, land taxes, and contributions to state disability insurance funds are all tax-deductible. Non-deductible taxes include federal income taxes, social security taxes, state or local gasoline taxes, federal excise taxes, customs duties, and federal estate and gift taxes.

Line 11. Deduct all of the state and local taxes that you have paid during the year, including those that were withheld from your paychecks and estimated tax payments that were paid during the year. Add all of these amounts from your W-2's and put the total on line 11. For example, if you live in New York City, you will be paying New York State income tax as well as New York City income tax. The total amount of state and city taxes that you paid during the year as shown on W-2 statements would go onto line 11.

Line 12 asks for real estate taxes that were paid during the taxable year, that is, only amounts that were paid from January through December. Only the *owner* of real property can deduct real estate taxes. Line 12 can include more than one property, but it's a good idea to break down the taxes paid for each different property on the dotted lines next to line 12. Also, if a portion of real estate taxes paid was for rental property, show the proration on line 12 and take only the portion that went for your personal residence. For example, you own a duplex and live in one of the apartments. Claim fifty percent on your Schedule E as a rental expense, and then the other fifty percent on line 12 of Schedule A. Write in "at ½" on the dotted lines beside line 12, and then put in the fifty percent amount. It's important to show the IRS the percentage or proration you are using.

Line 13a. General sales tax refers to all of the sales taxes you paid on living expenses during the year. The figure to be put on line 13a is based on your total income and the size of your family. In computing the amount, take into account *all* of your income for the year, including your taxable income as well as non-taxable amounts, such as welfare payments, social security benefits, sixty percent of capital gains, inheritances, etc.

There are two ways to compute the amount of the general sales tax deduction. The way used most often is simply to turn to the general sales tax tables found in the back of the Federal Income Tax Forms booklet, and look up the amount under the figures for your state. If your state has no sales tax, smile and go on to Interest Expense.

If you have been keeping records and receipts throughout the entire year for all of the sales taxes you have paid, and that amount is higher than the figure given in the appropriate sales tax table, then claim the amount you actually paid. It's a good idea to write in the word "actual" on line 13a, and then put in the total amount.

Be careful to read the fine print under each of the state sales tax tables to see if you can add in any additional amounts to your general sales tax deduction. For example, residents of the San Francisco Bay Area can add an additional eight per cent to the amount shown on the table, because they must pay an additional one-half percent more sales tax on items than the residents of other parts of California. Many urban counties in the United States have similarly higher sales tax rates.

Line 13b. In most states, when you purchase a motor vehicle you will pay state sales tax on it. Such amounts of sales tax are deductible in addition to the amounts found in the general sales tax tables. Motor vehicles include autos, trucks, motorcycles, mobile homes, campers, boats, planes, RVs, etc. Enter such amounts on line 13b.

Line 14. Personal property tax refers to taxes paid on the value of consumer goods

ITEMIZED DEDUCTIONS—SCHEDULE A

and other property that have not already been deducted on lines 12 or 13b.

If the state in which you live imposes a vehicle registration tax, the part that is based on the value of the vehicle is tax-deductible. If part of the tax is based on vehicle age or weight, however, that part cannot be deducted. Put the amount of tax based on the value of the vehicle on line 14.

On *line 15* put in the amount of any other types of taxes that are deductible. For example, stock transfer taxes and sales taxes that were paid on materials and supplies in the construction of a new house should be put onto line 15. Identify the nature of the tax paid next to the amount.

Line 16. Total the amounts on lines 11 through 15 to arrive at the amount of your total deduction for taxes.

INTEREST EXPENSES

Interest expense can be defined as money that you have spent for the use or forbearance of money. When you borrow money and are charged a certain amount, that is, "points," or pay a certain rate or percentage of interest, the dollar amounts you pay are tax-deductible. The principal portion of your load payments, the amount that goes to pay the original money that was borrowed, is not tax-deductible.

Generally, interest paid is deductible in three cases—where the money was borrowed for personal use, for rental or royalty property, or for your business. Schedule A is for claiming the deductions for interest that was paid on personal items, Schedule E is for rental or royalty interest, and Schedule C is for business interest. Therefore, on Schedule A we are concerned only with interest expenses related to your personal, family, and living purposes.

Line 17 asks for interest paid during the year on a home mortgage loan. If you lived in more than one house during the year and paid interest on mortgages for each one, show the amount of interest for each house on the dotted lines beside line 17. If a portion of your house is claimed as rental property on Schedule E, deduct only that portion of the total interest that pertains to your personal use on Schedule A. Write in "at" and the percentage used in calculating that amount on the dotted lines.

If you have purchased a house during the tax year, then there may be additional amounts to be claimed as interest expenses. Read the escrow papers and other closing documents to see if any other interest payments were paid at the time you purchased the house. For example, there may have been prepaid interest charges. These are tax-deductible.

Everyone who borrows money on a house from a commercial lender receives a yearly loan statement indicating exactly how much interest was paid on the loan during the year. Check to see that you received such a statement, and use it to determine the exact amount of interest expenses. If a private person rather than a commercial lender is holding the note, be certain that you both agree as to the amount of interest that has been paid during the year. The holder of the note must declare the same amount as income, and an inconsistency in the amounts can trigger a tax audit.

Line 18 asks for the total amount of interest you paid during the year to banks, department stores, and other businesses that have credit card or charge card plans. I don't like the idea of lumping together several different amounts into one large figure. I suggest that you put in the amount of interest for each of your credit cards along with the name of the business under the "other" section on line 19.

Line 19. This is the place to list all of your charge cards, finance charges, and personal loans. Write in the name of each bank, company, or person to whom you made interest payments, and then the amount paid to each one. If you have too many for the room provided on Schedule A, then write in "see attached" and include a sheet of paper with a specific list of names and amounts. In case of credit cards with short names, you may be able to list more than one on a line. Write in the name of each credit card on the dotted lines, put the amount paid close to it, and then put the total for the number of credit cards on a particular line in the proper amount column.

The following is a discussion of the various types of interest expenses.

Loan Origination Fees, Sometimes Called "Points." When you purchase a home and take out a new mortgage rather than assume an existing mortgage, the bank or other mortgage lender may charge you a loan origination fee. This fee is tax-deductible on Schedule A, if the house is used as a personal residence.

Loan origination fees are often 1-1/4% to 1-1/2% of the principal amount of the mortgage. In the last few years, however, these fees have increased a great deal. In some cases, people are paying from two to five points, or 2 to 5% of the principal amount. The IRS states that you are able to deduct loan origination fees only to the extent that they are normal for your area. In other words, if, in the area where you live, banks ordinarily charge only two per cent as a loan origination fee, but you are charged five per cent, you would then be able to deduct only two per cent as a loan origination fee. On the other hand, since these fees have gone up so drastically, and since interest rates have fluctuated so much recently, there is a real question as to what "normal" really means. I suggest that you claim the entire loan origination fee, but be prepared to answer questions in case of a tax audit.

In the escrow papers or other closing documents that you receive when purchasing a house, the amount of any loan origination fee should be listed. Simply look for that amount and put it on line 19 of Schedule A and write in "loan origination fee" or "points." and the name of the bank or other lender to which you paid the fee.

Loans. All interest paid on loans is tax-deductible. These can be loans from a bank or finance company or from a private person. If you are not given a statement of the exact amount of interest that you paid on the loan during the year, you can calculate the amount yourself, if the loan agreement calls for simple, rather than compound, interest. To calculate the amount of interest expense for the year, take the amount of money that you originally borrowed, and multiply it by the interest rate percentage. Then divide that amount by the number of months the loan will be outstanding, and multiply that amount by the number of months during this tax year that you have made payments on the loan. For example, say you borrowed $2,800 at 18% interest for thirty-six months, beginning in March of the taxable year, and you make ten monthly payments. The calculation would be: $2,800 x .18 = $504; $504 ÷ 36 = $14; $14 x 10 = $140. You've paid $140 in interest expenses this year, and that is the amount of your tax deduction.

Interest Paid on Charge Accounts, Etc. Interest paid on charge accounts, credit cards, installment purchases, and finance charges is all tax-deductible. List each company to which you paid interest separately and put down the amount paid to each on Schedule A. Each company or store should send you a statement showing the total finance, or interest, charges that you paid during the year. If you haven't received these statements, call the stores, banks, loan companies, etc. and get the information.

Today, a majority of Americans are buying things on time and paying tremendous amounts of interest. The IRS norms for interest expenses are fairly high, and it is quite rare for a taxpayer who uses Schedule A to claim little or no interest expense. This is also one area that is usually not audited, because most taxpayers fit well within the norms. Before you fill out your tax returns, be sure to gather all of the necessary information regarding your interest expenses for the year. Take full advantage of this excellent tax deduction.

On *line 20,* simply total the amounts on lines 17 through 19. This amount will be your total interest expense.

CONTRIBUTIONS

Contributions of money, property, or services are tax-deductible if they are donations to *qualified* organizations. Most commonly, this means churches, charities, educational institutions, and recognized non-profit organizations such as symphony orchestras, hospitals, and scientific research laboratories. You must have donated to an organization that is *qualified* by the IRS. If an organization is not recognized by the IRS to be tax-exempt, then amounts of money given to it are not tax-deductible.

Line 21a asks for the amount of cash contributions that you have made during the year for which you have cancelled checks or receipts. For example, you give $200 to the Boy Scouts of America and you have your cancelled check. On line 21a put in that amount together with any other cash contributions for which you have receipts or cancelled checks.

Beginning in 1981, if you have given $3,000 or more to any one organization, then you must put in the name of the organization and the amount donated on line 21b. I suggest that you write "see attached" near line 21b and send in proof of any such donation.

Line 21b. List each qualified charity, organization, or religious organization to which you have contributed during the year but have no receipt or cancelled check to prove the amounts claimed. Often the church collection plate may be the recipient of such unrecorded contributions. Many people give approximately $2.00 a week or $104.00 for the year. It is advisable to write in the specific name of each religious organization and of each different charity that you have given money to, and the specific amounts given to each.

You can also deduct out-of-pocket expenses incurred while rendering services for charitable organizations, as long as you're not being paid a salary by that organization. This can include automobile mileage, at 9 cents a mile, transportation fares, and meals and lodging while away on charitable services. Be careful that everything is documented, and get letters explaining your voluntary work from the organizations involved. You may want to attach a separate sheet of paper explaining in detail the trips and transportation expenses involved in any charitable contributions of services.

Line 22. "Other than cash" contributions usually means clothing, furniture, and appliances that you have donated during the year. It's a good idea to write in the name of the organization and the specific value of the item donated. For example, write in "The Salvation Army—$175.00."

The amount put down in the "other than cash" category is determined by the fair market value of the item donated. The fair market value is how much an item is worth at the time it was donated. You can have the charity determine its fair market value and give you a receipt or statement to that effect. You can also have an appraiser determine the item's value, and the appraisal fee also will be tax deductible as well, under "miscellaneous deductions." You, yourself, can determine the value, within reason.

For example, you donate a color TV to The Salvation Army. You purchased the TV for $500 five years ago. Its fair market value is determined as of the time you donate it. The Salvation Army gives you a receipt stating that the TV is worth $50. That $50 is the amount that is tax-deductible and is put onto line 22.

If the total amount on line 22 is greater than $200.00, you are required to attach a statement describing the items you have donated and declaring the value of each one. Write in the words "see attached" on line 22, and then, on a separate sheet of paper, list each item and its fair market value. If possible, you should also send in copies of verifying statements from each charitable organization.

Line 23. The maximum amount that can be deducted for contributions is fifty percent of your adjusted gross income. However, if the items donated are capital-gain property, or if the organization is not fully qualified, a thirty percent or twenty percent limitation may apply.

If you have more than the applicable limit during a taxable year, you can carry over the excess amounts to returns filed in succeeding tax years. For example, in 1981 the total amount of your contributions is $20,000, and your adjusted gross income for that year is $30,000. If these amounts were given to a church or other fully qualified organization, the most you could deduct would be $15,000 for 1981. The $5,000 excess amount can then be deducted in 1982 or future years by putting it onto line 23, a "carryover from prior years." You would continue the carryover until the total amount of excess contributions is used up.

Line 24. Total lines 21a through 23 to arrive at your total contributions on line 24.

Most taxpayers give a few hundred dollars each year in deductible contributions, generally between one and two percent of their adjusted gross income. If you claim deductions greater than two per cent of your adjusted gross income for charitable contributions, be certain that you can document all of your donations. Nevertheless, if your contributions are within the one to one and one-half percent range, you shouldn't have any problems with tax audits.

There are many people who give one-tenth, a tithe, of their income to religious or charitable organizations. In this case, I would strongly advise sending in photocopies of receipts, cancelled checks, or other proof of donations with the tax return. Again, write in "see attached" on lines 21 or 22 of Schedule A.

Beginning in the 1982 taxable year, there will be a charitable contribution write-off even if you don't itemize deductions on Schedule A. There will be a special tax credit, which is a direct reduction of tax, of up to $25 for charitable donations from taxpayers who do not itemize deductions. In subsequent years the credit limitation will be increased. Remember, though, that this new credit does not apply to your 1981 tax return.

CASUALTY OR THEFT LOSSES

A casualty is considered a complete or partial destruction, or loss, of property caused by a sudden, unexpected, or unusual identifiable event. Examples of casualty losses are: damage from hurricanes, tornadoes, floods, fires, storms, shipwrecks, or accidents. Damages resulting from an accident to your automobile, which is not willfully caused, are also in this category.

A theft is considered an unlawful taking or removing of your property or money with the intent of keeping you from having it. Money or property taken by larceny, robbery, embezzlement, extortion, kidnapping, and blackmail are examples of theft. When money or property has been merely mislaid or mysteriously disappears, it is not considered a theft loss. Such cases may qualify as a casualty loss, but only if it is sudden, unexpected, and unusual in nature, and results from an identifiable event.

When deducting casualty or theft losses, I feel you should always report them in a special way. The IRS provides a supplemental form, Form 4684, for supplying the information needed to deduct these losses. This form, however, is difficult to understand and does not provide enough space to describe the average occurrence. Therefore, I feel that it should not be used. I suggest you create your own form, a statement that describes the property and its value, and gives the details of the casualty or theft. An example is shown below.

For every item that is stolen or destroyed, fill in the appropriate information in each column. Describe each item, for example, "color TV." Write down the date you acquired it, meaning the month and year you bought it, or inherited it, or were given it. The cost is the amount that you paid for it, or its value at the time you inherited it or received it.

The fair market value of an item is determined as of the time that it was stolen or destroyed. For example, a color TV cost $500 when it was new, but it had gone down in value $200, and its fair market value at the time of loss was $300. On the other hand, say you purchased a diamond ring twenty years ago for $1,000, and its fair market value is now $10,000. It has appreciated by $9,000 during the years. Fair market value can be determined by qualified appraisers or

ITEMIZED DEDUCTIONS—SCHEDULE A

STATEMENT OF CASUALTY OR THEFT LOSSES
IN LIEU OF FORM 4684

Name as shown on Form 1040 _____ Social Security No. _____

	Description of Property	Date Acquired	Cost or Other Basis	Fair Market Value	Deducted Loss
1.	color TV	6/2/80	$500	$300	$300
2.	diamond ring	12/25/61	$1,000	$10,000	$1000

On September 29, 1981, our home at 1492 Elm Street was broken into and robbed of the items described above. The incident was reported to the police on the same day. Our home and its contents were not insured at the time of this incident. The stolen items have not been recovered.

---

retailers, or, in most cases, by you. In the case of a large tax loss based on a casualty or theft loss, it is always helpful to have a professional to back you up. You should do some research to determine the fair market values of items involved in a casualty or theft, and keep a record of your findings.

The deductible loss is the *lower* of the cost or the fair market value of an item. In other words, on the $1,000 ring above, you can deduct only $1,000, even though it was worth $10,000 when it was stolen. For an item that has depreciated or decreased in value, then you must deduct only its fair market value at the time it was destroyed or stolen. The color TV above that cost $500 five years ago was worth only $300 when it was destroyed in a fire. You can deduct only $300 as a casualty loss.

In the case of theft of a car or damage resulting in its total destruction, the Blue Book value usually determines your tax deduction. For example, you have a 1980 model car that was totally destroyed, and not covered by insurance. You can determine its fair market value, and the amount that you can deduct as a casualty loss, by finding out its Blue Book value. You can ask almost any new or used car dealer to look up your car in the Blue Book to find out its value at the time it was destroyed. Be sure to get the *retail* and not the wholesale figure. When you receive reimbursement from insurance or other sources for a loss, the amount of reimbursement must be subtracted from the loss. The difference, if any, is tax-deductible.

However, for each casualty or theft occurrence, $100 must be subtracted from the total amount of the loss. If, for example, the total loss from a theft was $89, you would not be able to take a theft loss deduction. If the loss was $575, then you could deduct only $475.

The IRS now states on Schedule A that you must submit Form 4684 when you claim a casualty or theft loss of $1,000 or more, or if certain other situations apply. I suggest that you prepare a substitute form of your own, as described above, in lieu of Form 4684, for *any* amounts of casualty or theft losses.

On *line 25* put in the total amount of your loss, for a casualty or theft, before receiving any type of reimbursement. Write in "see attached" and then prepare the casualty or theft statement described above on a separate sheet of paper.

On *line 26* put in the total amount of insurance or other reimbursement that you received for the casualty or theft. If you were not covered by insurance be sure to write that fact on your casualty or theft statement.

Line 27. Subtract the amount on line 26 from that on line 25.

Line 28. Put in $100 for each incident involved unless the amount on line 27 is lower. $100 must be subtracted from *all* personal casualty or theft incidents.

Line 29. Subtract the amount on line 28 (usually $100) from that on line 27. The remaining amount is your total casualty or theft loss deduction.

In some years, casualty or theft losses can be a large part of your itemized deductions. Be careful to describe each item damaged or lost, and claim the proper losses. You may have to submit several pages, with dozens of items listed. Immediately after discovering a casualty or theft, you should report it to the police. Try to get a police report, a file number, or a docket number, and begin to compile your statement of loss. If appropriate, you may also want to take pictures of the damages. Send in the pictures with the tax return and keep copies for yourself. The IRS is likely to audit large losses if they are not reported properly. Be sure to report them correctly and send in proof with your return.

MISCELLANEOUS DEDUCTIONS

Here is an area where many people fail to take full advantage of all of their possible legitimate itemized deductions. Many of the allowable deductions are unknown to most taxpayers, and the IRS doesn't go out of its way to inform the American people of them. To save money, it is important that you know about all of these deductions, and when and how to use them. We will go through each and every miscellaneous deduction, explaining the do's and don'ts of them.

It is interesting to note that under miscellaneous deductions the IRS has listed only two specific deductions on Schedule A—union dues and tax return preparation fee. On my list of miscellaneous deductions near the beginning of this chapter there are more than twenty different possibilities listed.

Line 30a. Union dues includes all union dues that you, and your spouse, on a joint return, paid during the year, whether or not you are still working at that job or profession. It also includes any amounts of money paid for union initiation fees and union assessments incurred during the year.

Line 30b. Put in the total amount, if any, you have paid someone to prepare your tax return during the taxable year. Include transportation and telephone expenses connected with having your return prepared.

Line 31 is where you should list all other miscellaneous deductions. Be sure to list them separately, along with the amounts for each. If there is not enough space on Schedule A, then use a separate sheet of paper and write in "see attached" on line 31. On that sheet of paper list all of your miscellaneous deductions, and put the total amount onto line 31 of Schedule A.

Now, let's discuss each of the other miscellaneous deductions and explain them in detail.

Employment agency fees that you paid during the year to obtain employment are tax-deductible on line 31. Like most of the other miscellaneous itemized deductions, these expenses have to be job-related. If this amount is substantial, you should send in proof of payment with the tax return.

Uniforms or specific clothing used solely for your job or profession, that are purchased during the year may be deductible. To be able to deduct the expense of a uniform or other work clothes, they must be worn specifically and only for your occupation. You cannot also wear this clothing outside of your job, in public, except perhaps on your way to and from the jobsite. Therefore, it should have some kind of insignia or other special distinction about it. In deducting uniform or other work clothes expenses, be sure to write in "not for general wear" next to the word "uniforms" or "work clothes." You thereby tell the IRS that these clothes are worn specifically and only for your occupation. If you can qualify for the uniform deduction, you will also be able to deduct all of the laundry and cleaning costs involved.

The IRS often audits uniform deductions. Be careful in taking this deduction. If it is well known that in your line of work or profession people usually wear uniforms, then you shouldn't have any problems in taking the deduction. For example, if you are a policeman and have to buy your own uniforms, the IRS is not likely to challenge your deduction. However, just because your employer requires you to wear a certain type of clothing, you are not necessarily allowed to deduct the expenses of such clothing. The key is that the clothing can be worn only on your job, and not in public for general wear. You may, though, be able to deduct certain other clothing expenses under the category of "protective clothing."

Protective clothing is anything that must be worn to protect yourself from the hazards of your specific job or occupation. For example, people who work outside need rain gear, hats, galoshes, etc. Items such as laboratory coats, gloves, steel-toed shoes, etc. can all be tax deductible here. In other words, you must wear these items for safety reasons while on your job. This is a category that many industrial workers can take advantage of.

Safety equipment is also job-related. If your job requires special equipment, be sure to save the receipts, and deduct your purchases unless your are reimbursed by your employer. Hard hats, safety goggles, etc. are deductible if they are specifically required by your employer and are not used outside work. Remember to be consistent with your occupation title and with items you have been deducting previously.

Tools, equipment, and supplies are common expenses. Pens and pencils, small work tools, etc. may qualify for this deduction. You should collect all receipts for such items throughout the year so that you can feel confident about claiming these deductions.

Teachers, for example, can deduct the cost of an attache case and all of the money spent for prizes, games, and activities for their students. Pens, paper, records, film, tapes, movies, and any other expenses incurred in teaching students are tax-deductible on line 31 of Schedule A.

Carpenters, mechanics, etc. should deduct the cost of all small tools and equipment, including hammers, pencils, tool boxes, etc. The key is that the expenses must be related to your occupation.

Professional organization expenses can be deducted by professional, technical, or highly skilled wage earners, especially those that are not members of trade unions. Included here are organization dues, the expenses of attending meetings, or convention costs related to the organizations. Do not, however, include any amounts that have already been claimed on Form 2106. It is a good idea to list the name of each professional organization to which you belong, but you can just abbreviate. For example, a school teacher might belong to the NEA and the ATSS.

Professional and trade publication subscription costs may be deducted by many people. Any books, magazines, periodicals, newsletters, or other publications that are related to your present job can be deducted on line 31. For example, auto mechanics may be able to deduct mechanics' manuals that are not furnished by the employer. If you have paid for such subscriptions and you can show that the publications are directly related to your work, then they can be tax-deductible.

Education expenses should be claimed in detail on Form 2106, under Parts II and III, as has been explained above in Chapter 12. Write in "see Form 2106" next to "education expenses" on Schedule A. This can be a very significant deduction, sometimes in the thousands of dollars. Fill out Form 2106, put in all the required information, and don't hesitate to take full advantage of this deduction.

Unreimbursed business expenses is a sort of

catch-all for amounts paid for job-related expenses. Examples of such expenses are a teacher who gives money to her students for an educational purpose and never gets any of it back, or an employee who lays out his own money for his employer's benefit and is not reimbursed. It's very important to keep records of these amounts throughout the year so that you don't forget them at tax time, and also so you can document these expenses if you are audited.

Safe deposit box fees are tax-deductible on line 31.

Fees paid for investment counseling are tax-deductible. Such counseling can include real estate appraisal fees, inspections, consultation costs, or engineering reports. For example, you purchase a new home and have an engineering inspection made. That inspection would be considered investment counseling, and would be tax deductible here.

Tax guides and publications, such as this book, are also tax-deductible. Write in "tax books" and put in the total amount.

You may have invested in the stock market or other types of securities, and pay counselors for advice on what to buy and when to sell. Or, you may subscribe to various business or financial newsletters, and refer to them for advice on investments. If you can show that specific expenses are needed to guide you in your investments, then they would be tax-deductible.

Telephone expenses are tax-deductible only if they are specifically required, but not paid for, by your employer for your job. In this case, you may want to get a written statement to that effect from your employer and to send in a photocopy of it with your return. You can deduct only the amount of the phone bills that relate directly to your job. Therefore, in most cases, you can claim only a portion of the telephone bills as an itemized deduction. For example, you may deduct one-half of the basic monthly charge, and all of the long-distance calls that were made specifically for your job. Make sure that you write in "telephone as required by my employer."

A library can be depreciated only if the books are directly related to your job or profession, such as reference works used by professionals to maintain and improve their skills and knowledge. The books may have been purchased in earlier years, perhaps before you began your present vocation— while in school, for example. Usually, a library is depreciated over three years, at one-third of its total value for each year. Estimate the total value of your library at the time of the end of the present tax year and then take that percentage for this year. Show the IRS your calculations. For example, if you are depreciating your library over three years, write in "at one-third." The key is that you must be in a profession that would be able to depreciate a library, for example, a professor, doctor, engineer, or clergyman.

Depreciation on major tools is similar to that of a library. The tools must be owned and used by a skilled worker in his trade or business. Carpenters, mechanics, machinists, etc. may be able to claim depreciation in this category, provided these tools are used directly by them on their job. Obviously, you can't depreciate or deduct the cost of another person's tools, only your own. Determine the useful life of each major tool and depreciate each one over that period of time, as is explained in Chapter 7. Do not deduct amounts for any tools that already have been deducted under the category of tools, equipment and supplies.

Transportation to a second job or job site is deductible if it is done in the same day. You can deduct such expenses either on Schedule A or on Form 2106 as an adjustment to income. I prefer claiming them on Form 2106 as that will lower your adjusted gross income and thus allow you to claim more in medical deductions on Schedule A. Determine your total expenses in traveling from the first job or job site to the second. Generally, you are allowed to claim twenty cents per mile for the first 15,000 miles, and eleven cents per mile for all mileage in excess of that.

Malpractice insurance permiums for a professional person who is a wage earner are tax-deductible on line 31.

Any physical examinations required, but not paid for, by your employer are tax-deductible on line 31.

Certain child adoption expenses are deductible. Beginning in the 1981 taxable year you can deduct up to $1,500 for qualified expenses connected with adopting a child with "special needs." Such a child is one who can qualify for adoptiion assistance payments under Section 473 of the Social Security Act. Deductible expenses include necessary adoption fees, legal fees, court costs, and any other items that are directly related to the child's adoption.

Home office expenses are a very risky deduction, and one that the IRS has been challenging frequently during the past few years. Until a few years ago, even wage earners were able to deduct a portion of their home or apartment expenses. For example, many teachers, technicians, and nurses were able to claim a home office expense deduction. In the past few years the IRS has made the requirements for taking this type of deduction much more difficult. Now, most wage earners are unable to qualify for it.

In order to claim the home office deduction, your office at home has to be the place where you do *all* of your work. Your patients, clients, or customers have to meet and deal with you there. This requirement eliminates almost all teachers, engineers, and other professionals.

The only wage earners who still may be able to deduct home office expenses are sales people who do business at home. They may work for a national company that does not have an office in their region, and are required to work out of their house. They can then deduct a portion of the expenses of their house or apartment, and can even include areas used for storage of their products.

If you are going to take a home office deduction, be sure to document it along with your tax return. On a separate sheet of paper, write in your name and your social security number, and title it "home office expenses." Then, write in "As my employer does not provide a facility available to conduct my business and work, I am required to set aside a portion of my house (or apartment) as a home office on a permanent basis as follows:"

You must then determine the percentage of your home that is used as an office. For example, you use twenty-five percent if you have a four room apartment and you use one room as your home office. You can then also deduct one-fourth of the utilities expenses, and one-fourth of the rent. If you own your own home, you would only be able to deduct one-fourth of the principal amount paid on a mortgage loan during the year. Remember, the interest payment is deductible on line 17 of Schedule A, and, therefore, cannot be deducted again on line 31. Furthermore, any amounts that have been claimed as home office expenses in your personal residence cannot be deferred from taxation on Form 2119. When the house is sold, you'll be required to pay capital gains tax on the portion that has been taken as a home office expense. My advice is to avoid taking a home office deduction unless you are self-employed. For wage earners, the IRS has virtually eliminated this deduction.

SUMMARY OF ITEMIZED DEDUCTIONS

Lines 33 through 38. Put in the totals for each of the different categories of itemized deductions, such as medical and dental expenses, taxes, etc.

On *line 39*, add all of the amounts from Lines 33 to 38.

On *line 40* put in either $3,400, $2,300, or $1,700, the standard deduction amounts that depend on your filing status. In order to be able to itemize deductions, the amount on line 39 must be greater than the amount on line 40.

Line 41. The difference of line 40 from line 39 is the total amount of your itemized deductions. Take the amount on line 41 and transfer it to line 32b on page 2 of Form 1040. If that amount is "0" or a negative number, then you are not able to itemize deductions and you automatically must take the standard deduction. Since the standard deduction is already figured into the tax tables and tax rate schedules, no amount is needed on line 33 for it.

Your itemized deductions should reflect your occupation, filing status, number of exemptions, and overall financial status. People who own homes with large mortgages generally have high itemized deductions. Single taxpayers who rent dwellings generally have lower itemized deduction totals.

Every American taxpayer is unique. Make an effort to understand all of the different types of deductions, and take full advantage of them. If you have a substantial income, say more than $20,000 a year, then you should be able to itemize deductions. Be sure to claim all of your miscellaneous deductions, all of your charitable contributions, all interest expenses, and all of the state and local taxes that you've paid during the year. All such payments are allowable deductions, but it's up to you to claim them.

PART V
DETERMINING YOUR TAX

CHAPTER FOURTEEN

☆

Computing Your Tax Liability

On *line 32b* of Form 1040, enter the amount from line 41 of Schedule A. If you are not able to itemize deductions, then put in "0."

If you have unearned income, such as interest or dividend income, and you are claimed as a dependent on your parents' tax return, check the box under line 32b. If you received more than $1,000 of unearned income and are claimed as a dependent on your parents' tax return, (unless you are a full-time student), you may have to file a tax return.

Line 32c. Subtract the amount on line 32b from line 32a.

On *line 33*, put in the amount that results from multiplying $1,000 by the total number of exemptions claimed on line 6e of Form 1040.

On *line 34,* subtract the amount on line 33 from the amount on line 32c. The remainder is your *taxable income* for the year.

TAX TABLES

Once most taxpayers have computed their taxable income on line 34 of Form 1040, they simply look up the amount of tax in the tax tables provided in the Federal Income Tax Forms booklet. The tax tables are used for people who—

• File in the status of single, married filing separate return, or head of household, and the amount on line 34 is $20,000 or less

• File in the status of married filing joint return or qualifying widow(er) with dependent child, and the amount on line 34 is $40,000 or less

• Are *not* able to income average, using Schedule G, or to use Form 4726, Maximum Tax on Personal Income.

If you are able to use the tax tables, find the one that is appropriate for you, based on your filing status and the amount on line 34. Find the amount of your tax from the tax tables and put that amount on line 35 on page 2 of Form 1040, and check the box labeled "Tax Tables."

TAX RATE SCHEDULES X, Y, AND Z

The tax rate schedules are also found in your tax booklet, right after the tax tables. Schedule X is to be used by single taxpayers, Schedule Y by married taxpayers and qualifying widow(ers), and Schedule Z by heads of household. Do the mathematics required by the tax rate schedule appropriate to your filing status, and put that amount on line 4. This amount will then be put onto line 35 on page 2 of Form 1040. Be sure to check the box on line 35 marked "Tax Rate Schedule X, Y, or Z."

If you can qualify for income averaging, then check the box on line 35 marked Schedule G and compute your tax using the income averaging method. Income averaging is discussed later in this chapter.

Form 4726 is for computing the maximum tax on personal service income. It is rarely used, but is needed by people with a very high taxable incomes who are not able to income average. If you meet the requirements of the maximum tax, fill out Form 4726 and compute your tax on that form. The tax as computed on Form 4726 goes onto line 35 of Form 1040, and you check the box labeled Form 4726.

INCOME AVERAGING— SCHEDULE G

Many American taxpayers have never heard

of income averaging, or, even if they have, they know very little about it. More people in my tax classes ask for information about income averaging than any other tax provision. It is widely misunderstood. In fact, Schedule G is a fairly easy form to fill out, and it can easily save you a bundle of tax money. Everyone should be well aware of Schedule G, and, if you are not sure that it will work for you, fill it out to see if it will save you money.

Often, when people discover the benefits of income averaging, they realize that they could have qualified for it in previous taxable years. Fortunately, it may not be too late. You can amend a tax return any time during a three-year period following its due date. If you find that you can save money by income averaging on a past tax return, fill out Schedule G for that taxable year and Form 1040X. You will then be able to get an additional refund from the IRS. The instructions for Form 1040X are discussed in Chapter 20.

What exactly *is* income averaging? The purpose of the law is to even out your income tax when you happen to strike it rich or begin to make a lot of money after several years of lower income. When your *taxable income* increases by a certain percentage over the similar amounts for the previous four taxable years, then you can average your income over five years and thereby lower the tax for the current year. Your taxable income is not your total income, but is the amount from line 34 on page 2 of Form 1040. In other words, taxable income includes all wages, self-employment profits or losses, and capital gains or losses, reduced by adjustments to income and itemized deductions, minus $1,000 times the number of exemptions claimed. If your taxable income has increased significantly over the last four years, then you may be able to income average and save some money.

Because of inflation, and in families in which both spouses are now working, many taxpayers will have much higher taxable income for 1981, and will be able to income average. In the last couple of years, I completed more Schedules G than in all previous tax seasons combined. With the high rate of inflation, and because more and more husbands and wives are both working, taxable incomes have increased and the number of people qualifying for income averaging has also increased.

To qualify for income averaging, you, and your spouse if you are filing a joint return, must meet two basic requirements. First, you must have been a citizen or resident of the United States throughout the entire taxable year, and you cannot have been a non-resident alien at any time during the last five taxable years.

The second requirement is that you must have furnished at least fifty percent of your own support in each of the previous four taxable years, unless you are over age twenty-five by the end of the current taxable year. This means that taxpayers who have been claimed as dependents on their parents' tax returns within the previous four years may not be able to income average this year. But if you were not claimed as a dependent by your parents, if you had no substantial income, and if you supplied over fifty percent of your own support during those years, then you can still income average.

In order to fill out Schedule G you need to have certain information from the four previous taxable years, including your taxable income for those years. Therefore, you must have copies of your tax returns for those four years. If you do not have them, you may need to request them from the IRS. Contact your local IRS office. They will send you copies of past returns for a charge of about $1.00 or $1.50 per return. If you are not able to obtain copies of previous tax returns in time to file your tax return for 1981 by April 15, 1982, you should file the return on time without using income averaging. When you finally get copies of the previous returns you need, and have all of the other information necessary to income average, file an amended tax return on Form 1040X, use Schedule G to recompute your tax for 1981, and claim a tax refund. It is better to do this than to file a tax return late.

If you owe no tax for 1981 anyway, you could also apply for a two-month extension of time to file your return on Form 4868, and complete Schedule G when you obtain all of the information you need.

FILLING OUT SCHEDULE G

Let's go step-by-step through Schedule G, Income Averaging. This is another IRS form that looks much more complicated than it really is. The key to filling out Schedule G is to understand which amounts from your past four years' tax returns should be put in on line 1 of Schedule G. Once those amounts are determined, the rest of the form is straight mathematics, and is very easy to complete. The best, and easiest, way of filling it out is as follows: First, put the amount from line 34 of Form 1040, your taxable income for 1981, onto *line 6* of Schedule G.

Line 1, columns (a) through (d). In order to income average on a 1981 tax return, you need to transfer the amounts of your taxable income from line 34 of Forms 1040 for the years 1977 through 1980 onto line 1 of Schedule G. If you have filed Form 1040A (the short form) during any of those years, transfer the amount on line 10 or 11 of Form 1040A to Schedule G in the appropriate column on line 1.

A problem may arise in calculating these amounts if this year's filing or marital status is different from that of any of the previous four years. Your filing status must be consistent for the four previous years in order to income average. For example, if your 1981 filing status is married filing joint return, then the taxable income of the four previous years must also reflect the same filing status. If you were not married, or were married to a different person, then you have to recompute your taxable income for you and your present spouse. If, for example, John and Mary were married in 1979 and are presently filing a joint tax return, John's taxable income and Mary's taxable income for the years 1977 and 1978 would be combined. If John and Mary filed a joint return in 1979, the amount on line 34 of Form 1040 for 1979 would be correct.

If John had been married to Sally in 1977, and they were divorced in 1978 and then John married Mary in 1979, it would be a little more complicated. John's 1977 taxable income would have to be separated from Sally's, and John's taxable income would have to be combined with Mary's in 1977 and 1978. The point here is that the filing status must be consistent, so you may have to separate one spouse's income in previous years from the other's, or add separate incomes together. It all depends on your 1981 filing status.

In community property states, such as California, even more adjustments may be required. Since in community property states both the husband's and the wife's earned income belongs equally to each spouse, use the *higher* amount of either your taxable income or one-half the combined taxable income of you and your ex-spouse. So, for example, if in 1977 John and Sally lived in California, and John's taxable income was $5,000 and Sally's was $20,000, then John's taxable income on Schedule G for 1981 would be $12,500—fifty percent of the couple's taxable income. If you are married and filing a separate return, you must report the difference between your personal earnings and your half of the community's total earnings, if your personal earnings are lower. The difference is called "excess community income," the amount of which goes onto line 9 of Schedule G. Such an amount would lower this year's averageable taxable income.

Line 2a. Under columns (c) and (d), 1977 and 1978, multiply the total number of exemptions you claimed in those years by $750 and put the product on line 2a.

Line 2b. Under columns (a) and (b), 1979 and 1980, multiply the total number of exemptions claimed by $1,000 each and put the product on line 2b.

Line 3. By subtracting $1,000, or $750, from the amounts on line 1, you are calculating your taxable income for each of the previous four years. That amount can be "0," but it cannot be a negative number.

SCHEDULE G
(Form 1040)
Department of the Treasury
Internal Revenue Service

Income Averaging

▶ See instructions on back.
▶ Attach to Form 1040.

OMB No. 1545-0074

1981
20

Name(s) as shown on Form 1040 | Your social security number

Base Period Income and Adjustments	(a) 1980	(b) 1979	(c) 1978	(d) 1977
1 Enter amount from: Form 1040—line 34 Form 1040A (1977 and 1978)—line 10 Form 1040A (1979 and 1980)—line 11 . .				
2 a Multiply $750 by your total number of exemptions each year, 1977 and 1978 .	/////	/////		
b Multiply $1,000 by your total number of exemptions each year, 1979 and 1980 .			/////	/////
3 Taxable income (subtract line 2a or 2b from line 1). If less than zero, enter zero . .				
4 Income earned outside of the United States or within U.S. possessions and excluded under sections 911 and 931				
5 Base period income (add lines 3 and 4) . .				

Computation of Averageable Income

6 Taxable income for 1981 from Form 1040, line 34 . . . . 6 _____
7 Certain amounts received by owner-employees subject to a penalty under section 72(m)(5) . . . . 7 _____
8 Subtract line 7 from line 6 . . . . 8 _____
9 Excess community income . . . . 9 _____
10 Adjusted taxable income (subtract line 9 from line 8). If less than zero, enter zero . . . . 10 _____

11 Add columns (a) through (d), line 5, and enter here . . . . |11| |
12 Enter 30% of line 11 . . . . 12 _____
13 Averageable income (subtract line 12 from line 10) . . . . 13 _____

If line 13 is $3,000 or less, do not complete the rest of this form. You do not qualify for income averaging. 🇬

Computation of Tax

14 Amount from line 12 . . . . 14 _____
15 20% of line 13 . . . . 15 _____

16 Total (add lines 14 and 15) . . . . 16 _____
17 Excess community income from line 9 . . . . 17 _____

18 Total (add lines 16 and 17) . . . . 18 _____
19 Tax on amount on line 18 (see caution below) . . . . 19 _____
20 Tax on amount on line 16 (see caution below) . . . . |20| |
21 Tax on amount on line 14 (see caution below) . . . . |21| |
22 Subtract line 21 from line 20 . . . . |22| |

23 Multiply the amount on line 22 by 4 . . . . 23 _____
   Note: *If no entry was made on line 7 above, skip lines 24 through 26 and go to line 27.*
24 Tax on amount on line 6 (see caution below) . . . . |24| |
25 Tax on amount on line 8 (see caution below) . . . . |25| |

26 Subtract line 25 from line 24 . . . . 26 _____
27 Add lines 19, 23, and 26 . . . . 27 _____
28 Multiply line 27 by .0125 . . . . 28 _____
29 Tax (subtract line 28 from line 27). Enter here and on Form 1040, line 35 and check Schedule G box . . 29 _____

Caution: Use Tax Rate Schedule X, Y, or Z from the Form 1040 instructions, but do not use the Tax Computation Worksheet on that page. Do not use the Tax Table.

For Paperwork Reduction Act Notice, see Form 1040 instructions.

343-064-2

COMPUTING YOUR TAX LIABILITY

Line 4. If you have received income within the previous four years that has been earned outside the United States or within U. S. possessions, and that income has been excluded under Internal Revenue Code Sections 911 or 931, then put in those amounts on line 4. This will apply to relatively few taxpayers each year.

Line 5. Your "base period income" is obtained by adding lines 3 and 4 in each of the columns.

Line 6 has already been discussed. It is the amount on line 34 of Form 1040 for 1981.

Line 7. In the unlikely event that you have received money from annuities or certain life insurance contracts covered by Internal Revenue Code Section 72(m)(5), put the total amount on line 7.

On *line 8* subtract the amount on line 7 from the amount on line 6.

Line 9 asks for the amount of excess community income, which is discussed above. For further information, see the instructions for Schedule G, or request Publication 506 from the IRS to determine the exact computation of excess community income. For most taxpayers the amount on line 9 will be "0."

On *line 10,* subtract the amount on line 9 from the amount on line 8. If it should be a negative number, enter "0."

On *line 11,* add all of the amounts on line 5, columns (a) through (d), and enter the total.

On *line 12,* multiply the amount on line 11 by 30%.

On *line 13,* subtract the amount on line 12 from that on line 10. This amount is your "averageable income."

If the amount on line 13 is $3,000 or less, you will not benefit from income averaging, and there is no reason to complete the rest of the form or to send it in along with your tax return.

On *line 14,* copy the amount on line 12 above onto line 14.

On *line 15* multiply the amount on line 13 by 20%.

On *line 16* add the amounts on lines 14 and 15.

On *line 17* put in the amount, if any, of excess community income from line 9. For most taxpayers, the amount will be "0."

On *line 18* add the amounts on lines 16 and 17 and put the total here.

Line 19. With the amount on line 18 in mind, go to Tax Rate Schedule X, Y, or Z. You cannot use the Tax Tables. Remember, Tax Rate Schedule X is for single people, Y is for married couples, and Z is for heads of household. Calculate the tax on the amount on line 18, and put the amount on line 19.

Line 20. For most taxpayers, the amount on line 20 will be the same as the amount on line 19. Simply copy that amount onto line 20. If, however, the amount on line 16 is different from the amount on line 18, then calculate the tax on the amount on line 16, again using Tax Rate Schedules X, Y, or Z.

On *line 21* take the amount on line 14 and, using the Tax Rate Schedules, calculate the tax on that amount.

On *line 22* subtract the amount on line 21 from that on line 20.

On *line 23* multiply the amount on line 22 by 4. If you have not put any amount on line 7 above, skip lines 24 through 26 and go directly to line 27.

Line 24. This line is filled out only if you received amounts covered by section 72(m)(5) of the Internal Revenue Code, as discussed above. Calculate the tax, using the Tax Rate Schedules, on the amount on line 6.

On *line 25* calculate the tax on the amount of excess community income on line 8, if any.

On *line 26* subtract the amount on line 25 from that on line 24.

Line 27. This amount will be your tax for 1981, using Schedule G, Income Averaging. Take the amount on line 27, enter it on line 35 of Form 1040, and check the box labeled "Schedule G." This is your basic income tax for 1981. Compare this amount with the tax on the amount on line 34 of Form 1040, using the appropriate tax table or tax rate schedule as though you did not income average. You can then determine how much money you have saved by income averaging.

You can continue to income average on Schedule G each year for as long as your average income is above the minimum amount. That is, as long as the difference between the current year's taxable income and thirty percent of the total of the last four years' taxable incomes is greater than $3,000, income averaging will continue to save you money. Some people have been told wrongly that income averaging can be used only once every four years. That is absolutely not true. Many people can save hundreds, if not thousands, of dollars by income averaging.

Be careful of hiring professional tax preparation firms to do income averaging on your tax return. They often charge extra, sometimes $50 or $100, to fill out Schedule G. Be sure that you are getting your money's worth. Don't pay somebody $50 to do income averaging when it will save you only $45. You should do it yourself. For most taxpayers, it's very easy.

THE MAXIMUM TAX

Another supplemental form used to compute your tax is Form 4726, Maximum Tax on Personal Service Income. This form is used by people who have very high salaries, profits from a business or profession, and other *personal service income*. If you think this form might be beneficial to you, compute your tax using it to see if it can save you some money. If you use Form 4726, you cannot also income average on Schedule G. You must choose one form or the other, whichever one will allow you to pay the least amount of tax.

The basic rule of Form 4726 is that there is a legal limit to the amount of tax that can be imposed on *personal service income*. No more than fifty percent of such "earned" income can be taken by the government, whereas up to seventy percent of "unearned" income, such as interest and dividends, may be taken.

1981 is the last taxable year for which Form 4726 will be needed, because, beginning in 1982, the very highest income tax bracket will be fifty percent. The maximum tax will then be unnecessary, and has been repealed by the Economic Recovery Tax Act of 1981.

Personal service income includes amounts of money or property received as wages, salaries, tips, self-employment income, professional fees, bonuses, commissions, sweepstakes prizes, and certain payments from pension or annuity plans.

You cannot use the fifty percent rate limit if you qualify for filing in the status of married filing joint return, but you elect instead to file in the status of married filing separate tax return. Get a copy of Form 4726 and carefully read the instructions as to how and when to use it, and how to fill it out. The amount on the bottom line of Form 4726 will go onto line 35 of Form 1040.

YOUR TAX AND ADDITIONAL TAXES

Now we will return to Form 1040.

On *line 35* put in the amount of your tax as you have calculated it using either the Tax Tables, the Tax Rate Schedules, Schedule D, Schedule G, or Form 4726. Check the appropriate box for the particular table, schedule, or form you used.

Line 36 is used to report several additional taxes that may be due. They all, however, are extremely rare, and for most taxpayers will not apply. In fact, some of the forms mentioned here are very difficult to obtain from the IRS.

Form 4972. The only form mentioned on line 36 that may have some use to more than just a handful of American taxpayers is Form 4972, the Special 10-Year Averaging Method.

As already mentioned, the special 10-year averaging method applies to taxpayers who receive lump sum distributions from qualified retirement plans. Instead of declaring such income on line 20 of Form 1040 "other income," you can fill out Form 4972 and use the Special 10-Year Averaging Method to save money. This form can be used only once every ten years.

Any amount of a lump sum distribution that is declared as a capital gain distribution on line 13 of Form 1040, must be added into the calculations of the special ten-year averaging method. Try doing it both ways. If you receive a large lump sum distribution, fill out Form 4972 to see what your tax is. Then determine your tax by putting the amount of the ordinary income portion of the lump sum distribution on line 20 of Form 1040, and the capital gain part on line 13, and see what that tax would be. Use the method that will allow you to pay the least amount of tax.

Form 4970. This form is used by people who receive an accumulated distribution from a trust. It is another form of income averaging, but involves only a distribution from a trust. Most taxpayers will never need this form.

Section 72[m][5] Penalty Tax. Internal Revenue Code section 72(m)(5) contains a ten percent penalty that applies to taxpayers who are owner-employees under an annuity plan or life insurance contract and who receive premature distributions from such plans or contracts. If you are in this rare category and have received amounts that are subject to this penalty, declare the amount of the penalty on line 36.

Line 37 of Form 1040. On this line, add the amounts on lines 35 and 36 to arrive at your total tax.

CHAPTER FIFTEEN

☆

Tax Credits

Tax credits directly reduce your tax liability. A tax *credit* lowers the amount of your tax dollar for dollar, whereas a tax *deduction* merely lowers your taxable income, and you save only a percentage of each dollar you deduct. Many taxpayers are unaware of tax credits, and, therefore, lose money on each year's tax return. Become familiar with them, and know how each one may apply to you.

We shall discuss each tax credit on page 2 of Form 1040.

CONTRIBUTIONS TO CANDIDATES FOR PUBLIC OFFICE.

This tax credit, entered on line 38, is limited to $50 for unmarried taxpayers and married couples filing separate returns, or $100 for married couples filing joint returns. You may claim fifty percent of all amounts given to candidates for public office up to the applicable $50 or $100 limit. This is a good, simple tax credit and if possible should be taken advantage of. If you do claim this tax credit, I recommend that you check the box labeled "yes" on page 1 of Form 1040 in the section entitled "Presidential Election Campaign." By checking yes, you tell the IRS that you are politically involved, and, more importantly, your return shows consistency.

CREDIT FOR THE ELDERLY— SCHEDULES R AND RP

Under certain conditions, taxpayers who receive pensions or annuities can get a tax credit by filling out Schedules R or RP. If you can qualify for this tax credit, the IRS computer will fill out this schedule for you, if you prefer. Put in your name and social security number, check the correct box for filing status and age, and fill in line 2a if Schedule R is applicable, or lines 1, 2, and 5 if Schedule RP is applicable. However, I suggest that you fill it out yourself. You'll probably do a more accurate job than the IRS computer.

Schedule R. This schedule is used by taxpayers who are sixty-five or over. For a married couple filing a joint return, if either spouse is sixty-five or over you can use either Schedule R or RP, but the spouse who is under sixty-five must have had pension or annuity income from a public retirement system.

Filing status and age. Check the appropriate box. Note that you can qualify for this credit if you are filing in the status of married filing separate return, if you and your spouse have not lived together at any time during the taxable year. Also note that if you have received non-taxable pension payments, such as social security benefits, of $3,750 or more, or if the amount of your adjusted income from Form 1040, line 32a, is $17,500 or more, you are not able to claim the Credit for the Elderly, and you should not file this schedule.

Line 1. Put in the appropriate amount based on the box under filing status that is checked—box A, B, C, or D.

Line 2a. Put in the amount that you have received as a pension or annuity under the Social Security Act or under the Railroad Retirement Acts. If none, put in "0."

On *line 2b,* put in the amount from Form 1040, line 32a.

On *line 2c*, enter $7,500 if you checked box A, $10,000 if you checked boxes B or C, or $5,000 if you checked box D.

Schedules R & RP (Form 1040)	**Credit for the Elderly**	OMB No. 1545-0074
Department of the Treasury Internal Revenue Service	▶ See Instructions for Schedules R and RP. ▶ Attach to Form 1040. ▶ Schedule RP is on back.	1981 21

Name(s) as shown on Form 1040	Your social security number

Please Note: *IRS will figure your Credit for the Elderly and compute your tax. Please see "IRS Will Figure Your Tax and Some of Your Credits" on page 3 of the Form 1040 instructions and complete the applicable lines on Form 1040 and Schedule R or RP.*

Should You Use Schedule R or RP?

If you are:	And were:	Use Schedule:
Single	▶ 65 or over	R
	▶ under 65 and had income from a public retirement system	RP
Married, filing separate return [1]	▶ 65 or over (unless joining in the election to use Schedule RP with your spouse who is under 65 and had income from a public retirement system)	R
	▶ under 65 and had income from a public retirement system (unless your spouse is 65 or over and does not join in the election to use Schedule RP)	RP
Married, filing joint return	▶ both 65 or over	R
	▶ one 65 or over, and one under 65 with no income or income other than from a public retirement system	R
	▶ both under 65 and one or both had income from a public retirement system	RP
	▶ one 65 or over, and one under 65 with income from a public retirement system	R or RP [2]

[1] You can take the credit on a separate return ONLY if you and your spouse lived apart for the whole year. See "Purpose" in Schedules R&RP instructions for limitation.
[2] Figure your credit on both schedules to see which gives you more credit.

Schedule R — Credit for the Elderly—For People 65 or Over

If you received nontaxable pensions (social security, etc.) of $3,750 or more or your adjusted gross income (Form 1040, line 32a) was $17,500 or more, you cannot take the credit for the elderly. Do not file this schedule.

Filing Status and Age (check only one box)
- A ☐ Single, 65 or over
- B ☐ Married filing joint return, only one spouse 65 or over
- C ☐ Married filing joint return, both 65 or over
- D ☐ Married filing separate return, 65 or over, and did not live with spouse at any time in 1981

1 Enter: { $2,500 if you checked box A or B / $3,750 if you checked box C / $1,875 if you checked box D } **1**

2 a Enter amounts you received as pensions or annuities under the Social Security Act or under the Railroad Retirement Acts (but not supplemental annuities), and certain other exclusions from gross income (see instructions). If none, enter zero **2a**

  b Enter amount from Form 1040, line 32a . . **2b**

  c Enter: { $7,500 if you checked box A / $10,000 if you checked box B or C / $5,000 if you checked box D } . **2c**

  d Subtract line 2c from 2b. If line 2c is more than line 2b, enter zero **2d**

  e Enter one-half (½) of line 2d **2e**

3 Add lines 2a and 2e. (If line 3 is the same or more than line 1, you cannot take the credit; do not file this schedule. If line 3 is less than line 1, go on to line 4.) **3**

4 Subtract line 3 from line 1 . . . . **4**

5 Multiply line 4 by 15% (.15) **5**

6 Enter amount of tax from Form 1040, line 37. (If this amount is zero, you cannot take the credit; do not file this schedule.) **6**

7 Enter the amount from line 5 or line 6, above, whichever is less. This is your **Credit for the Elderly**. Enter the same amount on Form 1040, line 39. . . . . ▶ **7**

For Paperwork Reduction Act Notice, see Form 1040 Instructions. 343-065-1

TAX CREDITS

Schedules R&RP (Form 1040) 1981
OMB No. 1545-0074

Name(s) as shown on Form 1040 | Your social security number

Schedule RP — Credit for the Elderly—For People Under 65 Who Had Pension or Annuity Income from a Public Retirement System — **21**

If you are under 72 and received nontaxable pensions (social security, etc.) of $2,500 or more or your earned income (salaries, wages, etc.) was $3,950 or more, you cannot take the credit for the elderly. Do not file this schedule.

Name(s) of public retirement system(s)

Filing Status and Age (check only one box)

- A ☐ Single, under 65
- B ☐ Married filing joint return, one spouse is under 65, and that person had income from a public retirement system. (If you checked this box and had community property income, see Community Property Income on page 26 of the instructions.)
- C ☐ Married filing joint return, both under 65. (If you checked this box and had community property income, see Community Property Income on page 26 of the instructions.)
- D ☐ Married filing separate return, under 65, and did not live with your spouse at any time in 1981.
- E ☐ Married filing separate return, 65 or over, did not live with your spouse at any time in 1981, and you are joining with your spouse in electing to use Schedule RP.

RP

Column (b)—Fill out column (b) whether you file a separate or joint return.
Column (a)—Fill out column (a) if you file a joint return. Use it only to show amounts for:
- The wife, if both of you were under 65, or
- The spouse who was 65 or over.

	(a)	(b)
1 Enter: $2,500 if you checked box A / $3,750 if you checked box B or C. Allocate this amount between you and your spouse, but do not enter more than $2,500 for either of you. It will generally be to your benefit to allocate the greater amount to the spouse with more retirement income. / $1,875 if you checked box D or box E		
2 Enter:		
a Amounts you received as pensions or annuities under the Social Security Act or under the Railroad Retirement Acts (but not supplemental annuities), and certain other exclusions from gross income (see instructions). If none, enter zero. — **2a**		
b Earned income such as wages, salaries, fees, etc. you received (does not apply to people 72 or over). (See page 26 of instructions for definition of earned income.):		
(i) If you are under 62, enter earned income that is over $900 — **2b(i)**		
(ii) If you are 62 or over but under 72, enter an amount that you will figure as follows: If earned income is $1,200 or less, enter zero. If earned income is over $1,200 but not over $1,700, enter one-half of the amount over $1,200. If earned income is over $1,700, enter the amount over $1,450. — **2b(ii)**		
3 Add lines 2a and 2b. — **3**		
4 Subtract line 3 from line 1. (If the result for either column is more than zero, go on. If the result for either column is zero or less, do not complete the rest of the lines in that column. If the result for both columns is zero or less, you cannot take the credit; do not file this schedule.) — **4**		
5 Retirement income:		
a If under 65— Enter only income from pensions and annuities under public retirement systems (e.g. Federal, State Governments, etc.) that you received as a result of your services or services of your spouse that you reported as income. Do not enter social security, railroad retirement or certain other payments reported on line 2a. — **5a**		
b If 65 or over— Enter total of pensions and annuities, interest, dividends, proceeds of retirement bonds, and amounts you received from individual retirement arrangements and individual retirement annuities that you reported as income, and gross rents from: Schedule E, Part I, columns A–C, line 3a. Also include your share of gross rents from partnerships and your share of taxable rents from estates and trusts. — **5b**		
6 Enter amount from line 4 or line 5, whichever is less. — **6**		
7 Add amounts in columns (a) and (b) of line 6. Enter total here. ▶ **7**		
8 Multiply line 7 by 15% (.15). — **8**		
9 Enter amount of tax from Form 1040, line 37. (If this amount is zero, you cannot take the credit; do not file this schedule.) — **9**		
10 Enter the amount from line 8 or line 9, above, whichever is less. This is your **Credit for the Elderly.** Enter the same amount on Form 1040, line 39. ▶ **10**		

For Paperwork Reduction Act Notice, see Form 1040 Instructions. ☆ U.S. GOVERNMENT PRINTING OFFICE : 1981—O-343-065

343-065-1

On *line 2d,* subtract the amount on line 2c from that on line 2b. If the result is a negative number, then enter "0."

On *line 2e,* enter one-half the amount on line 2d. If line 2d is "0," then, of course, line 2e would also be "0."

On *line 3*, add the amounts on lines 2a and 2e. If Line 3 is equal to or more than the amount on line 1, you will not be able to claim this tax credit.

On *line 4,* subtract the amount on line 3 from the amount on line 1.

On *line 5*, multiply the amount on line 4 by fifteen percent (.15).

On *line 6*, enter the amount on line 37 of Form 1040. If this amount is "0," you cannot take the credit.

On *line 7,* enter the amount on line 5 or line 6, whichever is less. This will be your credit for the elderly. Then take the amount on line 7 and transfer it onto line 39 of Form 1040.

Schedule RP. This schedule is used by taxpayers who are *under* age sixty-five and have received pension or annuity payments from a public retirement system, such as a federal, state, or local government pension plan. If you are married, filing a joint return, and one spouse is under sixty-five and is in a public retirement system, then you also can use this schedule. Once you elect to use Schedule RP, then both you and your spouse must use it. Neither can elect to use Schedule R if the other uses Schedule RP. Therefore, taxpayers in this situation should fill out both Schedules—R as well as RP—and file the one that results in the greater tax credit. You should also use Schedule RP if your spouse is deceased and was in a public retirement system.

If you are under seventy-two years of age and have received at least $2,500 in non-taxable amounts from pension plans, such as social security, or if your earned income—salaries, wages, etc.—is $3,950 or more, you are not able to take this tax credit.

Filing status and age. Check the appropriate box. If you live in a community property state, disregard the community property laws in filling out Schedule RP. Put in the exact amounts received by each spouse, and do not divide everything equally. Also, if you are in the filing status of married filing separate return, then to qualify for this tax credit, you and your spouse cannot have lived together for any time during the taxable year.

On *line 1*, enter the appropriate amount based on the filing status box you have checked. If you checked either box B or C you can divide the $3,750 between you and your spouse, except that not more than $2,500 can be given to either spouse. As the IRS points out, you should give the greater amount to the spouse who has the most retirement income.

On *line 2a*, put in any amounts you have received as payments from social security or under the Railroad Retirement Acts. Do not put in amounts received as lump-sum death benefits, child's insurance benefit payments that you may have received as a child's guardian, or non-taxable pensions and annuities.

Line 2b applies to people who are under age seventy-two. If you are under age sixty-two, take the total amount of earned income (i.e., wages, salaries, fees, etc.) and subtract from that amount the sum of $900. Put the remainder on line 2b(i).

If you are over age sixty-two but under age seventy-two, then determine the amount as follows:

If your earned income is $1,200 or less, put in "0."

If your earned income amount is between $1,200 and $1,700, subtract $1,450 from the total and enter one-half of that figure on line 2b(ii).

If the amount of your earned income is more than $1,700, subtract $1,450 from the total and enter that figure on line 2b(ii).

On *line 3*, add the amounts in lines 2a and b.

On *line 4*, subtract the amount on line 3 from the amount on line 1. You cannot show a negative number in either of the columns. If a negative number results from the subtraction, enter "0" and do not complete the rest of that column. If the result in both columns is "0," you are not able to claim the tax credit.

On *line 5a*, if you are under age sixty-five, put in the amount of payments you have received from pensions and annuities under a public retirement system. Do not put in any amounts for social security or railroad retirement payments.

Line 5b applies to taxpayers age sixty-five or over. Put in the total amount of pensions, annuities, interest, dividends, proceeds of retirement bonds, amounts that you have received from IRAs and annuities that you have reported as income, and the total gross rents from Schedule E, Rent and Royalty Income or Loss. Also include in that amount your share of gross rents from partnerships and your share of taxable rents from estates and trusts.

On *line 6*, enter the amount on either line 4 or line 5, whichever is less.

On *line 7*, add the amounts in columns (a) and (b) of line 6 and put in the total.

On *line 8*, multiply the amount on line 7 by fifteen percent (.15).

On *line 9*, enter the amount of tax from Form 1040, line 37. If that amount is "0," you will not be able to claim this tax credit.

On *line 10*, put in the amount from either line 8 or line 9, whichever is the lower amount. This will be your "Credit for the Elderly." Take the amount from line 10 and put it onto line 39 of Form 1040.

CREDIT FOR CHILD AND DEPENDENT CARE EXPENSES— FORM 2441

In order to be able to claim the tax credit for care of a child or dependent, certain criteria must be met. The first is that you maintain a household for the dependent(s) or child(ren). Maintaining a household means that you are paying for more than half the cost of keeping up the house. You must be gainfully employed, or in active search of gainful employment during the same period for which child care expenses are claimed, or a full-time student at an educational institution. You can also claim the credit if you are incapable of self-care during the period of child care.

If you are married, then you must file a joint tax return, unless during the last six months of the taxable year, your spouse was not a member of your household and you met the requirements for filing in the status of head of household. (See page 39 for information on the requirements for that filing status.) On the joint return you can claim only the child care expenses for the period of time in which both spouses met the above requirements.

There is no maximum income limitation, as there used to be until a few years ago. Instead, there is what is called an "earned income limitation" under which you cannot claim more money as a credit than you have earned as income in the form of wages, salaries, self-employed income, etc., or, if married, the amount earned by the spouse with the lower earned income.

If you were a full-time student, or incapable of self-care, then the earned income limitation is $166 a month for one child. If you can claim two or more children's expenses, then that limitation is $333 per month. If both spouses fall into this category, then the limitations are doubled for each month.

The basic age limitation for your dependent child is fifteen. You can claim expenses, though, for other dependents over fifteen, or for a person you can claim as a dependent as long as he or she doesn's earn $1,000 or more, if he or she is physically or mentally incapable of self-care. You can also deduct expenses for a spouse who is physically or mentally incapable of self-care.

FILLING OUT FORM 2441

Line 1 asks for information concerning each qualifying person whose expenses for child or dependent care you are claiming as a tax credit. Write in the name, date of birth, relationship, and months that each person has lived with you. In most cases, that means the name or names of your children, their dates of birth, their relationship to you, i.e., son or daughter, and 12 months, if they have lived with you for the entire year.

On *line 2*, fill out columns (a) through (e)

Form **2441**	**Credit for Child and Dependent Care Expenses**	OMB No. 1545-0068
Department of the Treasury Internal Revenue Service	▶ Attach to Form 1040. ▶ See Instructions below.	**1981** 26

Name(s) as shown on Form 1040 | Your social security number

1 See the definition for "qualifying person" in the instructions. Then read the instructions for line 1.

(a) Name of qualifying person	(b) Date of birth	(c) Relationship	(d) During 1981, the person lived with you for:	
			Months	Days

2 Persons or organizations who cared for those listed on line 1. See the instructions for line 2.

(a) Name and address (If more space is needed, attach schedule)	(b) Social security number, if applicable	(c) Relationship, if any	(d) Period of care		(e) Amount of 1981 expenses (include those not paid during the year)
			From Month—Day	To Month—Day	

To Figure Your Credit, You MUST Complete ALL Lines That Apply

3 Add the amounts in column 2(e) **3**
4 Enter $2,000 ($4,000 if you listed two or more names in line 1) or amount on line 3, whichever is less **4**
5 Earned income (wages, salaries, tips, etc.). See the instructions for line 5. An entry MUST be made on this line.
   (a) If unmarried at end of 1981, enter your earned income . . . .
   (b) If married at end of 1981, enter:
      (1) Your earned income . . . $ _____   Enter the lesser
      (2) Your spouse's earned income $ _____   of b(1) or b(2) . . ▶ **5**
6 Enter the amount on line 4 or line 5, whichever is less **6**
7 Amount on line 6 paid during 1981. An entry MUST be made on this line . . . . ▶ **7**
8 Child and dependent child care expenses for 1980 paid in 1981. See instructions for line 8 . . . **8**
9 Add amounts on lines 7 and 8 . . . . **9**
10 Multiply line 9 by 20 percent **10**
11 Limitation:
   a Enter tax from Form 1040, line 37 . . . . **11a**
   b Enter total of lines 38, 39, and 41 through 43 of Form 1040 . . **11b**
   c Subtract line 11b from line 11a (if line 11b is more than line 11a, enter zero) **11c**
12 Credit for child and dependent care expenses. Enter the smaller of line 10 or line 11c here and on Form 1040, line 40 . **12**

13 If payments listed on line 2 were made to an individual, complete the following: Yes   No
   (a) If you paid $50 or more in a calendar quarter to an individual, were the services performed in your home? . . . .
   (b) If "Yes," have you filed appropriate wage tax returns on wages for services in your home (see instructions for line 13)? . . . .
   (c) If answer to (b) is "Yes," enter your employer identification number . . . . . . ▶

if you have paid any persons or organizations to care for your child or dependent. List each person's name, or the name of each organization, separately. If there is not enough space on Form 2441 for all of the information, then attach a separate schedule.

In *column a* write in the names and addresses of the persons or organizations you paid.

In *column b* put in their social security numbers, but *only* if child or dependent care services were performed in your house and the person performing such services is employed by you. This is not often the case, thus do not put in anyone's social security number unless you actually employed such a person.

In *column c* describe the relationship to you of the persons who perform the services of caring for your child or dependent. If the person is not related to you, write in "none." Remember that the person who provides care and who has received payments from you must declare such income on his or her income tax return.

In *column d* put in the beginning and ending months and days of the period in which child and dependent care expenses were incurred during the taxable year. Remember that you can deduct such expenses only during periods in which you and your spouse, if married, were working or actively looking for work, or you were a full-time student or were incapable of taking care of the child or dependent.

In *column e* put in the total amount of expenses paid or incurred and not yet paid to each person or organization during 1981. For example, during the last week of December, 1981, you incurred child care expenses, but you did not actually pay the child-care person until January of 1982. Nevertheless, include those expenses in the total for 1981, even though they ordinarily would not be claimed until 1982 under the cash method of accounting.

On *line 3*, add all of the amounts in column 2(e).

On *line 4*, put in the amount on line 3, but only up to $2,000 if you claim one dependent person, or up to $4,000 if you claim more than one dependent person.

Line 5. This is a very important amount on Form 2441. If you are unmarried at the end of the year, put in the total amount of your earned income, such as wages, salaries, tips, and self-employed income. Income from dividends, interest, annuities, pensions, etc. is not included in earned income.

If you are married as of the end of the year, put down the smaller amount of either your earned income or that of your spouse. For example, your earned income is $15,000 and your spouse's is $10,000. Put in $10,000 on line 5.

On *line 6*, put in the amount from line 4 or line 5, whichever is smaller.

On *line 7*, put in the portion of the amount on line 6 that was actually paid during 1981. In other words, any expenses that were incurred but not paid during the year should not be included. If all expenses were in fact paid during the year, put in the total amount.

On *line 8*, put in the amount of any child care expenses that were incurred in 1980 but were actually paid in 1981.

On *line 9*, add the amounts from lines 7 and 8.

On *line 10*, multiply the amount on line 9 by 20% (.20).

Line 11. This is where you calculate your child and dependent care expenses limitation.

On *line 11a*, enter the amount on line 37 on page 2 of your Form 1040. On *line 11b*, enter the total of the amounts on lines 38, 39, 41, 42, and 43 of Form 1040. On *line 11c*, subtract the amount on line 11b from that on line 11a. If the amount is a negative number, enter "0."

On *line 12*, enter the smaller of the amount on line 10 or the amount on line 11c. That figure is your child care and dependent care expense tax credit. Transfer the amount on line 12 to line 40 on page 2 of Form 1040.

Line 13. If you have declared payments to an individual on line 2, then you must answer two questions and supply further information.

Line 13a. If you paid $50 or more in a calendar quarter to any individual, you are asked whether or not the services were performed in your home. If the answer is "yes" then you are responsible for filing the appropriate wage tax returns and for paying social security taxes. In other words the IRS is saying that if the work is done in your house, the person who is doing that work is in your employ. Therefore, you are required as an employer, to fill out all the necessary forms, make quarterly tax payments, and pay social security taxes on behalf of your employee. However, if the child and dependent care services are performed outside your house, you should answer "no" to the question on line 13a.

On *13c*, if you've answered "yes" to the question on line 13b, put in your Employer I.D. number. If you have not been assigned an I.D. number, request and complete Form SS-4, and write in "applied for" on line 13c.

USING FORM 2441 PROPERLY

The most important aspect in using the tax credit for child and dependent care expenses is whether or not you meet the employment, full-time student, or disabled qualifications. The law allows this tax credit in order to enable you and your spouse to work, to look for work, or to be a full-time student. Therefore, you must approach Form 2441 with that in mind. If, for example, you are married and file a joint return, and one spouse works during the day and the other at night, you probably would not be able to claim this credit. Always keep in mind the basic tax law pertaining to child and dependent care expenses, in case you are audited.

The child and dependent care expense tax credit can be a beneficial tax write-off for young couples or single parents who are not able to itemize deductions or claim any other type of tax write-off. This tax credit can save money for such people. Many times taxpayers with lower incomes are advised simply to fill out the short form, Form 1040A, but in doing so they are not able to claim the tax credit for child and dependent care expenses. Whether you do your taxes yourself or have a professional do them for you, be sure to claim this tax credit if you qualify. In fact, if you discover that you were qualified in the past but did not claim the credit, file an amended return on Form 1040X for each possible prior year, and claim refunds of taxes paid. Otherwise, you are *losing* on your income taxes. Amended returns are discussed in Chapter 20.

INVESTMENT TAX CREDIT—FORM 3468

Investment Tax Credits are granted to encourage the purchase of new or used "tangible personal property" used in a trade or business. They may be claimed by taxpayers who are self-employed as sole proprietors, by beneficiaries of trusts and estates, by members of partnerships, or by corporations. A tax *credit*, as opposed to a tax *deduction*, directly reduces your tax bill, and is not dependent on your tax bracket in order to save you money. Tangible personal property basically means machinery and equipment, such as automobiles, trucks, and business machinery, and it can even include things such as paintings or an aquarium as decorations for an office. The main thing that does not qualify for the investment credit is a building.

Beginning with the 1981 taxable year, you can choose one of two methods of claiming an investment tax credit. The first method involves depreciating property using the new ACRS method of depreciation, or cost recovery. (See pages 65—68 for a discussion of ACRS.) When you use the ACRS method, and the property qualifies for an investment tax credit, fill out *line 1* of Form 3468. If the property has a recovery period of three years, you can claim a tax credit of 6% of its total cost, whether it is new or used property. For example, say you purchased a used automobile for your business for $6,000 in November, 1981. You can depreciate it over three years, using the ACRS method, and claim a tax credit of $360 on your 1981 tax return. If new or used property is depreciated over five or more years, using the ACRS method, the investment tax credit is 10% of its total cost.

If you chose *not* to use the ACRS method of depreciation, the amount of the investment tax credit is calculated on *line 3* of Form 3468 as follows:

• If the item is depreciated during a useful life of three to five years, then you may claim a 10% tax credit of one-third of the total cost.

• If the item has a useful life of five to seven years, you may claim a 10% tax credit of two-thirds of its total costs.

• If the item has a useful life of seven or more years, you may claim a 10% tax credit of 100% of its total cost.

For example, you purchase an automobile for your sales business on December 31, 1981 for $12,000. If you elect to depreciate the car over seven years, you could claim a tax credit on your 1981 tax return of $1,200—10% of its total cost.

If you instead elect to depreciate this same car over a three year period, the tax credit would be $400—10% of one-third of its total cost.

An important point here is that, even though you purchased the car on the last day of the taxable year, you are still able to reduce your taxes by up to $1,200.

The two methods of claiming the tax credit presents you with a trade-off between taking depreciation deductions for an item over a longer period of time, or claiming a greater tax credit immediately.

TAX CREDITS

Form 3468
Department of the Treasury
Internal Revenue Service

Computation of Investment Credit
▶ Attach to your tax return.
▶ Use separate Schedule B (Form 3468) to figure your tentative business energy investment credit.

OMB. No. 1545-0155

1981
27

Name | Identifying number as shown on page 1 of your tax return

Part I — Elections (Check the box(es) below that apply to you (see Instruction D).)

A The corporation elects the basic or basic and matching employee plan percentage under section 48(n)(1) . . . . ☐
B I elect to increase my qualified investment to 100% for certain commuter highway vehicles under section 46(c)(6) . . . . ☐
C I elect to increase my qualified investment by all qualified progress expenditures made this tax year and all later years . . . . ☐
Enter total qualified progress expenditures included in column (4), Part II ▶..............................
D I claim full credit on certain ships under section 46(g)(3). (See **Instruction B** for details.) . . . . ☐

Part II — Qualified Investment

Figure your qualified investment in new or used investment credit property acquired or constructed and placed in service during the tax year. The qualified investment for qualified progress expenditures and qualified rehabilitation expenditures is allowed in the tax year the expenditure is incurred or in the case of self-constructed property the year the expenditure is chargable to a capital account for the property.

For certain taxpayers, the basis or cost of property placed in service after February 18, 1981, is limited to the amount the taxpayer is at risk for the property at year end. See Instruction E.

Note: *Include your share of investment in property made by a partnership, estate, trust, small business corporation, or lessor.*

1 Recovery Property	Line	(1) Recovery Period	(2) Unadjusted Basis	(3) Applicable percentage	(4) Qualified investment (Column 2 × column 3)
New	(a)	3-Year		60	
	(b)	Other		100	
Used	(c)	3-Year		60	
	(d)	Other		100	

2 Total—Add lines 1(a) through 1(d) **2**

3 Nonrecovery Property	Line	(1) Life years	(2) Basis or cost	(3) Applicable percentage	(4) Qualified investment (Column 2 × column 3)
New	(a)	3 or more but less than 5		33⅓	
	(b)	5 or more but less than 7		66⅔	
	(c)	7 or more		100	
Used	(d)	3 or more but less than 5		33⅓	
	(e)	5 or more but less than 7		66⅔	
	(f)	7 or more		100	

4 Total—Add lines 3(a) through 3(f) **4**
5 New commuter highway vehicle—Enter total qualified investment. (See **Instruction D**) . . . **5**
6 Used commuter highway vehicle—Enter total qualified investment. (See **Instruction D**) . . . **6**
7 Qualified rehabilitation expenditures incurred before January 1, 1982, for: (see specific instructions)
  (a) Improvements with 5 or more but less than 7 years—Enter 66⅔% of expenditures . . . **7(a)**
  (b) Improvements with 7 or more life years—Enter 100% of expenditures . . . . **7(b)**
8 Total qualified investment in 10% property—Add lines 2, 4, 5, 6, 7(a) and 7(b). (See instructions for special limits) . **8**
9 Enter 100% of qualified rehabilitation expenditures incurred after December 31, 1981, for: . .
  (a) 30-year old buildings **9a**
  (b) 40-year old buildings **9b**
  (c) Certified historic structures (Enter the Dept. of Interior assigned project number ....) **9c**
10 Total qualified investment—Add lines 8, 9(a), 9(b), and 9(c) **10**

Part III — Tentative Regular Investment Credit

11 10% of line 8 . . . . **11**
12 15% of line 9(a) **12**
13 20% of line 9(b) **13**
14 25% of line 9(c) **14**
15 Corporations electing the basic or basic and matching employee plan percentage for contributions to tax credit employee stock ownership plans—Check box A above (see **Instruction D**)
  (a) Basic 1% credit—Enter 1% of line 10 . . . . **15a**
  (b) Matching credit (not more than 0.5%)—Enter allowable percentage times adjusted line 10 (attach schedule) . **15b**
16 Credit from Cooperative—Enter regular investment credit from cooperatives **16**
17 Current year regular investment credit—Add lines 11 through 16 . . . . **17**
18 Carryover of unused credits **18**
19 Carryback of unused credits **19**
20 Tentative regular investment credit—Add lines 17, 18, and 19, enter here and in Part IV, line 21 . **20**

For Paperwork Reduction Act Notice, see page 2.

Form **3468** (1981)
343-160-1

Form 3468 (1981)   Page **2**

Part IV   Tax Liability Limitations

21 Tentative credit from Part III, line 20	21
22 (a) Individuals—Enter amount from Form 1040, line 37, page 2 . . . . (b) Estates and trusts—Enter amount from Form 1041, line 26, page 1 . . . . (c) Corporations—Enter amount from Schedule J (Form 1120), line 3, page 3 . . . . . (d) Others—Enter tax before credits from your return	22
23 (a) Credit for the elderly (individuals only) . . . . 23(a)	
(b) Foreign tax credit . . . . 23(b)	
(c) Tax on lump-sum distribution from Form 4972 or Form 5544 . 23(c)	
(d) Possessions corporation tax credit (corporations only) . . . 23(d)	
(e) Section 72(m)(5) penalty tax (individuals only) . . . . . 23(e)	
24 Total—Add lines 23(a) through 23(e)	24
25 Subtract line 24 from line 22	25
26 (a) Enter smaller of line 25 or $25,000. See instruction for line 26	26(a)
(b) If line 25 is more than line 26(a), and your tax year ends in 1981, enter 80% of the excess (if your tax year ends in 1982, enter 90% of the excess)	26(b)
27 Regular investment credit limitation—Add lines 26(a) and 26(b)	27
28 Allowed regular investment credit—Enter the smaller of line 21 or line 27	28
29 Business energy investment credit limitation—Subtract line 28 from line 25	29
30 Business energy investment credit—Enter amount from line 14 of Schedule B (Form 3468) .	30
31 Allowed business energy investment credit—Enter smaller of line 29 or line 30	31
32 Total allowed regular and business energy investment credit—Add lines 28 and 31. Enter here and on Form 1040, line 41; Schedule J (Form 1120), line 4(b), page 3; or the proper line on other returns	32

Paperwork Reduction Act Notice.—The Paperwork Reduction Act of 1980 says we must tell you why we are collecting this information, how we will use it, and whether you have to give it to us. We ask for the information to carryout the Internal Revenue laws of the United States. We need it to ensure that you are complying with these laws and so that we can figure and collect the correct amount of tax. You are required to give us this information.

343-160-1

An automobile was used as the example above because, as stated earlier, you can depreciate an automobile over as little as three years. In certain cases, though, you may want to assign a longer useful life to an auto in order to claim a higher investment tax credit. How should you determine the useful life? If this year's tax liability is going to be significantly higher than it will be during the next few years, then you may want to take the higher tax credit, and depreciate the item over seven years. But, if you feel that you need greater business deductions in the next couple of years, then you may choose to depreciate the car over only three years and claim a smaller investment tax credit. These are the overall factors, and when you do your tax return, each one should be taken into consideration.

Another important factor affecting the investment tax credit is the carryback and carryforward provisions. What that means is that if a tax credit is greater than your total tax liability, you can carry the unused portion back three years and claim the tax credit for those past years, and you can carry the tax credit forward for the next seven years. For example, if you bought a machine for your business for $100,000, you may qualify for an investment tax credit of

$10,000. If your total tax liability for this year is only $8,000, you could go back three years to claim the additional $2,000 from taxes that you have already paid, or you could carry it forward for the next seven years until you've used up the entire $10,000 tax credit.

Wealthy taxpayers in the United States have greatly benefitted from the investment tax credit for years. However, few tax preparers have understood the credit until the last few years. Today, if you go to a branch of a national tax preparation firm as a self-employed taxpayer, the chances are that you'd not be advised properly as to the investment tax credit. In the last few years, more and more taxpayers have begun to take advantage of it.

With the passage of the Economic Recovery Tax Act of 1981, the laws concerning the investment tax credit have been greatly liberalized. In order to get the full 10% investment tax credit, the property now must be depreciated over only a five-year period. For eligible property in the three-year recovery class, a 6% investment tax credit is available.

The allowance for eligible used property also has been increased, from $100,000 to $125,000 in 1981, and to $150,000 in 1985 and thereafter.

Investment tax credits and net operating losses can now be carried forward for fifteen years, instead of seven years, and this period is retroactive, to allow further carryovers for loss and credit carryforwards that were due to expire in 1981. There are new rules that prevent a taxpayer from claiming a tax credit unless he or she is personally liable for repayment of loans taken to purchase otherwise eligible equipment, and when family members loan money to the taxpayer. These are part of the "at-risk" rules that are too complicated for the scope of this book.

If you have claimed an investment tax credit for property, and you sell or trade it before the end of its "recovery period," you are required to pay an additional tax. For example, if you have taken an investment tax credit on 100% of the cost of a machine and you establish a useful life for it of at least seven years, and then you dispose of the machine after only three years, you would have to pay back some of the tax credit that you took in the year of purchase. This increase in tax is calculated by filling out Form 4255, Recapture of Investment Credit, and the amount is entered on line 50 of Form 1040.

Under the newEconomic Recovery Tax Act, if qualified property is disposed of prior to the end of its recovery period, the investment tax credit is recaptured by allowing only a two percent credit for each year the property was held. There is no recapture, that is, no increase in tax on line 50, if the property is held for at least five years before it is sold. If the property is being depreciated over a three-year period, then it must be held for at least three years.

BUSINESS ENERGY INVESTMENT TAX CREDIT

Beginning in 1980, a new Business Energy Investment Credit was established. This credit is calculated on Schedule B of Form 3468. The Business Energy Investment Credit allows you to claim 15% of the total cost of qualified energy equipment investment. If you've purchased solar or wind power generating equipment, ocean thermo equipment, or geothermo equipment, be certain to claim your 15% tax credit.

REHABILITATION EXPENDITURE TAX CREDIT

For rehabilitating a non-residential building, *beginning after 1981*, there will be a three-tier investment tax credit, as follows:
- 15% for improving buildings that are at least thirty years old
- 20% for structures at least forty years old
- 25% for certified historic structures

In each case, the rehabilitation must be "substantial." These are terrific tax incentives.

FOREIGN TAX CREDIT
FORM 1116

The foreign tax credit is a tax reduction based on any income taxes you have paid to the government of another country. To qualify for this credit, the tax that was paid to another country must have been based on earned income that was also taxable on your United States income tax return. Therefore, any amounts of income that are excludable under the Internal Revenue Code cannot be figured into the foreign tax credit.

Form 1116 must be filled out in order to claim the credit on line 42 of the 1040. One problem that you may have in filling out this form is converting foreign currencies into U.S. dollar amounts. Before you fill out Form 1116, be sure to find out all of the appropriate exchange rates and convert the foreign sums into U.S. dollars.

Since a relatively small percentage of taxpayers ever earn money abroad, we will not discuss this tax credit in detail.

WORK INCENTIVE TAX CREDIT (WIN)

This tax credit can be claimed by self-employed taxpayers who employ WIN (Work Incentive Program) people in their businesses. WIN is a federal and state government program that attempts to help unemployed persons find jobs by allowing a special tax credit to employers who hire them. If you can qualify, fill out Form 4874 and take full advantage of this tax credit. The amount of the credit is entered on *line 43* of Form 1040.

You may be able to claim a credit of 35% of the first $6,000 of wages that you pay to each eligible non-business employee. The maximum amount of non-business wages on which you may claim this credit is $12,000.

JOBS CREDIT—FORM 5884

The jobs credit is also available to self-employed taxpayers who have hired certain qualified employees during the taxable year. The credit is based on employee wages subject to F.U.T.A., the unemployment compensation system. If you meet all the requirements, you may take advantage of the jobs credit. You must fill out Form 5884 in order to do so. The amount goes onto *line 44* of Form 1040.

RESIDENTIAL ENERGY CREDITS—
FORM 5695

The energy credits came into effect a few years ago, and for many American taxpayers it can be a very nice tax write-off. For an energy tax credit involving your personal residence, Form 5695 must be filled out and attached to your tax return. The house must be located in the United States, and it must be your principal residence—the main place where you and your family live. A summer or vacation home would not qualify. However, you do not have to own this house or apartment, you can be a tenant. You must be living in it, and you must be the one who has paid for the energy-saving devices that form the basis of the credit.

There are basically two types of energy credits that may be claimed, one that involves costs for home energy conservation, and one that involves costs for renewable energy source property. Energy conservation includes expenses for insulation, storm or thermal windows, caulking, weather stripping, etc. Renewable energy source items include solar, wind, and geothermal energy devices. These items can heat or cool your principal residence or provide hot water or electricity for it. Items such as solar panels installed on roofs, heat exchangers, windmills, etc. would be included as renewable energy source items.

You are not able to take an energy tax credit for items such as carpeting, drapes, wood paneling, etc. On the reverse side of Form 5695 is a list of all of the items that are eligible, and the items that aren't. Go through the list to see what you may be able to deduct.

Filling Out Form 5695. Part I of Form 5695 deals with energy conservation costs. You can claim the total expenses of purchasing and installing these items. However, you are not able to claim any expenses involved in repairing or maintaining them.

Line 1. In order for you to be able to

TAX CREDITS

Form **5695**	**Residential Energy Credit**	OMB No. 1545-0214
Department of the Treasury Internal Revenue Service	▶ Attach to Form 1040. ▶ See Instructions on back.	**19****81** 33

Name(s) as shown on Form 1040 | Your social security number

Enter in the space below the address of your principal residence on which the credit is claimed if it is different from the address shown on Form 1040.

If you have an energy credit carryover from a previous tax year and no energy savings costs this year, skip to Part III, line 24.

Part I Fill in your energy conservation costs (but do not include repair or maintenance costs).

1 Was your principal residence substantially completed before April 20, 1977? . . . . ▶ ☐ Yes ☐ No

Note: You MUST answer this question. Failure to do so will delay the processing of your return. If you checked the "No" box, you CANNOT claim an energy credit under Part I and you should not fill in lines 2 through 12 of this form.

2 a Insulation . . . . | 2a |
  b Storm (or thermal) windows or doors . . . . | 2b |
  c Caulking or weatherstripping . . . . | 2c |
  d A replacement burner for your existing furnace that reduces fuel use . . . . . . | 2d |
  e A device for modifying flue openings to make a heating system more efficient . . . . | 2e |
  f An electrical or mechanical furnace ignition system that replaces a gas pilot light . . . . | 2f |
  g A thermostat with an automatic setback . . . . | 2g |
  h A meter that shows the cost of energy used . . . . | 2h |
3 Total (add lines 2a through 2h) . . . . | 3 |
4 Enter the part of expenditures made from nontaxable government grants and subsidized financing . . | 4 |
5 Subtract line 4 from line 3 . . . . | 5 |
6 Maximum amount of cost on which credit can be figured . . . . | 6 | $2,000 | 00
7 Enter the total energy conservation costs for this residence from your 1978, 1979, and 1980 Form 5695, line 2 . . . . | 7 |
8 Subtract line 7 from line 6 . . . . | 8 |
9 Enter the amount of nontaxable government grants and subsidized financing entered on line 4 . . . | 9 |
10 Subtract line 9 from line 8. If zero or less, do not complete the rest of this part . . . . . . | 10 |
11 Enter the amount on line 5 or line 10, whichever is less . . . . | 11 |
12 Enter 15% of line 11 here and include in amount on line 23 below . . . . | 12 |

Part II Fill in your renewable energy source costs (but do not include repair or maintenance costs).

13 a Solar _____ | 13 b Geothermal _____ | 13 c Wind _____ | Total ▶ | 13d |
14 Enter the part of expenditures made from nontaxable government grants and subsidized financing . . | 14 |
15 Subtract line 14 from line 13 . . . . | 15 |
16 Maximum amount of cost on which credit can be figured . . . . | 16 | $10,000 | 00
17 Enter the total renewable energy source cost for this residence from your 1978 Form 5695, line 5 and your 1979 and 1980 Forms 5695, line 9 . . . . | 17 |
18 Subtract line 17 from line 16 . . . . | 18 |
19 Enter the amount of nontaxable government grants and subsidized financing entered on line 14 . . . | 19 |
20 Subtract line 19 from line 18. If zero or less, do not complete the rest of this part . . . . . | 20 |
21 Enter the amount on line 15 or line 20, whichever is less . . . . | 21 |
22 Enter 40% of line 21 here and include in amount on line 23 below . . . . | 22 |

Part III Fill in this part to figure the limitation

23 Add lines 12 and 22. If less than $10, enter zero . . . . | 23 |
24 Enter your energy credit carryover from a previous tax year. Caution—Do not make an entry on this line if your 1980 Form 1040, line 47, showed an amount of more than zero . . . . | 24 |
25 Add lines 23 and 24 . . . . | 25 |
26 Enter the amount of tax shown on Form 1040, line 37 . . . . | 26 |
27 Add lines 38 through 44 from Form 1040 and enter the total . . . . | 27 |
28 Subtract line 27 from line 26. If zero or less, enter zero . . . . | 28 |
29 Residential energy credit. Enter the amount on line 25 or line 28, whichever is less. Also, enter this amount on Form 1040, line 45. Complete Part IV below if this line is less than line 25 . . . . . | 29 |

Part IV Fill in this part to figure your carryover to 1982 (Complete only if line 29 is less than line 25)

30 Enter amount from Part III, line 25 . . . . | 30 |
31 Enter amount from Part III, line 29 . . . . | 31 |
32 Credit carryover to 1982 (subtract line 31 from line 30) . . . . | 32 |

For Paperwork Reduction Act Notice, see instructions on back.

343-210-1

claim the energy tax credit, your principal residence must have been substantially completed before April 20, 1977. If it is newer than that, you are not able to claim an energy credit for energy conservation items. Check "yes" or "no" in the boxes provided at the right side of this section.

On *Lines 2a through h*, Put in the total amounts that you have spent on the items listed. For example, you may have spent $500 for insulation. Put that amount on line 2a.

On *line 3*, add the amounts that were put in lines 2a through 2h.

The rest of the questions asked in Part I of Form 5695 are fairly simple and straightforward. Simply put in the appropriate amounts, if any, and proceed to the next part.

In *Part II* you will report your renewable energy source costs. Again, do not include expenses for repairs and maintenance. You can include only the costs of purchasing and installing renewable energy source items, such as solar, geothermal, and wind items.

In *Part III* you calculate your energy credit and your energy credit limitation. On *line 24*, put in the amount that you were credit carryover from a previous taxable year. A carryover is an excess amount, greater than the amount that you were allowed to claim in a previous year, and you can now claim it in this year. For example, you were entitled to a $200 energy credit in 1980, but were not able to deduct all $200 of it because your total tax laibility was only $100. The other $100 is a carryover amount and would be claimed on your 1981 return on line 24 of Form 5695.

Fill out the rest of Part III and enter the amount on *line 29* on line 45 of Form 1040. Also, you must fill out Part IV of Form 5695 if line 29 is less than line 25.

Part IV is used to figure your carryover to the 1982 taxable year. That amount, if any, will go onto next year's return, again on Form 5695. Don't forget about it next year, or you will not realize the full benefit of the residential energy tax credit.

Remember that the energy credit limitation is based on your principal residence. If you use up the tax credit for one residence and then move to a different residence, you may be able to claim up to the maximum credit again on that different residence. If, in one year, you have two different principal residences, and you have energy conservation costs for each, you should fill out a separate Form 5695 for each residence. Then, enter the total amount of costs on all of the Forms 5695 only line 23 of one of the Forms 5695. Write in the space above Line 23 on that form, "more than one principal residence." Then be sure to attach all of the forms to your tax return.

When you sell a principal residence on which you have claimed an energy credit, you may have to reduce the basis of the residence by the total amount of the energy credits that you have taken. This is done only if the items for which you have taken the credit have been used to increase the basis of the principal residence. In other words, you spend $2,000 on insulation, and you claim a tax credit of $300. You then sell the house, and in computing the basis of the residence sold, you add the $2,000 insullation expenses. You would then have to subtract the $300 energy tax credit, allowing you to increase the basis of the principal residence by only $1,700.

YOUR TOTAL TAX CREDITS

On *line 46* of Form 1040, add all of the amounts on lines 38 through 45 to arrive at your total tax credits.

On *line 47*, subtract the amount on line 46 from that on line 37. The difference is your tax liability reduced by your tax credits. You can easily see the direct benefit of being able to claim tax credits.

CHAPTER SIXTEEN

☆

Other Taxes

Lines 48 through 54 of Form 1040 involve other taxes that must be added to your tax liability. Much of the information asked for does not apply to most taxpayers. Just skip any lines that do not apply to you, and don't worry about them.

SELF-EMPLOYMENT TAX—SCHEDULE SE

We have already discussed Schedule SE in detail on page 70. Self-employment social security taxes are payable when you show net profits of over $400 in sole proprietorships (Schedule C), partnerships, joint ventures, etc.

MINIMUM TAX—FORM 4625

Line 49a of Form 1040. A minimum tax is an additional tax imposed on certain types of income that are given preferential treatment by the tax code. These types of income include capital gains, stock options, income offset by depletion, amortization of specified investments, and accelerated depreciation. Form 4625, Computation of Minimum Tax—Individuals, applies to the above items of income except capital gains. If you have *tax preference* items that total more than $10,000, or $5,000 if filing in the status of married filing separate returns, then you must fill out Form 4625. Even if you are not subject to any additional tax, you must still fill out the form. Actually, relatively few taxpayers have substantial tax preference income.

ALTERNATIVE MINIMUM TAX—FORM 6251

Line 49b of Form 1040. The alternative minimum tax is an additional tax that is imposed on long-term capital gains if they exceed $10,000 or $5,000 if filing in the status of married filing separate returns, and in the case of very large itemized deductions. You must report the long-term capital gain deduction, your adjusted itemized deductions, and your adjusted gross income minus your itemized deductions from line 33 on Form 1040, your zero bracket amount, and your personal exemptions. It does not involve capital gains on the sale of a personal residence. Request copies of Form 6251 and Publication 525 in order to determine if you are liable for the alternative minimum tax.

TAX FROM RECOMPUTING PRIOR YEAR INVESTMENT CREDIT—FORM 4255

Line 50 of Form 1040. If you have previously taken an Investment Tax Credit, and you dispose of the property before the end of the determined useful life, then you are required to pay back some of the tax credit you claimed. For example, if you claimed a tax credit on a machine used in your business that had a useful life of seven or more years, and then sold that machine two years later, you would have to pay back some of the tax credit. You determine the exact amount by filling out Form 4255. You would have taken a tax credit of 10% of the total cost of the machine, based on depreciating it over a useful life of at least seven years. Because you used the machine only for two years, you would have to return some of the money you saved by claiming the tax credit.

With the Economic Recovery Tax Act of 1981, credits are recaptured by allowing only

SCHEDULE SE	Computation of Social Security Self-Employment Tax	OMB No. 1545-0074
(Form 1040)	▶ See Instructions for Schedule SE (Form 1040).	1981
Department of the Treasury Internal Revenue Service	▶ Attach to Form 1040.	22

Name of self-employed person (as shown on social security card)	Social security number of self-employed person ▶	

Part I — Computation of Net Earnings from FARM Self-Employment

Regular Method

1 Net profit or (loss) from:
   a Schedule F (Form 1040) **1a**
   b Farm partnerships **1b**
2 Net earnings from farm self-employment (add lines 1a and 1b) **2**

Farm Optional Method

3 If gross profits from farming are:
   a Not more than $2,400, enter two-thirds of the gross profits . . . .⎫
   b More than $2,400 and the net farm profit is less than $1,600, enter $1,600 . . . .⎭ . . . **3**
4 Enter here and on line 12a, the amount on line 2, or line 3 if you elect the farm optional method . **4**

Part II — Computation of Net Earnings from NONFARM Self-Employment   **SE**

Regular Method

5 Net profit or (loss) from:
   a Schedule C (Form 1040) **5a**
   b Partnerships, joint ventures, etc. (other than farming) **5b**
   c Service as a minister, member of a religious order, or a Christian Science practitioner. (Include rental value of parsonage or rental allowance furnished.) If you filed Form 4361 and have not revoked that exemption, check here ▶ ☐ and enter zero on this line **5c**
   d Service with a foreign government or international organization **5d**
   e Other (specify) ▶ _____ **5e**
6 Total (add lines 5a through 5e) **6**
7 Enter adjustments if any (attach statement, see instructions) **7**
8 Adjusted net earnings or (loss) from nonfarm self-employment (line 6, as adjusted by line 7). Enter here and on line 12b. (Note: If the amount on line 8 is less than $1,600, you may wish to use the nonfarm optional method instead. See instructions.) **8**

Nonfarm Optional Method (Use only if your earnings from nonfarm self-employment are less than $1,600 and less than two-thirds of your gross nonfarm profits.)

9 **a** Maximum amount reportable under both optional methods combined (farm and nonfarm) . . **9a** $1,600 00
   b Enter amount from line 3. (If you have no amount on line 3, enter zero.) **9b**
   c Balance (subtract line 9b from line 9a) **9c**
10 Enter two-thirds of gross nonfarm profits or $1,600, whichever is smaller **10**
11 Enter here and on line 12b, the amount on line 9c or line 10, whichever is smaller **11**

Part III — Computation of Social Security Self-Employment Tax

12 Net earnings or (loss):
   a From farming (from line 4) **12a**
   b From nonfarm (from line 8, or line 11 if you elect to use the Nonfarm Optional Method) . . **12b**
13 Total net earnings or (loss) from self-employment reported on lines 12a and 12b. (If line 13 is less than $400, you are not subject to self-employment tax. Do not fill in rest of schedule) **13**
14 The largest amount of combined wages and self-employment earnings subject to social security or railroad retirement taxes for 1981 is **14** $29,700 00
15 **a** Total FICA wages (from Forms W-2) and RRTA compensation **15a**
   b Unreported tips subject to FICA tax from Form 4137, line 9 or to RRTA **15b**
   c Add lines 15a and 15b **15c**
16 Balance (subtract line 15c from line 14) **16**
17 Self-employment income—line 13 or line 16, whichever is smaller **17**
18 Self-employment tax. (If line 17 is $29,700, enter $2,762.10; if less, multiply the amount on line 17 by .093.) Enter here and on Form 1040, line 48 . . . . **18**

For Paperwork Reduction Act Notice, see Form 1040 Instructions.

OTHER TAXES

a 2% credit for each year the property was held. In other words, you'll get a credit of 10% of an item's total cost if you keep the property for at least five years. If you dispose of the property before the five years is up, you can keep 2% of that 10% tax credit for each year you actually held the property. For example, you have a $1,000 tax credit on property with a useful life of five years. If you sell in four years, then only 80% of that credit is allowed, and you must pay an additional tax of 20% of the $1,000 tax credit, or $200. Compute this additional tax by filling out Form 4255 and attaching it to Form 1040.

SOCIAL SECURITY [FICA] TAX ON TIP INCOME NOT REPORTED FORM 4137

Line 51a of Form 1040. Form 4137 is used primarily by cab drivers, waiters, waitresses, etc., who collect tips but the total is not figured into their gross wages on a W-2 statement. The amount of tip money first should be recorded on line 20 of Form 1040, "other income," and then you should fill out Form 4137 to determine the additional amount of social security taxes you owe, if any.

UNCOLLECTED EMPLOYEE SOCIAL SECURITY TAX ON TIPS

Line 51b of Form 1040. The amount that is to be reported on line 51b will be shown on your W-2 statement. Basically, this applies to people who have tip income and whose employers have estimated the social security taxes on their tips. The uncollected and unpaid amount must therefore be put onto line 51b. You must pay this amount even if you have no other tax liability and would not otherwise have to file a tax return.

TAX ON AN INDIVIDUAL RETIREMENT ACCOUNT [IRA]— FORM 5329

Line 52 asks for the amount of additional tax based on premature withdrawals of funds in an individual retirement account. If you open an IRA, you are allowed to claim your deposits as an adjustment to your income. If you withdraw money from the IRA before you reach age 59½, you are required to pay an additional tax based on the amount withdrawn. Fill out Form 5329 to determine that amount. In most cases, the tax will be 10% of the amount that you have prematurely withdrawn.

ADVANCE EARNED INCOME CREDIT [EIC] PAYMENTS RECEIVED

Line 53 of Form 1040. If you have received payments in advance on an earned income credit through your employer, the total amount should be reported on line 53. The total should be shown on your W-2 statements. Simply transfer that amount onto line 53.

TOTAL TAX

Line 54 of Form 1040 is the most important line on your entire tax return. This is the amount of your total tax liability for the year. The matter of whether you will get a large refund or no refund, or whether you will have to pay an additional amount of money to the IRS, is of secondary importance to the amount shown on line 54. Winning on your income taxes does not necessarily mean getting a large refund. It means having the smallest amount on line 54 that is legitimately possible.

CHAPTER SEVENTEEN

☆

Payments of Tax

REFUND OR BALANCE DUE

On *lines 63 through 66* of Form 1040, you will determine the amount that the IRS owes you, or the amount that you owe them. To me, the actual amount in this section is relatively insignificant. The most important amount on the tax return is line 54, your total tax liability. That is the exact amount of income tax that you owe for the taxable year. A refund means only that you have paid the IRS too much money during the year. All they are doing is giving you back some of your own money, perhaps a year later, when it is worth less.

Receiving a refund is in fact losing money. You have been paying the IRS all year long, and any money that you get back now, without any interest, is worth less—because of inflation, and because you were not able to do anything with it during the year. If you had taken the amount of your refund and simply put it in the bank, you'd be better off. Between the loss of income from investment of your refund and the fact that you are getting it a year later, you are probably losing a minimum of 20% on that money.

A great tax mistake that many people make is to think they have done well if they get a large refund. It is not the amount of the refund that really counts, but, rather, the amount of the actual tax liability. To better understand this principle, decide which one of these two situations you would rather be in:

• Taxpayer A has a tax liability of $5,000, and has paid in $9,000 during the year. He will therefore receive a $4,000 refund.

• Taxpayer B is not going to get a refund, and, in fact, is going to have to pay an additional $500.

If may sound terrible to have to pay even more to the IRS, but taxpayer B's total tax liability is actually only $3,000. Since he paid in only $2,500 during the year, he'll have to pay an additional $500 with his tax return.

Taxpayer B is obviously in a better tax position. His total tax liability is lower, and he was able to invest more of his money during the year. Taxpayer A was forced to allow the government to use his money during the year.

Line 63. If the amount on line 62 is greater than that on line 54, then you will receive a refund from the IRS. Put the amount of that difference onto line 63.

Line 64. If you want the amount on line 63 refunded to you, then put that same amount onto line 64. *If you do not put any amount onto line 64, the IRS will not send you any refund.*

Line 65. If, instead of receiving the full amount of your refund now, you want to have all or part of it applied to your tax liability for the next year, then put the desired amount onto line 65.

Line 66. If the amount on line 54, your total tax liabilty, is greater than the amount on line 62, your total payments, then you owe the IRS additional money. That difference goes onto line 66.

PENALTIES AND EXEMPTIONS FORM 2210

If the amount that you owe the IRS on line 66 is greater than 20% of the total payments that the IRS received, interest on the underpayment will be charged. The amount credit worksheet" found in your federal income tax forms booklet. Then look up the amount of the credit allowed in the tax table entitled "earned income credit table." Put that amount onto *line 57* on Form 1040.

AMOUNT PAID WITH FORM 4868

Line 58 of Form 1040. Form 4868 is the "Application for Automatic Extension of Time to File U.S. Individual Income Tax Return." If you are not able to file on time, i.e., by April 15, then you can file Form 4868 for an extension of time to file. If you expect to receive a tax refund, or if you owe no tax at all, then all you have to do is fill out the form and send it in.

However, if you expect to owe money to the IRS and want to avoid the costly penalties for late payment of tax, then send in the amount you expect to owe along with Form 4868. Do not forget to declare on line 58 any amounts you sent in along with Form 4868.

EXCESS FICA OR RRTA TAX WITHHELD

Line 59 of Form 1040. As already discussed in Chapter 6, there is a specific limit to the amount that must be paid into FICA (social security) or RRTA (railroad retirement) systems. Any amount over that limit is refundable as a tax payment. If you have had more than one employer during the taxable year, you should check to see if too much money for FICA taxes was taken out of your paychecks. Go through your W-2 statements, total up all of the FICA taxes that were taken out, and see if the limit for the taxable year has been exceeded. Remember, each spouse's limits are separate, because social security taxes are imposed on each individual taxpayer. The limit for each year changes. For 1981 the limit is $2,762.10, based on $29,700 in wages.

CREDIT FOR FEDERAL TAX ON SPECIAL FUELS AND OILS— FORM 4136 OR 4136-T

Line 60 of Form 1040. There is a special tax credit treated as a payment for people who use gasoline, diesel fuel, special motor fuels, lubricating oil, "gasohol," and aviation fuels in the operation of non-highway vehicles. Non-highway uses involve farming, boating, aircraft, etc. If your business involves such vehicles, fill out the appropriate information on Form 4136, or Form 4136-T, and take full advantage of this tax payment. The credit is generally about two cents a gallon for gasoline and six cents a gallon for lubricating oil.

REGULATED INVESTMENT COMPANY CREDIT—FORM 2439

Line 61 of Form 1040. If you have invested in a regulated investment company that has withheld tax on any distributions allocated to you as capital gain dividends, then you will receive a copy of Form 2439 from the company. The amount that the company has paid to the IRS is treated as a tax payment by you, and, therefore, you will get that amount back as a refund. Simply copy the amount from Form 2439 and put it onto line 61 of Form 1040. Attach a copy of Form 2439 to your tax return.

TOTAL PAYMENTS

Line 62 of Form 1040. Add all the amounts on lines 55 through 61, and put the total here.

CHAPTER EIGHTEEN

☆

The Bottom Line

On *lines 55 to 62* of Form 1040, you record all the tax payments that you have made during the taxable year. Such payments include income taxes that have been withheld, estimated tax payments, and amounts paid in conjunction with an application for an extension of time. Be certain to put down all such amounts. The credit for federal tax on special fuels and oils, and the earned income credit are claimed in this section as well.

TOTAL FEDERAL INCOME TAX WITHHELD

On *line 55* of Form 1040 simply copy the amount in the box entitled "Federal Tax Withheld" on your W-2 statement or put in the total of such amounts if you have more than one W-2 statement. If you are filing a joint return, add up the amounts from both your and your spouse's W-2 statements.

ESTIMATED TAX PAYMENTS

Line 56 asks for the total amount of estimated tax payments that you have sent in to the IRS during the taxable year, usually in four quarterly installments—on April 15, June 15, September 15 of 1981 and January 15 of 1982. Estimated taxes are most commonly paid by self-employed people who do not have taxes withheld by an employer. Instead, they must estimate what their income tax will be for the year and then send in payments of income tax in four installments during the year. Estimated taxes must be paid on time in order to avoid the penalty for late payment that the IRS charges. For more information, see the section on Form 1040ES in Chapter 20.

Also, include on line 56 any amount that has been credited from last year's tax return to this year's.

EARNED INCOME CREDIT

Line 57. The earned income credit came into effect a few years ago and can be very beneficial to lower income people. In order for you to be eligible for this credit, your total earned income, that is, income earned only from wages, self-employment, or professional fees, or your adjusted gross income on line 32a of Form 1040, must be under $10,000. Do not include income from interest, dividends, pensions, or gain from real estate sales, etc. as part of the earned income figure. The amount of either your earned income or your adjusted gross income, whichever is larger, is used to compute your earned income credit.

The other eligibility requirement for this credit is that you must have maintained a household during the entire year for yourself, and your spouse, if married, and for a child who is under nineteen years of age or is a full-time student (meaning a student for at least five months during the year). This child does not have to be claimed as your dependent in order for you to qualify. If the child is over age nineteen and disabled, and you can claim him or her as a dependent, then you also will be able to qualify. If you are married you must file a joint return in order to get this credit.

The maximum amount of the earned income credit is $500. Even if you have no tax liability and have not paid anything into the tax system, you can still get this earned income credit.

To determine the amount of your earned income credit, fill in the "earned income of the underpayment is determined by a quarterly assessment of your tax payments. The point is that the IRS wants its money all during the taxable year and not just at the end of the year.

In the last few years many taxpayers have been claiming large numbers of personal withholding exemptions during the taxable year, on the W-4 statements that are given to an employer by an employee. By claiming more exemptions, employees have less money withheld from their paychecks, and they have higher take-home pay. Some people have claimed as many as ninety-nine exemptions during the year, or even claim to be exempt, on their W-4 statements. When these people file their tax returns, however, they owe large sums of money to the IRS and have to pay an additional interest penalty for late payment of tax.

Since in the past the interest rate charged by the IRS has been only 12%, a low rate by today's standards, many people feel that it is good planning to have the use of the money during the year and pay the penalty later. The IRS, however, is going to try to stop this practice by raising the interest rate.

The new interest rate for underpayment of tax will be about 18%. It will be based on the prime rate in effect in September of each year. This will make it unprofitable to create an underpayment of tax through exaggerating the number of exemptions on Form W-4. In addition, a civil penalty of $500 will be imposed beginning in 1982 for making a statement with respect to withholding exemptions for which there is no reasonable basis. There will also be a criminal penalty of $1,000 and/or imprisonment of not more than one year in the case of willfully supplying false or fraudulent information, with respect to withholding of tax from wages. Therefore, you should not follow the advice of people who advise you to exaggerate the number of withholding exemptions you claim.

If you receive a large refund year after year, however, you definitely should increase the number of exemptions claimed during the year to reduce the withholding from your paycheck. But, on the other hand, don't reduce your withholding so much that you wind up having to pay an interest penalty to the IRS. The ideal situation is to owe very little, or to break even on lines 63 and 64 of Form 1040. That way, you can put all of your money to work all year long, and you won't have to pay any interest penalty to the IRS.

Computing Your Penalty. Form 2210 or 2210F can be completed in order to compute your own interest penalty, if applicable. I usually feel no duty to fill out these forms. Sometimes a return will slip through the computer without it picking up the fact that you owe a penalty. Therefore, the penalty may not have to be paid.

Even if the IRS does determine that you owe a penalty, there is no real advantage to your filling out Form 2210. Let the IRS do the dirty work and compute the penalty for you.

YOUR CHECK OR MONEY ORDER

Be sure to write your social security number on the check or money order that you send to the IRS, because the IRS only knows you as a number. If you don't identify yourself with your number, your check may be lost in the bureaucratic shuffle.

SIGNATURES

After you have completed Form 1040 and all of the applicable supplemental forms, you, and your spouse, if you are filing jointly, must sign the tax return and date it. The husband's signature goes on the left and the wife's on the right. If the return is not signed they will not be processed by the IRS and will be returned to you.

At the bottom of page 2 of Form 1040 are spaces for a paid tax preparer's signature, I.D. number, and address. If you pay someone to prepare your tax return, be sure he or she signs it and puts in his or her social security number, address, etc.—the law requires it. If the preparer does not do this, you should not pay him or her, and you should not file the return as prepared by that person.

THE FINAL STEPS

After all forms are completed and signed, make photocopies of every part of your tax return, including your check to the IRS, if any. Keep these copies with your tax records for at least ten years, and refer to them whenever you do tax planning.

PART VI
OTHER RETURNS, FORMS, AND CONSIDERATIONS

CHAPTER NINETEEN

☆

State and Local Tax Returns

After you have finished your federal tax return, do the state and, where necessary, the local (or city) return. Some (wonderful) states do not impose a state income tax. However, if you have received sufficient income from sources within a state that does impose an income tax, then a tax return must be filed.

Generally, there are three types of state tax returns: The regular, full-year resident return; a non-resident return for taxpayers who earned income in the state but who do not reside in it; and a part-year resident tax return for people who have moved either into that state or out of it during the taxable year.

If you move from one state to another during the taxable year, then you may be required to file at least two separate state tax returns. The tax on each return is prorated, based on the amount of income received in that state and the length of time you resided in it. Be sure to get the appropriate forms, information, and instructions for the tax returns of each state involved.

Each state that imposes an income tax has a different set of procedures and laws. Most states use the same basic types of forms and procedures as the federal government, but each has its own peculiarities. Some states may allow certain itemized deductions that the federal law does not, or some states may grant tax credits rather than tax deductions for various items. The point here is that, by doing the federal return first, you will have most of the information you will need to do your state return. Find out the specific differences in forms and procedures for the state return, and then do it after you have finished the federal return.

In some areas, including New York City and Detroit, there are also city or local income tax returns to be filed. If you live in such an area or earn income there, then you are required to file another tax return. Again, be sure to get the appropriate forms and information well before such returns are due.

CHAPTER TWENTY

☆

Additional Tax Forms

There are two other important tax forms of which everyone should be well aware. These forms are not filed with your regular Form 1040. They can be used at any time during the year, and you should know how and when to file them.

FORM 1040ES—ESTIMATED TAX PAYMENTS AND WORKSHEET

Form 1040ES, the Declaration of Estimated Tax for Individuals, is used by taxpayers who are required to make payments of their own federal income taxes throughout the year. Estimated tax must be paid by people who are self-employed, who have high income from sources other than W-2 wages, or who do not have enough tax withheld from paychecks. The government wants its tax money all during the year and not afterwards, when you file your tax return. A penalty is charged if you owe the IRS more than 20% of the amount they received in tax payments during the year. To avoid this penalty, fill out Form 1040ES, and send in tax payments on or about April 15; June 15, September 15, and January 15.

There are two parts of Form 1040ES. The first part is a worksheet on which you compute the amount of estimated tax you will pay for the year. Before April 15 you must estimate your tax for the entire taxable year, and then determine how much in estimated taxes you must send to the IRS.

To compute the amount that should be paid in these installments, you must imagine how you think next year's tax return will look. Using estimated amounts of income, deductions, tax credits, etc., determine what next year's tax liability will be. Obviously, this will not be exact, and it can change drastically during this year. If necessary, you can, at any time, change the amount of your estimated tax payments to be either higher or lower, or not to make any additional estimated payments for the taxable year.

The second part of Form 1040ES contains four declaration-vouchers that must be filled out when you send in your estimated tax payment. Be sure to put in the correct social security numbers and amounts, and sign each declaration-voucher. The amount of each payment is based on your estimated tax worksheet, but can be changed for any quarterly statement.

If you file your tax return by February 2 of the following year and pay the total amount owed for the taxable year, you do not also have to send in the fourth declaration-voucher of your estimated taxes.

FORM 1040X—AMENDED U.S. INDIVIDUAL TAX RETURN

After a federal tax return is filed, any information on it can be changed, or amended, by filling out Form 1040X. You have three years in which to file an amended return from the due date of the original tax return. In other words, a tax return for 1981 can be amended any time before April 15, 1985.

There are many instances in which it is necessary or desirable to amend your tax return. Some of the most common instances are:

• You or a professional tax preparer put down an incorrect amount;

• After reading this book, you realize that you can qualify for additional tax deductions or tax credits, or that you should have itemized deductions;

Form 1040X — Amended U.S. Individual Income Tax Return
(Rev. November 1980)

Department of the Treasury — Internal Revenue Service

This return is for calendar year ▶ 19___ , OR fiscal year ended ▶ _____, 19___.

Please print or type

Your first name and initial (If joint return, also give spouse's name and initial)	Last name	Your social security number
Present home address (Number and street, including apartment number, or rural route)		Spouse's social security no.
City, town or post office, State, and ZIP code		

Enter below name and address as shown on original return (if same as above, write "Same"). If changing from separate to joint return, enter names and addresses used on original returns. (Note: *You cannot change from joint to separate returns after the due date has passed.*)

a. Service center where original return was filed

b. Has original return for the year being changed been audited? . . . . ☐ Yes ☐ No
If "No," have you been advised that it will be? . . . . ☐ Yes ☐ No
If "Yes," Identify IRS office ▶

c. Filing status claimed. (Note: *You cannot change from joint to separate returns after the due date has passed.*)
On original return . ▶ ☐ Single ☐ Married filing joint return ☐ Married filing separate return ☐ Head of Household ☐ Qualifying Widow(er)
On this return . . ▶ ☐ Single ☐ Married filing joint return ☐ Married filing separate return ☐ Head of Household ☐ Qualifying Widow(er)

Income and Deductions

	A. As originally reported or as adjusted (See Instructions)	B. Net change—Increase or (Decrease)—explain on page 2	C. Correct amount
1 Total income (see instructions)			
2 Adjustments to income (see instructions)			
3 Adjusted gross income (subtract line 2 from line 1)			
4 Deductions (see instructions)			
5 Subtract line 4 from line 3			

Note: *If this return is for 1977 or later and you use the tax tables, do not complete line 6 or take the general tax credit. Instead, enter on line 8, the tax on the income you reported on line 5.*

6 Exemptions from page 2, line 5			
7 Taxable income (subtract line 6 from line 5)			

Tax Liability

8 Tax (see instructions) (method used in column C ....)			
9 Credits (such as residential energy credits, credit for the elderly—see instructions)			
10 Subtract line 9 from line 8			
11 Other taxes (such as self-employment tax, minimum tax—see instructions)			
12 Total tax liability (add line 10 and line 11)			

Payments

13 Federal income tax withheld and excess FICA and RRTA tax withheld			
14 Estimated tax payments			
15 Earned income credit			
16 Credits for Federal tax on special fuels, regulated investment company, etc.			
17 Amount paid with Form 4868 (application for automatic extension of time to file)			
18 Amount paid with original return, plus additional tax paid after it was filed			
19 Total of lines 13 through 18, column C			

Refund or Balance Due

20 Overpayment, if any, as shown on original return
21 Subtract line 20 from line 19 (see instructions)
22 **BALANCE DUE.** If line 12, column C is more than line 21, enter difference. Please pay in full with this return
23 **REFUND** to be received. If line 12, column C is less than line 21, enter difference

Please Sign Here

Under penalties of perjury, I declare that I have filed an original return and that I have examined this amended return, including accompanying schedules and statements, and to the best of my knowledge and belief this amended return is true, correct, and complete. Declaration of preparer (other than taxpayer) is based on all information of which the preparer has any knowledge.

Your signature _____ Date _____
Spouse's signature (if filing jointly BOTH must sign even if only one had income)

Paid Preparer's Use Only

Preparer's signature and date	Check if self-employed ☐	Preparer's social security no.
Firm's name (or yours, if self-employed) and address	E.I. No. ▶	
	ZIP code ▶	

BE SURE TO COMPLETE PAGE 2

Form **1040X** (Rev. 11–80)

ADDITIONAL TAX FORMS

Form 1040X (Rev. 11-80) Page 2

Part I — Exemptions (See Form 1040 or Form 1040A Instructions)
If exemptions are unchanged or are decreased, do not complete lines 6 and 7.

	A. Number originally reported	B. Net change	C. Corrected number
1 Exemptions—yourself and spouse, 65 or over, blind			
2 Your dependent children who lived with you			
3 Other dependents			
4 Total exemptions (add lines 1 through 3)			
5 Multiply $1,000 ($750, if 1978 or prior) by the total number of exemptions claimed on line 4. Enter this amount here and on page 1, line 6			

6 Enter first names of your dependent children who lived with you, but were not claimed on original return:

Enter number ▶ ☐

7 Other dependents not claimed on original return:

(a) Name	(b) Relationship	(c) Number of months lived in your home	(d) Did dependent have income of $1,000 ($750, if 1978 or prior) or more?	(e) Did you provide more than one-half of dependent's support?

Enter number ▶ ☐

Part II — Explanation of Changes to Income, Deductions, and Credits
Enter the line reference from page 1 for which you are reporting a change and give the reason for each change. Attach applicable schedules.

Check here ▶ ☐ if change pertains to a net operating loss carryback, an investment credit carryback, a WIN credit carryback, or a jobs credit carryback.

Part III — Presidential Election Campaign Fund
Checking below will not increase your tax or reduce your refund.

Check here ▶ ☐ if you did not previously want to have $1 go to the fund but now want to.
Check here ▶ ☐ if joint return and if spouse did not previously want to have $1 go to the fund but now wants to.

☆ U.S. GOVERNMENT PRINTING OFFICE: 1980-O-313-455 58-0401110

- You want to change the number of exemptions that were claimed;
- You qualify for income averaging but didn't file Schedule G along with the original return;
- You inadvertantly didn't include all of your income (you may come across an additional W-2 statement).

Be very cautious and accurate when you file Form 1040X. Since there are relatively few similar forms filed, it is much easier for the IRS to scrutinize it. Do not file an amended return unless you are absolutely certain that you can back up any changes made. Be sure to fill out all of the necessary supplemental forms, such as Schedule A or Schedule G, and send them in with Form 1040X. Explain all of the changes made on Part II on page 2 of Form 1040X, and use additional paper or documents if necessary.

I would not amend a tax return unless a substantial amount of money is involved. The most common reason for filing an amended return is to claim a refund after income averaging. With income averaging, the IRS cannot usually dispute the additional refund. If you amend returns in order to take advantage of income averaging, be sure to fill out Schedule G and any other form that may have been required in a particular taxable year.

Answer all of the questions and complete all parts of Form 1040X, even if they are not affected by the changes that you are making. Be sure to fill out the back of the form, Parts I and II, and clearly write an explanation for your changes. Also, if applicable, write in "see attached" on Part II and then include all the additional forms or documents with it.

Form 1040X basically requires you to repeat information as it was reported on your original tax return, and then show the information as it should be reported after the amendments are made. Column a is for the amounts on the original return, and Column c is for the amounts as they should now be, whether they are being changed or are the same. In Column b, show the difference between the amounts in Column a and Column c.

If you do not have a copy of your original tax return, then get a photocopy from the IRS. Be sure to down the exact original, amounts. Don't make any estimates. Fill in Form 1040X, line by line, and then compute the amount of your additional refund or payment due to the IRS.

APPENDIX

Forms and Schedules—A Summary

The following is a list of the various forms and schedules that might apply to most American taxpayers. Become acquainted with each one, and imagine how it might apply to you, specifically.

FORMS

Form W-2. This is a statement that every wage earner receives shortly after the end of the calendar year from each employer. On it it contains information about the total wages that were paid, the amount of federal taxes withheld, state taxes withheld, social security (FICA) taxes withheld, total FICA wages paid, etc. Gather all of these forms before you sit down to complete your tax returns.

Form W-4. This is a form that is completed by each employee and given to the employer. The information on this form will determine how much money will be withheld from each of your paychecks to be paid over to the IRS to cover your tax liability. By claiming a greater number of exemptions, less money for tax will be withheld. You can legally claim more exemptions on form W-4 than the actual number of dependents you have. You may claim additional exemptions if you expect to claim large deductions, such as high interest payments, on your return. If you have always claimed large refunds on your tax return, then your should increase the number of exemptions of Form W-4, have less tax withheld, and get higher take-home pay.

Form 1040. This is the basic tax form, popularly called the "long form." Everyone should use this form to file individual tax returns. Pages 34-35

Form 1040A. This is the so-called "short form." I recommend that no one should use it. If you do use this form, you will automatically pay the highest possible amount of tax. Almost no types of deductions can be claimed on this form.

Form 1040ES. This form is used to compute estimated tax payments.

Form 1040X. This form is used for amending, or changing, a tax return after it has been filed. Pages 184-185.

Form 1065. This is the basic tax form used by a partnership. Once this form is filled out, Schedules K-1 must be filled out and sent to each partner.

Form 1099. This is a form given to independent contractors or self-employed people who have done work for a company or another person and have earned more than $400 in a taxable year. The amount of payments shown on this form goes onto Schedule C.

Form 1099-DIV. This form shows you the total amount of dividends you received from a perticualr company during the taxable year. This amount goes onto line 8b of Form 1040, and, if over $400, onto Schedule B.

Form 1099-INT. This form tells you the total amount of interest you received during the year from one particular source. This amount goes onto line 8a of Form 1040, and, if over $400, onto Schedule B.

Form 1116. This form is used to claim the Foreign Tax Credit. If you have paid income tax to another country, then you may be able to reduce your U.S. income tax by filing this form.

Form 1310. This form is used by a person claiming a refund on behalf of a family member who has died during the year. Attach this form to Form 1040.

Form 2106. This form is used by wage earners who have employee business expense deductions. You can use this form to claim such expenses as an adjustment to income, even if you cannot itemize deductions on Schedule A. Pages 118-119.

Form 2119. This form is used in connection with Schedule D to defer the capital gain on the sale of a personal residence. Page 80.

Form 2120. This form is used to claim an exemption for a dependent where any one taxpayer has not provided 50% or more of the total support of the dependent. Only one taxpayer, however, can claim the dependent as an exemption. The person claiming the dependent as an exemption should fill out Form 2120 and have it signed by all the persons who provide partial support for the dependent.

Form 2210. Fill out this form to determine how much you owe the IRS in penalties for not paying in enough tax money during the taxable year. Also, use this form to assert any of the four exceptions that may allow you to avoid such penalties.

Form 2440. This form is used by taxpayers who are permanently disabled and are receiving disability pay. Page 127.

Form 2441. This forms is used to claim a tax credit for child and dependent care expenses. Page 160.

Form 3468. This form is used to claim a tax credit by self-employed people, sole proprietorships, partnerships, and corporations that have purchased expensive equipment and certain other items for their businesses. Pages 163-164.

Form 3903. This forms is used to claim an adjustment to your income, based on your having to move at least thirty-five miles because of a change in jobs or job location. It can be used whether or not you itemize deductions. Page 112.

Form 3903F. This form is similar to Form 3903, but is used when you move to a foreign country. Page 116.

Form 4137. This form is used to compute the additional social security tax on tip income that has not been reported to your employer.

Form 4625. This form is used to calculate the additional tax imposed in tax preference items such as stock options, allowances, amortization, accelerated depreciation, and large itemized deductions, when such items exceed $10,000 in a taxable year.

Form 4797. This form is supplemental to Schedule D and is used to determine capital gains and losses on the sale of rental property, businesses and farms, the amount of involuntary conversions, and gain or loss on the sale used in a trade or business. Pages 85-86.

Form 4868. This form is used to get an extension of time in which to file your tax return.

Form 4972. This form is used by taxpayers who receive a large lump-sum distribution from a pension plan. It is used to spread out the tax over a period of ten years.

Form 5329. This form is used to compute the additional tax imposed on the premature withdrawal of money from an individual retirement account (IRA). This tax applies only to people under age 59½.

Form 5695. This form is used to claim the tax credit for purchasing and installing energy-saving devices used in your personal residence, such as insulation, thermal doors or windows, and solar heating equipment. You can claim this credit whether you itemize deductions or not. Page 167.

Form 6251. This form is used to calculate the additional tax (the alternative minimum tax) that is imposed when you report more than $10,000 in long-term capital gains.

Form 6252. If you have sold property in an installment sale, fill out this form to determine the taxable percentage of the amount of each payment you receive.

TAX SCHEDULES

Schedule A. This schedule is used to report itemized deductions. The categories of expenses permitted to be deducted are medical expenses, taxes paid, interest expenses, charitable contributions, casualties and thefts, and miscellaneous deductions. Page 130.

Schedule B. This form is used to report interest and dividend income of $400 or more. Page 52.

Schedule C. This form is used by sole proprietorships only. On it, you report amounts of income, expenses, and depreciation, and determine your net profit or loss for the taxable year. Pages 57, 60.

Schedule D. This form is used when you invest in and then sell capital investments, such as real estate, stocks, bonds, etc. Pages 75-76.

Schedule E. This schedule is used to report income from pensions, annuities, rental property, royalties, partnerships, estates, trusts, and small business corporations. Pages 94-95.

Schedule F. This schedule is used by people who are involved in agriculture or who have any sort of farm income. It is used to determine the net profit or loss from farm operations.

Schedule G. This form is used for income averaging when your current year's taxable income is considerably higher than the average of the previous years' taxable income. Page 150.

Schedule R. This schedule is used by people age sixty-five or over who can qualify for the retirement income credit. Page 156.

Schedule RP. This schedule is used by taxpayers under age sixty-five who qualify for the retirement income credit. Page 157.

Schedule SE. This schedule is used by people who have $400 or more in net profit from self-employment income, sole proprietorships, partnerships, service as a minister, farm income, etc. It is used to calculate the amount of social security tax that is due. Page 170.

Index

Accelerated Cost Recovery System
  (ACRS)
 accelerated recovery, 65, 68
 defined, 65
 investment tax credit, 162
 salvage value, 65
 straight-line method, 65, 68
 recovery periods, 66, 68
 rental property, 101
 tables, 68
Accountants, 25
Accounting methods, 58
Accrual basis accounting, 58
Accuracy, responsibility for, 25
Adjusted gross income, 128
Adjustments to income 111-128
Adoption expenses, 143
Advance earned income credits
  received, 171
Alimony
 paid, 126
 received, 54
All-Savers Certificate, 51
Alternative minimum tax, 169
Alternative tax, 77
Amending returns, 181-186
Annuities
 fully-taxable, 92
 partially-taxable, 93
Audits
 causes of, 20
 informers, 20
 keys to winning, 21-22
 random selection, 20
 reasons for, 20
 repeat audits, 22
 strategy, 20-22
 timing of, 19
Auto expenses in business, 61
Averaging income, 147-152
Avoidance of taxes, 18-19
Bad debts, 72
Blindness exemption, 41
Books, 142
Business energy investment
  tax credit, 165
Business expenses, 61-63
Business income, 55-70
Capital gain distributions, 91
Capital gain or loss
 alternative tax, 77
 calculating, 77
 carryover of loss, 77
 long-term, 72-74
 nonbusiness bad debts, 72
 short-term, 71-73

Car expenses of employees, 120
Carryback of investment
  tax credit, 165
Carryback and carryforward
  of investment tax credit, 165
Cash basis accounting, 58
Casualty losses, 131, 138-140
Charge account interest, 136
Charitable contributions, 131, 136-138
Child adoption expenses, 143
Childcare expense tax credit, 159-162
Child support, 54
Church contributions, 136-138
Component depreciation, 100
Consistency on returns, 20, 23
Contributions, 136-138
Cost recovery, see Accelerated
  Cost Recovery System
Credits (tax credits), 155-168
Deferring capital gain, 79, 87
Dental expenses, 131-134
Dependent care expense
  tax credit, 159-162
Dependent exemptions, 41
Depreciation
 accelerated, 64
 ACRS, see Accelerated Cost
  Recovery System
 component, 100
 declining balance, 64
 rental property, 98-101
 straight-line, 64
 sum of years' digits, 64
 useful life, 65
Diaries, 27
Disability income exclusion, 126-128
Dividends, 53-54
Drugs, 132
Earned income credit, 173
Education expenses, 123-125
Elderly, tax credits for, 155
Electing out of installment
  method, 77
Employee business expense, 115-123
Employer I.D. number, 58
Employment agency fees, 140
Energy credits, 165, 166—168
Estimated tax payments, 173, 181
Evasion of tax, 18
Exchange of residence, 84
Exclusions
 dividends, 53
 interest, 50
Exemptions
 age, 41
 blindness, 41

(Exemptions, continued)
 children, 41
 excess, 175-176
 other, 42-43
Extension of time to file, 28
Fair market rent, 96
Farm income, 105
Fear of taxes, 17
FICA tax, excess, 174
Filing requirements, 27-28
Filing status, 37-41
Foreign moving expense, 115
Foreign tax credit, 166
Foreign taxes, 134
Form 1040—Chapters 4-18
Form 1040ES, 173, 181
Form 1040X, 182-183
Form 1099-DIV, 53
Form 1116, 166
Form 2106, 119-125
Form 2119, 79-84
Form 2120, 42
Form 2210, 175
Form 2440, 126-128
Form 2441, 159-162
Form 3468, 162-165
Form 3903, 111-115
Form 3903F, 115-116
Form 4136, 174
Form 4137, 171
Form 4255, 169, 171
Form 4562, 63, 66
Form 4625, 169
Form 4797, 84-87, 91
Form 4868, 28, 174
Form 5695, 166-168
Form 5884, 166
Form 6251, 169
Form 6252, 87-89
Form SS-4, 58
Form W-2, 48-50
Fuels and oils, credit for, 174
Head of household status, 39
Hobby expenses, 56
Home energy conservation, 166
Home office expenses, 58, 143
Income averaging, 147-152
Informers, 20
Installment sales, 87
Interest due to IRS, 175
Interest expense, 131, 135-136
Interest income, 50-51
Interest penalty for early
  withdrawal from savings, 126
Inventory valuation, 58
Investment counselling, 142

Investment tax credit, 104, 162-165
IRA (Individual Retirement Account), 126, 171
IRS, sources of information, 18
Itemized deductiions
  generally, 129-144
  casualty losses, 138-140
  contributions, 136-138
  interest, 135-136
  medical & dental expenses, 131-134
  taxes, 134-135
  theft losses, 138-140
Jobs credit, 166
Joint filing status, 38
Keogh accounts, 125
Late filing, 28
Ledgers, 26
Libraries, 142
Loan fees, 136
Local taxes, 179
Lump-sum distributions, 106
Malpractice insurance, 142
Maximum tax, 152
Meal and lodging reimbursement by employer, 107
Medical expenses, 131-134
Medicines, 132
Membership fees, 141
Minimum tax, 169
Miscellaneous deductions, 140-143
Moving expenses, 111-115
Multiple Support Declaration, 42
Non-taxable distribution, 53
Norms, 19
Outside salesperson's expenses, 122
Partnership income, 103
Penalties, 175
Pensions 92-93

Personal residence, see Residence
Points (loan fees), 136
Political contributions, 155
Profit-sharing distributions, 106
Protective clothing, 141
Qualifying widow(er) with dependent child, 40
Recordkeeping, 26-27
Refunds from IRS, 175
Refunds from state & local income taxes, 54
Regulated investment company credit, 174
Rehabilitation expenditure tax credit, 166
Renewable energy source costs, 168
Rental income, 93
Rental property
  ACRS, 101
  depreciation, 98-101
  expenses, 97
  income, 93
  sale, 84-87
Residence
  adjusted basis, 83
  adjusted saled price, 82
  gain, 82
  sale or exchange, 79
Residential energy credit, 166
Revolt by taxpayers, 19
Rounding off, 30
Royalty income, 93
RRTA withholding, 174
Safety equipment, 141
Salespersons' expenses, 122
Schedule A, 129-144
Schedule B, 50-51, 53-54
Schedule C, 55-70

Schedule D, 71-78
Schedule E, 93-104
Schedule G, 147-152
Schedule R, 155-158
Schedule RP, 157-159
Schedule SE, 70, 169-170
Self-employment income, 55-70
Self-employment tax, 70, 169
Senior citizen credits, 155-159
Senior citizen exemptions, 41
Separate returns, 38
Signatures, 176
Single filing status, 37
Small business corporations, 104
Standard deduction, 129
State & local taxes, 134, 179
Subchapter S corporations, 104
Supplemental gain or loss, 91
Tables, 147
Tax credits, 155-168
Tax-exempt savings certificate, 50
Tax guides, 142
Tax option corporation, 104
Tax preparers, 24-26
Tax rate schedules, 147
Tax tables, 147
Theft losses, 138-140
Time for filing, 27
Tip income, 106, 171
Tools, 141
Total income, 47-54, 107
Transportation expense, 61
Unemployment compensation, 105
Uniforms, 140
When to file, 27
Windfall profit tax, 104
Work incentive tax credit (WIN), 166